To Gerald
   From
      Mother.
March 4, 1953.

BURMA SURGEON

BURMA SURGEON

GORDON S. SEAGRAVE

LIEUT. COLONEL, M.C.
UNITED STATES ARMY FORCES IN
CHINA, BURMA, INDIA

PEOPLES BOOK CLUB EDITION
Published by
Consolidated Book Publishers, Inc.
by special arrangement with
W. W. NORTON & COMPANY, INC.

Copyright, 1943, by
W. W. NORTON & CO., INC.
70 Fifth Avenue, New York

This is a special edition for
THE PEOPLES BOOK CLUB
P. O. Box 6570A
Chicago, Ill.

This book is
manufactured under wartime conditions
in conformity with all Government regulations
controlling the use of paper
and other materials

PRINTED IN THE UNITED STATES OF AMERICA

TO

"TINY"

TO

BILL, PAUL, and TUN SHEIN

TED and BASAW

"UNCLE" GRINDLAY and MAJOR "BEAR"

and even

with my wholehearted admiration

TO

"GRANDDADDY JOE"

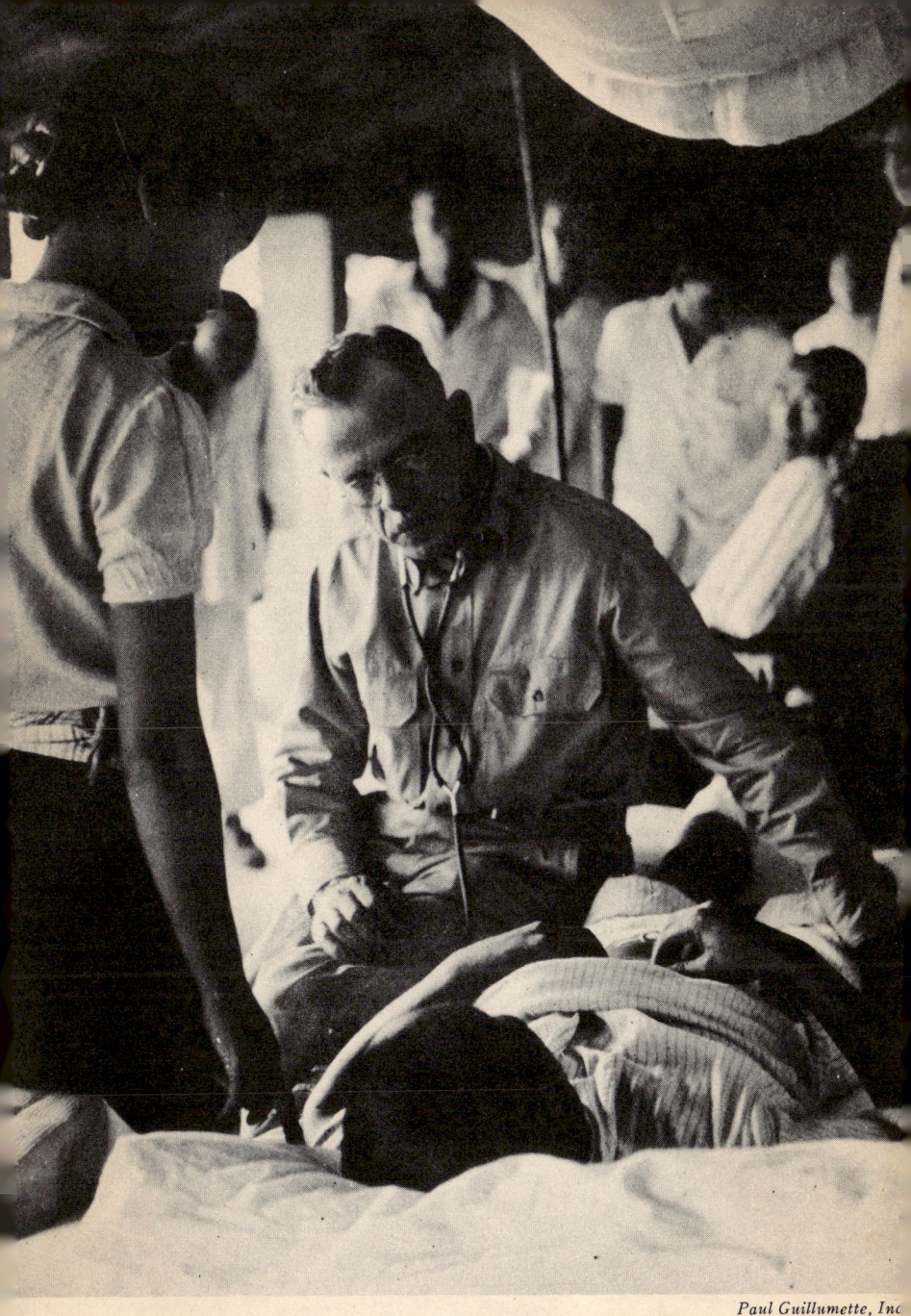

Dr. Gordon Seagrave Attending Wounded Chinese Soldier

The Hospital—Namkham

Dr. and Mrs. Seagrave with Their Two Young Boys

Frank Crane

Dancing Nurses in Burmese Court Dress

Shan Nurses in Men's Clothing for the "Sword Dance"

Frank Crane

Chit Sein "Miss Burma, 1942"
Bill Cummings

Karen Nurses and Dr. Ba Saw
Frank Crane

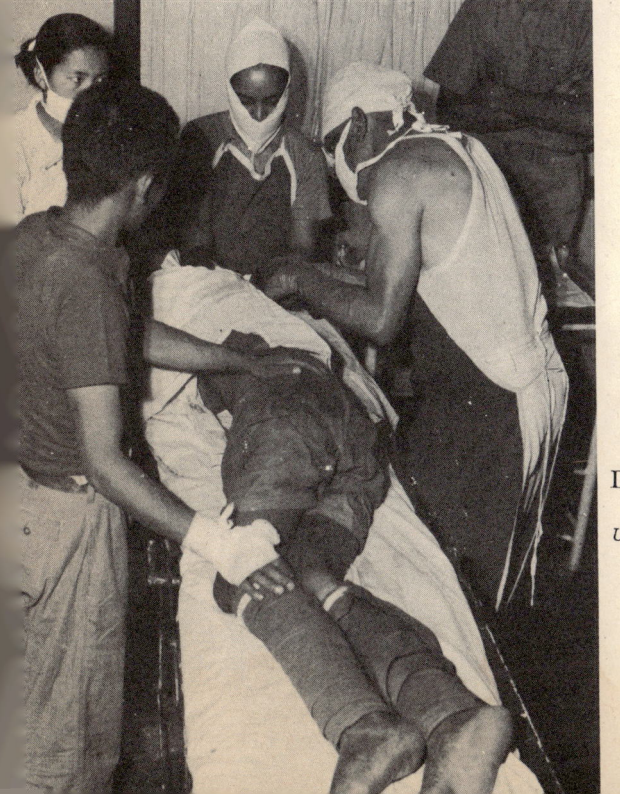

U. S. Army Signal Corps
Doctor and Nurses

Dr. Seagrave Operating during the Battle of Burma
U. S. Army Signal Corps

U. S. Army Signal C[orps]
The Doctor's Jeep

General Stilwell (right) a[nd]
General Sibert
U. S. Army Signal Corps

The Bazaar—Namkham

Photos H. Hoteko

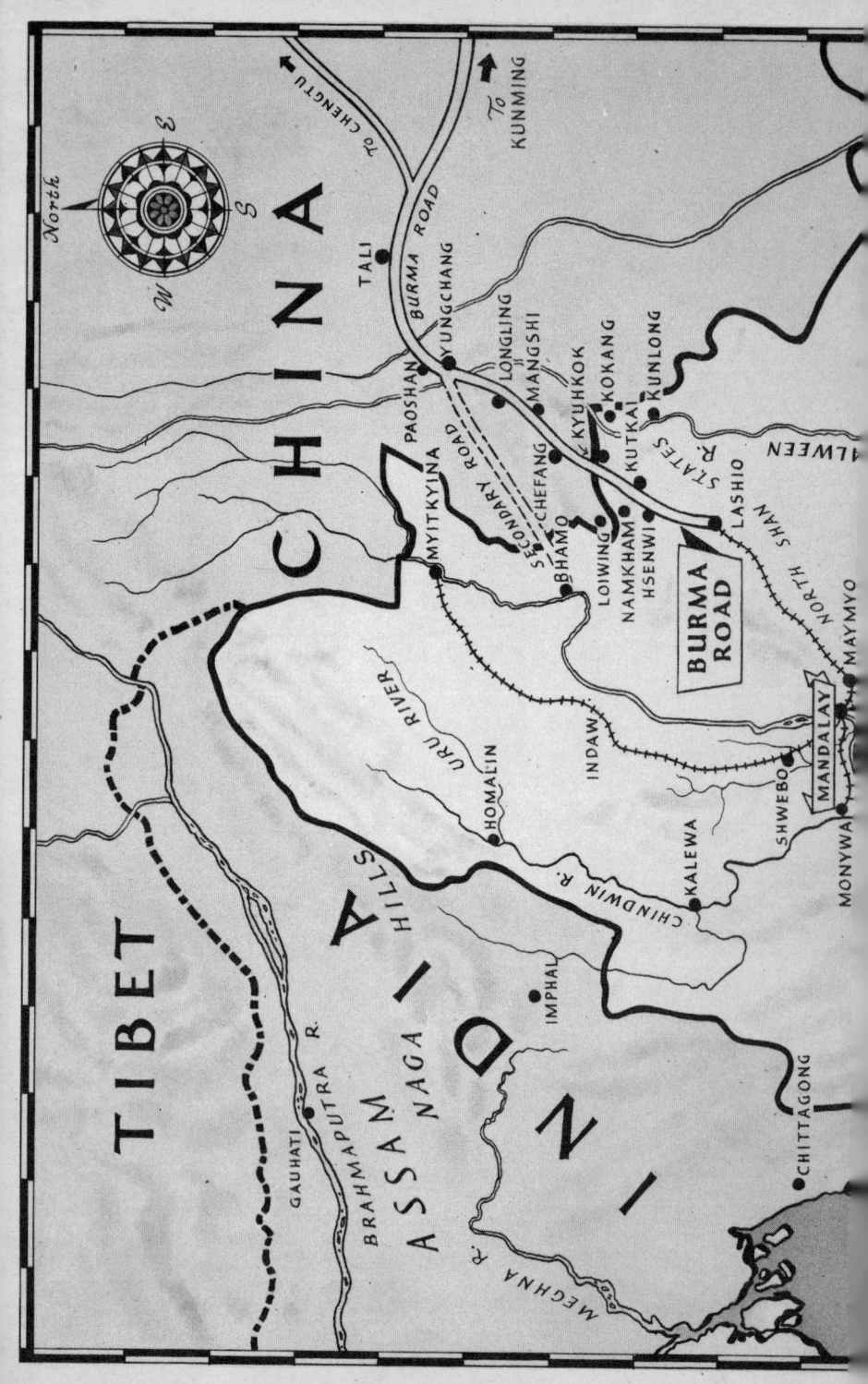

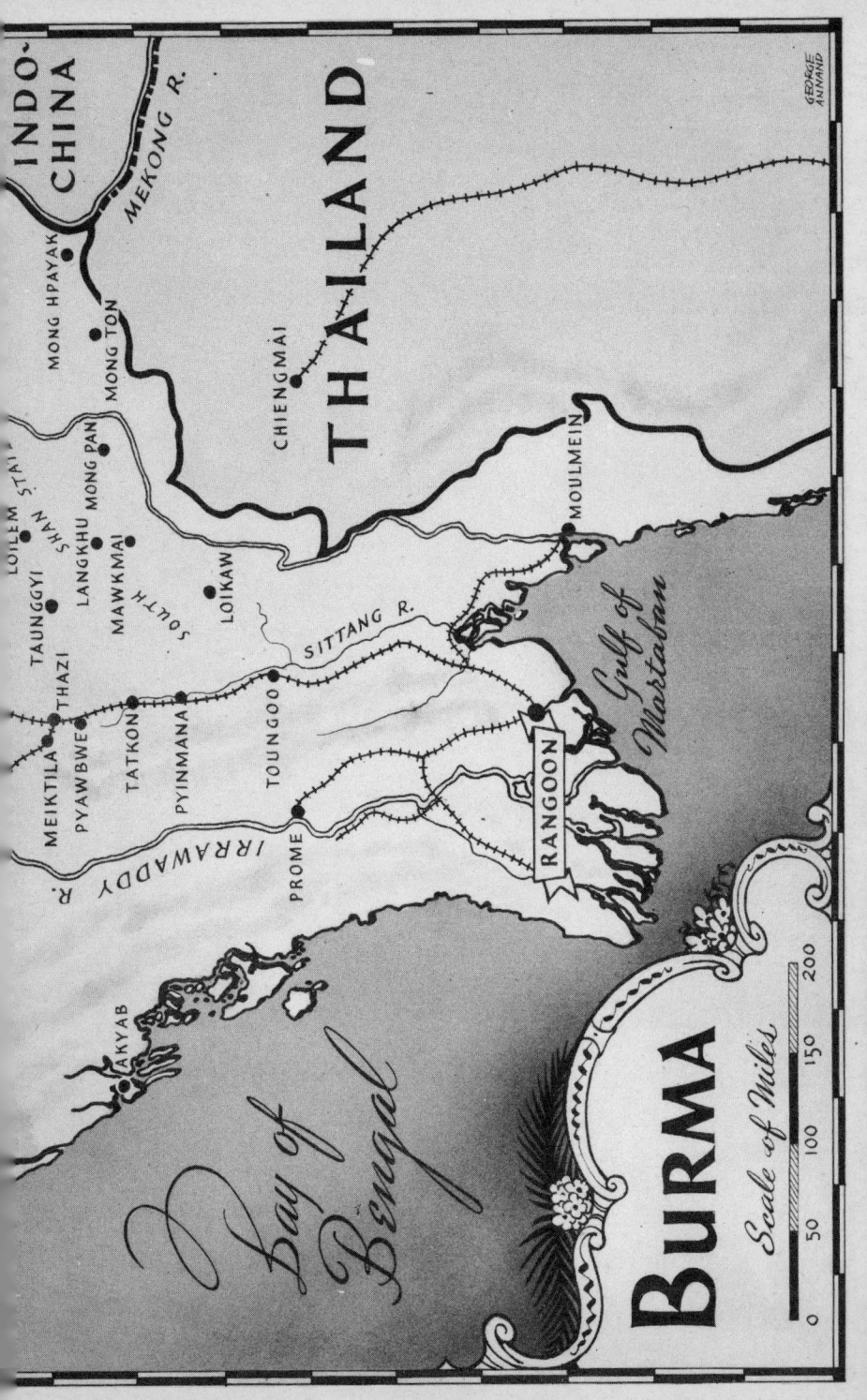

J. W. Decker
Salween River Gorge

ridge over the Salween
Frank Leckell

Making Raft Shelters on the Retreat

Official U. S. Army Photo

Official U. S. Army Photo

Dr. Seagrave Leading the Unit through the Jungle

Rest on the Retreat with Stilwell

Official U. S. Army Photo

H. Hoteko

After the Bombing—Loiwing

Airplane Factory after the Bombing—Loiwing (Mme. Chiang's Private Plane in Rear

H. Hoteko

U. S. Army Signal Corps

Dr. Seagrave at Emergency Hospital on the Toungoo Front

Nurses Doing Hospital Laundry

U. S. Army Signal Corps

Scenes on the Burma Road *Photos J. W. Decker*

Contents

PROLOGUE   11

PART I. BURMA MISSION

I	WE ARRIVE	23
II	OUR NURSES	33
III	WASTEBASKET SURGERY	49
IV	WE BUILD A HOSPITAL	70

PART II. BURMA ROAD

V	MUDHOLES AND PRECIPICES	79
VI	WE BUILD A NURSES' HOME	87
VII	JOURNEY TO KUNMING	98
VIII	THE PLAGUE	106
IX	MALARIA AND AIRPLANES	119
X	MEDICAL OFFICER ON THE BURMA ROAD	134

PART III. BATTLE OF BURMA

XI	THE BEGINNING	151
XII	LEND-LEASE TRUCKS	162
XIII	UNDER GENERAL STILWELL	174
XIV	HOSPITALS UNDER FIRE	187
XV	MEDICAL MAJOR	200
XVI	HELPING THE A.V.G.	213
XVII	FIRST RETREAT	219
XVIII	PULLING OUT	232
XIX	ON FOOT	243
XX	FLOATING DOWN THE URU	250

CONTENTS

XXI	OVER THE MOUNTAINS	258
XXII	THROUGH TO IMPHAL	268
XXIII	BILL'S STORY	278
XXIV	ASSIGNMENT IN ASSAM	283

Prologue

Rangoon, 1902—I was about five years old. A great hulking Irishman stamped up the steps to the huge verandah of the house my great-grandfather had built to live in when, after the second Burmese War, the British took over all of Lower Burma as far north as Toungoo. It was a huge house but it shook under the Irishman's footsteps. I came out to explore. The Irishman apparently loved children. He sat me on his lap and told me stories of wild jungles and great deeds: about service in the Royal Irish Constabulary as a young man; about his later adventures in Canada in the Royal Northwest Mounted Police; about stray rifle bullets that whizzed past him as he sat in his bungalow in the Shan States and that bored through the side of his bookcase; about the day his horse ran around the corner of a jungle path and almost plunged into a wild elephant, bucked and threw him to the ground; about walking sixty miles with both bones of his arm broken to find the nearest doctor. Then he grasped the top of a heavy dining-room chair in his teeth and swung it up over his head. I was fascinated! I tried it out on my tiny nursery chair, but it didn't work; my teeth couldn't have been much better then than they are now. Then he asked me for a glass of water to quench his thirst, and drank it down—standing on his head. I was completely overwhelmed!

After he had gone I asked my mother who the big chap was.

"He is Doctor Robert Harper, a medical missionary at Namkham on the border between the Northern Shan States and China."

That made it still more romantic.

"When I grow up I'm going to be a medical missionary in the Shan States," I declared.

Mother didn't say anything. The vaporizings of a five-year-old didn't worry her. After a few years her only son would undoubtedly become an evangelistic missionary to the Karens of Lower Burma like his father, grandfather and great-grandfather, and a smattering of uncles and aunts, great-aunts, and what not had been before him. Blood would tell.

Perhaps blood would have told if the Karens hadn't taken their new national religion so seriously. To them religion meant going to church on Sunday in a big way. Their chapel next door boasted the largest bell purchasable in America and they rang it twice for each service. Half-past five every Sunday morning it woke them up. Fifteen minutes later it told them to hurry along for the morning prayer service. At six o'clock it warned stragglers that the service was beginning. At seven the women had a special meeting to pray for the souls of their errant males. Then breakfast, then Sunday school, then the main service, followed by assorted Christian Endeavor meetings till nine o'clock at night.

My parents were very lenient. The only service I had to go to was at ten o'clock. Now a good Karen preacher almost always begins his sermons with the lapse from grace of Adam —it being Eve's fault, of course. An outline of the more dramatic sins of the poor Israelites follows, and then, after people have subsided into coma, he ends up with a little intricate exegesis of some of St. Paul's more difficult remarks.

I used to sit by my mother's side in the choir. All the Vintons who were missionaries to the Karens were musical, and so were the Karens. My father didn't have the Vinton voice, but he could wield a mean bass when he sat beside my uncle Vinton who was a basso profundo. My uncle Vinton's voice would come from his toes, some six feet two below his pith helmet, and fairly shock the natives. Those anthems were grand. Karen singing has even been known to convert a hard-boiled captain in the Medical Corps of the modern United States Army!

My father preached some of the most convincing, simply worded sermons I ever heard in English or Karen, and his prayers were poetry. But one day after a long-winded Karen sermon he stood up and prayed. I had been hoping for the best when the preacher sat down. This was too much, even if it was my father who was praying. I rolled the paper boat, which I had been making, into a wad and threw it at him in disgust. I hadn't meant to, but I hit him squarely on the cheek. The means I took to bring the meeting to a close were effective—very! So effective it still hurts me to sit down when I think of it.

My father never spanked me enough. If I'd been spanked as often as I deserved, I probably would never have grown to manhood.

I had three sisters, all older than I. Now that isn't right. If parents are going to divide their children eccentrically with regard to sex, the oddly-sexed one should be the eldest so that he will have some chance to lick the others when they gang up on him. That's what I did. I had three sons and one daughter, so I fathered the daughter first, and she can still hold her own though the eldest boy is about a foot taller than she is. But I had good training, taking on those three older sisters. I eventually stood up to my mother and dad and told them I was going to be a *medical* missionary—and made them like it.

Some time that same year a little girl was learning to toddle around in the not-very-famous city of Carlinville, Illinois, where her civil-engineer father was taking on more jobs than he could handle. She must have been "Tiny" then, and I bet she was cute. When I first saw her, some seventeen years later, she was, at least in my eyes, the glamor girl to end all glamor girls.

1909—The Atlantic was in a turmoil. I ate a ham sandwich as we pulled out of Southampton and my next meal—to stay down—was a banana as we passed the Statue of Liberty.

We settled down in the great and glorious university town of Granville, Ohio. Unfortunately, our house was surrounded by a yard sufficiently large for us to have a big garden. The fact that the garden was one mass of rocks didn't seem to matter to my father. Any future missionary, said he, should know how to lay his hand to anything. The more difficult and nasty jobs you could learn to handle, the better missionary you would be. So that was when I first learned to gather rocks. It was then, too, that I first learned how to handle women. My three sisters each had household jobs they had to do in rotation. One had to cook, one had to sweep, one had to do the washing. I had the garden. I bargained with Grace to do our jobs together, she to help me in the garden, and I to help her in the house. So I hitched her to the cultivator and made her

PROLOGUE

drag that plough while I pushed—if and when we hit a rock!

On my part I learned to cook, wash the dishes, sweep, do the laundry, and, all in all, become the ideal bridegroom.

I liked to rotate crops. One year I raised so many potatoes that we didn't have enough room in the cellar to store our winter coal. Another year I raised so many beans that the grocery stores were filled with them, and the price of beans on the Granville Stock Exchange crashed. That was the year appendicitis and tympanites became so fashionable in central Ohio.

Mother thought I was getting off too easily, so we began raising chickens for the market. Everyone helped me raise them, but I was the Lord High Executioner. I don't like chicken yet unless it is a strange chicken that has been butchered far, far away. The ducks and geese were worse. Without a sound they could stretch out their necks on the chopping block. I am still unable to do an amputation without a sob.

But it wasn't all easy. Granville knew about missionary children, and since we had come there for an education, education was what we should have. I still bear on my bruised carcass the marks of that education. As soon as I got into long pants I began to work for my board in the college girls' commons, waiting on tables, since my father, being a missionary, never had any spare cash. I got quite adept at the art. I could carry five full coffee cups in my bare hands without very much of the coffee slopping into the saucers. I could carry out all the dishes for eighteen girls on one tray without having a crash more often than once in two weeks. That was good training for my shoulders, so I decided to go out for pole vaulting. I became an expert. Once in Johns Hopkins, at the end of the first World War, I actually got a gold medal for pole vaulting. That night the Baltimore *Sun* gave me a good write-up: POLE VAULT—SEAGRAVE, JOHNS HOPKINS, FIRST. NO OTHERS RAN.

I earned my room rent by working in the college library, and my tuition by correcting papers for the English and/or Mathematics departments. That's how I became such a good teacher of nurses. I nursed a huge chap along who had failed his first semester's Virgil examination. By the end of the second semester he was so good he got an A and didn't have to take the examination!

1918—I was sick of the smells of the dissecting room at Johns Hopkins, smells that would empty the balcony around you if you went to a movie without a bath. I wanted some fresh air. I applied for and got a job at a summer camp in Lake Geneva, Wisconsin. I am glad I didn't know, in advance, what the job was going to be. At dawn we got up, fetched the tank car, went into all the cottage rooms and emptied the slop pails into the tank. But I used to come across a damsel there who was making up beds. Since 1902 she had been creating havoc on the farm her father bought for a hobby. When she wasn't hoeing the corn and the potatoes, she and her ten brothers and sisters had been generally raising Cain riding the horses bareback, falling out of trees, stealing apples and otherwise producing a crop of scars for identification purposes.

I had kept my fingers crossed whenever I cast my eye on these neurotic little creatures. I had seen many a first-flight missionary who had had to give up a grand job and come back to the States because his wife couldn't take it. But Tiny looked as if she could take it, with a little education! The only fault

PROLOGUE

I could find with her was that she didn't like rice, and a missionary must like rice *and* curry. Something had to be done, for Tiny was too good to miss. She undertook to educate me in the art of enjoying long walks, and I used the opportunity to cook her some picnic dinners of rice and curry and teach her to like it. I was the better teacher of the two. Tiny loves rice and curry and can cook a mean curry herself. I abominate my legs and continually hope and pray I never have to use them. If a Japanese bomb gets me, I hope it's in my legs!

It took me two summers of slop emptying to convince Tiny she couldn't do better than marry me and go to Burma, but it was worth it. Furthermore I became completely converted to modern plumbing, as you shall see.

1921—Tiny was going to have a baby. I decided to find out something about babies with a summer internship in the Pediatrics Hospital at Mt. Airy, Maryland. We had a grand time there till Tiny's father was killed by a Chicago and Alton train.

Then came my real internship at the Union Memorial Hospital in Baltimore. I didn't begin well. During our first emergency appendix a telephone call came telling me Tiny's pains had set in. Why do residents always get such a laugh out of an interne who is having his first baby?

Then I got into trouble showing off Leslie Mae to the hospital staff. The Chief Resident, like Queen Victoria, was not amused. He accused me of upsetting the hospital routine. Well, the future Prom Queen, May Queen, and College Annual Queen of her university ought to be allowed to upset the hospital routine! The other day my colonel looked long and closely at Leslie's picture. "Well," he said at last, "there is something about her eyes! Yes, I guess you are her father after all." I was glad of that. I had wondered about it myself!

But it was in the hospital that I learned the efficacy of prayer in the practice of medicine. In our first year at Hopkins we had an eccentric classmate whose name was—shall we say—Smith. He hadn't been able to make the grade and had taken a job about town. An ambulance brought him in one night with a physician's diagnosis of acute appendicitis. John M. T. Finney had been called to operate. Smith fell into the hands of Paul "Eggy" Sutton, my fellow interne. Eggy found Smith hadn't had a bowel movement for eight days so he decided to give the preoperative enema himself. He called Smith to the toilet and proceeded to mix the enema. A quart of soapsuds, half a bottle of glycerin, several ounces of turpentine, and, finally, a pint of peroxide went into the enema can.

"Now," said Eggy, "before I give you this powerful enema, old man, I think we'd better kneel and have a word of prayer together."

But Smith, popeyed, didn't even get a chance to kneel. He no longer needed the enema, nor the operation!

One day in the operating room there was comparative quiet, and the operating-room superintendent decided to clear out all the useless broken-down surgical instruments that could no longer be repaired. I happened in as she was having the orderly take away a wastebasketful of these instruments. Since I knew my Burman mission and the extent of surgical instruments I would find there, I asked for, and was given, that wastebasketful. With them all my surgical work was done for five years, in spite of the fact that they were broken and not mates. Many of the hemostats would not remain clamped but would

PROLOGUE

spring apart and permit large hemorrhages in the most embarrassing parts of the operations.

So in August, 1922, Tiny, Leslie Mae and I set sail for Burma, well equipped with shaving soap and toothpaste (which some fool told us couldn't be bought in Burma), with our wastebasket of surgical instruments, but, most of all, with dreams of the marvelous surgery we were going to do for the aborigines of the Shan States of Burma.

PART ONE
BURMA MISSION

I

We Arrive

BEFORE WE left Baltimore, we had been told that, because of my Karen missionary ancestors, we would be stationed in Loikaw, in the Karenni States, where the people understood the Sgaw Karen which I spoke before I learned English. We had accordingly studied up all the known facts about the Red Karens, the Padaungs who stretch the necks of their women with brass rings till they are about a foot long, about that special variety of Karens that does not permit its men to marry outside of their own village and is thereby rapidly dying out, and about the other funny people of the Karenni. When we reached New York we were told that the mission could no longer afford—the missionary revival that had followed the first World War had already lost momentum—to put a medical missionary at Loikaw, and we would have to go to Kengtung, the largest and easternmost Shan State that borders on China, Indo-China and Siam.

I didn't care. All I wanted was plenty of jungle and thousands of sick people to treat, preferably with surgery. Our luck broke when we changed steamers at Liverpool and found, as a fellow passenger, Mr. John Shaw, who had been the Burma government's assistant superintendent of Kengtung State. Mr. Shaw had a very attractive personality and spent a great deal of time on the long voyage telling us all he knew about Kengtung. Full of Kengtung dreams we finally disembarked in Rangoon, where Leslie and Tiny both promptly came down with dengue fever after the minimum incubation period of three days.

Dr. Harper was in Rangoon when we arrived. The mission committee had a session and Dr. Harper, for Namkham, and Dr. Henderson, for Kengtung, went into a tussle to see who could get us. Dr. Harper won by promising me his practice, all his good will, and a free hand, since he was going to retire permanently in the spring. The committee agreed and ordered me to Namkham. That seemed a most appropriate decision in view of my infantile fascination for Dr. Harper and all his works. The committee was anxious that Tiny remain in Rangoon till our son was born, two months later. But Tiny, in spite of dengue fever was so anxious to get to the place where we would at last have our own home that she voted to start at once.

We went by train to Mandalay and then by river steamer three days up the Irrawaddy to Bhamo. How the English do feed! At six o'clock one of the table boys comes banging on your door. You wake up with an angry start, open your door and he stalks in with tea, toast, and marmalade intended to give you sufficient strength to get up two hours later. At nine, before your toast has digested, you sit down to a five-course breakfast. The pain caused by the five courses has not disappeared at one o'clock, when the gong drives you to lunch and you plough through four more courses. At five o'clock there is a big tea to help you live through till dinner at eight or nine. By the third day I had an attack of hiccoughs that lasted five days!

Bhamo is a dirty town. We stayed there only long enough to

find mandarin chairs and carriers for Tiny as, of course, she ought not to ride sixty miles on a horse in her condition. The rest of us rode native ponies, and our equipment went up on mules.

We did twelve miles a day, spending the nights in government bungalows. The first day went well. It was all level plain, and the mules, the carriers, and our ponies stayed together in one large caravan. The second day was a long, steep climb. Knowing nothing about the Chinese, I was quite happy as our ponies took the lead. Tiny, in the meanwhile, was having her troubles. Our son was turning somersaults internally and our daughter was turning handflips externally. Leslie's antics constantly shifted the balance of the load and hurt the shoulders of the three Chinese carriers terribly. The Chinese cursed and swore, and Chinese is a wonderful language! They turned so sharply round the corners that though they all three had their feet on the road, Tiny was swung a yard out over the precipice. Then, suddenly, they set Tiny down in the middle of the virgin jungle and all three men disappeared to have a three-hour siesta with their opium pipes. It was the first time Tiny had been through Kachin country, and, until you know the Kachins, their fierceness terrifies you more than the tigers and leopards that howled around Tiny that day. Finally, when we were just preparing to send out a search party, she arrived in camp half dead from fright.

On the fourth day we crossed the great seven-mile-wide Shweli River plain and passed through Namkham Town up the hundred-foot climb to the Shan compound on the right and the Kachin compound on the left. Our hearts were pounding. What sort of setup were we going to find in this place where we were to spend twenty years? The hospital was a rotten wooden building with twenty wooden beds bare of all furnishings. The floor was stained with blood and pus and medicine, and was so rotten you had to step carefully not to break through. Nurses have, since then, scrubbed that floor so thoroughly and so often that the boards are about half as thick as when they were nailed down; yet the stains are still there, for the jungle wood is as porous as a sponge. The walls were covered with large red splashes of the saliva of betel-nut chewers. All the window ledges were covered with nasal secreta which the patients blow on their fingers and then carefully wipe off on the nearest projection.

There was one patient with a leg ulcer.

There was plenty of good will for Dr. Harper to turn over, but what is good will without patients? Yet if there was no medical work to do I could occupy my time elsewhere, for I had four grade schools, one silk-weaving school, one mulberry garden in which to raise silkworms, and one Shan Christian village to keep in order.

That night Marion and I broke down and sobbed in each other's arms.

The next morning we set our teeth and decided that if Namkham wasn't what we wanted it to be, we would get off to an early start and do something about it. I found a Karen preacher chap who spoke English and Shan well, and made him sit with me all day long and help me teach myself Shan. Poor Tiny never had any luck. You can't study Shan with a baby making havoc of your insides. Besides, until she married me, the poor girl had never been farther out of Illinois than that one corner of Wisconsin where we met. No American, unless he lives in the foreign quarters of our big cities, realizes there can really be such a stupid thing as a foreign language.

I got all the breaks. I had spoken Karen before I spoke English and had learned quite a few words of Burmese as a boy in school. Shan, though it had five different tones in which each word could be spoken—each tone with a different meaning—was quite easy for me. At the end of three months I preached my first Shan sermon. That was the worst sermon I ever heard preached in any language. You have to sing Shan, not speak it, and preferably your mouth should be full of betel nut as you sing. I persisted in singing my sermon in the wrong key!

Take the one word *hsu*. If you say it with an even sound it means "a tiger." If you say it gruffly, down in your belly, it means "straight." When you cut the word off sharp with an axe it means "coat." Sung on high C for a couple of measures it means "happy," and high C staccato means "buy."

Still, I thought I was pretty good. It was time now to kill two birds with one stone: give the accepted evangelistic type of missionary work a fair trial, and, incidentally, advertise Johns Hopkins. I gathered together a gospel team, loaded a mule with medicines, and started off on tour. At each village we called on the headman. He had to admit us, poor fellow, for I was white. When we announced free medicine for all sick, the villagers crowded in. It was too good to miss. We gave each patient just enough of the right medicine to make him want more. One patient didn't want more. He had pylorospasm and I had no belladonna, so I gave him three tablets of pure atropine and told him to take one after every meal and report to me how he felt the next day. He reported in great disgust. He had decided to hurry the cure by taking all three of those tiny tablets at once. His pylorospasm had been cured, but he hadn't been able to spit all day, no matter how much betel nut he chewed. He would, he said, like to have his spit and his pylorospasm back again!

After medicines were distributed, one of the preachers got up and started preaching; whereat, with one accord, everyone got up and went out.

We tried passing out tracts. That went over big. They wanted extra copies for the folks back home! Now we were getting somewhere at last! Or at least I thought so, until I saw them using the pages of the tracts to roll their huge cheroots. Smoking the gospel seemed to me a funny way to convert a man.

My luck was with me again, though, on that trip. A man came to me with tuberculous lungs. I went over him carefully and told him I was sorry, I couldn't do a thing for him. With those lungs he couldn't live more than a year. One year later, to a day, he died, and my reputation among the Shans was made!

Soon after that tour the Kachins threw a huge convention in their mission compound across the street. They had heard of the new doctor, so as soon as they had registered they came over to put me to the test. One man had a huge adenomatous goiter. "You'll have to have the thing cut out," I said, and nearly fainted when he replied, "All right, go ahead."

I ran up to the house.

"Tiny," I called, "I've got an operation to do. A goiter as big as a grapefruit. Will you give the anesthetic for me? I'll tell you what to do."

Tiny agreed. I got out my pressure cooker and sterilized some towels. The wastebasket instruments were put on to boil. Tiny got the chloroform bottle and started to pour. Then I began to cut; cut and tie, cut and tie. That's all there is to surgery. I cut darn near everything that man had in his neck before I got the goiter out. Then I sewed up his ribbon muscles and skin and sat down beside him to wait. When he was fully conscious I said, "Listen, fellow, I want you to promise me to lie flat on your back for several days. If you try to sit up your neck's going to fall apart. Understand?"

Yes, he understood. He would be a good boy.

Much relieved that he had not died on the table, I went up to breakfast. When I came down, half an hour later, he was already sitting up in bed.

The next morning I was called for an obstetrical case the other side of the river. As I rode up the street that afternoon, on my return, I saw the Kachin convention was having a feast out on the grass. Mr. Sword, the Kachin missionary, waved to me to come and join them. While I was waiting to be served, I looked around and saw a funny apparition. A Kachin man was standing near, dressed in a most extraordinary manner. As Kipling says, "Nothin' much before, an' rather less than 'arf o' that be'ind." He had a bandage around his neck. I looked again. Yes, there was my goiter patient! He had smelled the pork curry and had come across the street to get it. And yet he couldn't die!

This was the first time in northern Burma and the Shan States that a goiter had been successfully removed. People came in willing to take a chance at other operations. I remember a few key cases that opened up whole districts to a confidence in us. There was a cancer of the breast that had already reached the cauliflower stage but was not yet fastened irremovably to the chest wall. She was from Momeik State, down toward the Ruby Mines at Mogok. For years she spread the news of how her breast had been removed and skin from her leg grafted onto her bare chest in sheets! There was a woman with a sarcoma of the orbit pushing her eyeball way out of her head. We removed the eyeball and the tumor, and, until last year, she was still sending patients to us. A rich Chinese came down from Tengyueh, capital of Western Yünnan. He had been inexpertly operated on for amebic abscess of the liver, and the fistula had never closed. He wanted another operation, but we cured him with injections of emetine and irrigations of quinine and salvarsan. A high-class Kachin woman of wide influence had had one girl baby followed by several abortions, and wanted a boy badly. We removed a dermoid cyst of the ovary and a year later she did have a boy.

In lots of these cases we had the breaks. I had not had more than a minimum variety of operations on which to acquire experience under guidance in America, and I looked forward with dread to every new operation I had to do. But I never had any overwhelming love for a quitter. When a new operation needed to be done, I got out my books and studied every detail. Then I was profusely sick, went to bed on it, and the next morning, still nauseated, started operating. Somehow or other, the first three operations of each variety were more or less uncomplicated and the patients got along well. After that—God help me! But by that time I could feel confident that the reason the patient died was not all my fault, and I could continue trying to save lives.

Tiny is quite annoyed at the way I operate. She says that

all through my operations I am either praying out loud, singing, or swearing. She is wrong. They are all three just my peculiar way of praying.

In medicine, also, we had the breaks. I was called once to see the sawbwa of Chefang State in China who was "dying" of malaria. Chefang is now just a short trip by car on the Burma Road, but then it took me three days through mud up to the ponies' bellies. When I got there the prince had just about got control of his fever; but I gave him an intravenous injection of quinine and then, when all his lords and ladies gave me the credit for a marvelous cure, I just kept my mouth shut and smiled my gratitude; and patients began to pour in from Chefang State.

The same thing happened with the sawbwa of Mangshi, still farther north in China. He was dying of amebic dysentery, but a few injections of emetine followed by stovarsol tablets, and the patients began to come in droves six days by foot from Mangshi.

These Shan sawbwas are what Maurice Collis calls "Lords of the Sunset" in his book of that name. The Shan title, *Saohpa*, literally means "Lord of the sky or universe." In Burmese, this Shan title sounds like a very filthy female anatomical cuss word, so they smooth it out to *sawbwa*. In England these sawbwas would be dukes, earls, or baronets, according to the size of their respective states. *Mangshi* would be a duke, *Chefang* an earl, *Hsenwi*, in whose state Namkham lies, *Kengtung, Hsipaw, Momeik*—these would be dukes. *Tawngpeng, Yawngwhe, Lawksawk* (whose grand-daughter Louise is) would be earls. *Wanyin*, whose daughter Pearl is, and *Hopong* would be baronets. In the Shan States of Burma, the sawbwas are chiefs, but their work is supervised by British superintendents and assistant superintendents who are responsible directly to the governor and Defense Department of Burma and not to the Burmese congress.

A year later, when we had developed the hospital to a point where patients were really coming for treatment, I received a letter. Dr. Harper, the writer said, would like to come back for another term at Namkham, so he was sure it was "God's Will" that I should move to Kengtung. How about it? I replied that it was the general consensus last year that it was "God's Will" that I should go to Namkham, and I was sure God didn't change his will so frequently—and I stayed on in Namkham!

2

Our Nurses

WITH SURGERY in the offing it was immediately apparent that we must have nurses. The hospital staff consisted of Tiny and myself, a Karen doctor, and a girl who had had a year of training in Rangoon. Our milkman's wife came running to me one morning to ask me to visit her husband who was sick with malaria. I rode out to their village on my pony and found him very seriously ill. He needed hospitalization. His wife and I managed to get him into my saddle, and, she propping him up on one side and I on the other, we transported him to the hospital without his falling off the pony. I put him to bed and gave him fifteen grains of quinine, for I believed in large doses in those days. My "nurse" was nowhere in evidence. Then I went home for dinner. When I came back an hour later I discovered to my horror that not only had my nurse come in and, seeing a fever case, given him ten grains of quinine, but my assistant doctor had turned up and given him fifteen grains more. The patient almost died of quinine poisoning, but it cured his fever!

We decided then and there that we would train our own nurses. We began with a Shan and a Kachin girl. The Shan girl was the daughter of the chief torture expert of the Chefang sawbwa. Mr. Sword, the Kachin missionary, kindly permitted me to have the Kachin girl, because she had failed all her examinations in school and so was of no further use to him. The language made things difficult. I taught the Shan girl in Shan and she taught the Kachin girl in Burmese! In our operations we had four languages, English, Burmese, Shan, and Kachin, going at once.

Shan girls were hard to obtain, so, after two years, we had one Shan and five Kachin nurses, and my Shan was practically useless. I started to study Kachin but gave it up at once. Kachin is a child's language compared to Shan. It is easy to learn because there isn't anything to it. It has no term for anything important. All the girls, however, had had to study Burmese in school, and Burmese is more expressive even than Shan. So I set myself to learning Burmese by the simple expedient of having the nurses teach me Burmese while I taught them nursing. It worked pretty well except in anatomy where the only names for the genitourinary organs with which the nurses were acquainted were the filthy terms that they had heard used in the bazaars when Burmese women cursed each other. Without realizing it, they were teaching me to be very proficient in profane Burmese.

Tiny had an awful time learning Shan sufficiently well to take the two examinations "required" of missionaries. She had acquired the colloquial quite readily in spite of handicaps, but somehow she always had a baby hanging around, which, plus her extensive duties in the hospital, kept her from getting the book work done. Finally she set her teeth, stayed up late nights, and, a week before John was born, passed both her examinations in Shan simultaneously with great credit. And then we stopped using Shan entirely in the hospital and used Burmese instead! For my part, there was a dearth of textbooks of nursing, and I had to set myself to writing one in Burmese. As it happened, one copy was brought out of Burma after the battle. The rest have been bombed to a pulp by the Japanese, and now the United States Air Force is accounting for any spare copies the Japs missed.

We needed to import a trained nurse from outside to teach general-nursing procedures. That was something I could not do myself, and Tiny had no time to give more than supervision to the class, aside from the fact that she didn't know Burmese. Our first imported nurse was a grand girl, but she was subject to the disease that spoils the work of so many persons in the Far East, namely, homesickness. She used to bathe the patients in her tears as she was caring for them. Our next effort was the nurse wife of an Indian doctor we had for a while. She developed tuberculosis and that was the end of her. Then we tried a couple of American nurses. The first lasted six days and the second six months. Our last effort was the most successful, a very fine Karen nurse named Lucy from Moulmein. She was with us for a long time until she and my Kachin doctor got into a fight, and then we lost both of them.

By this time our training school had reached government standards and obtained government recognition and our first class of English-speaking nurses had passed their state examinations with credit. The top girl in the class was a charming Shan girl named E Hla, with a first-class brain. All through her course her daily recitations and examinations had averaged well over 95 per cent. We put her in as head nurse and she was still head nurse at the time of the evacuation of Burma. During her first three or four years she was not of much assistance in disciplining the younger nurses who had been her schoolmates, but as the years passed her prestige throughout the country was so great that the pupil nurses began to recognize her for her real worth, and she never had to fret about loss of face. Then she married Ai Lun, a boy from a poor Shan family whom I was putting through medical college, and became forthwith an "old woman," with that title's corresponding sharp rise in prestige.

Unless you have seen the jungle races of the Shan States you cannot possibly grasp the problem of training nurses, nor yet appreciate the girls we have trained. We have girls of ten or twelve races continually represented in the school, each with their own language entirely unintelligible to the other race groups. Their only common language is Burmese which they learn in the school—and also in the bazaars—and in the whole history of the school we have had only four pupil nurses who were actually Burmese. The largest race group was Kachin, the next Shan, the next Karen, and then a smattering of other tribes, Hkamti, Padaung, Taungthu, Lahu, Red Karen, Black Karen, Maru, Atsi, Lashi, Pwo, Bghai, and Paku. There were two Indian girls and one Intha. There was one Hkun. The only race we wanted represented, but without success, was the Chinese.

Of them all, the Kachins were the most hopeless-looking when they came for training. The Kachins have a stocky, low-slung chassis, and are, by nature and preference, brigands. They migrated down, the last to come to Burma, from the Chinese-Tibetan divide. With their skill in the use of dahs they were fast chopping themselves southward through the Shans and Burmese, and if the British had not taken over Burma, they would by this time have been unquestioned masters of the country. They are intensely loyal to the British and make the best soldiers of all the Burma races. In the first World War they covered themselves with glory, and did not do so badly in the Battle of Burma, considering their equipment and training. But living in the mountaintops where it is cold and water very difficult to obtain, the Kachin villager never bathes unless someone puts it over on him. That happens three times in his life: once when he is born, once when he is married, and once when he dies. That means that only once in a lifetime does a normal jungle Kachin voluntarily take a bath. A missionary asked a villager once if he ever bathed and he replied, "Yes, teacher, twenty years ago I had a bath and a month later my uncle died. Five years later I had another bath and my cousin died. I haven't dared bathe since!" I never go to a Kachin church service if it can be avoided, for I do not possess a gas mask!

The Kachins of Burma are dying out 1 per cent per year, the chief causes being syphilis and gonorrhea. Syphilis makes Kachin women abort or give birth to dead or dying infants, and gonorrhea seals off their ovarian tubes and makes them sterile. In every normal Kachin home there is one special guestchamber. Kachin custom requires the family to furnish hospitality to all Kachin travelers whether they are acquaintances or not. If the visitor is not "hungry" he sleeps around the fireplace in the main room. If he is "hungry" he goes to the special room and the family have to furnish one of the daughters of the household to entertain him. Kachin boys and girls are supposed to experiment from the age of ten or twelve on. If one of the daughters is a bit shy her mother pushes her out of the house after dinner. A pregnancy makes the girl all the more desirable for marriage as she has proved herself to be not primarily sterile. Any Kachin will marry her happily whether he fathered the child or not.

Dr. Geis, one of the pioneer Kachin missionaries, told me he was convinced there was not a Kachin virgin in the country over ten or twelve years of age. I was horrified, but after a few years of gynecological practice I was sure he was right for that day. Since then a new generation of Christian Kachin girls has grown up. The Kachin missionaries had done a good job —an extraordinarily good job. The jungle Kachins, of course, heathen Kachins, are the same as before.

There is not nearly so much gonorrhea and syphilis among the Shans. They don't take their sex quite so seriously. Still there is some room for improvement. I was vaccinating some Shan children and the government vaccination register required the entry of the father's name. I asked the young mothers who the fathers were. They giggled.

"Good Lord, we don't know." They change husbands so frequently they cannot quite keep track.

Two Shan women were overheard fighting in the bazaar.

"You are not half as lovely as I am," said one. "You have only had three husbands, while I have had seven."

The people known as Shans were the original inhabitants of southern China. Driven out by the Chinese, they migrated west and south. One branch filtered into Siam and became the Siamese. Those that came into East Burma became the Shans, into West Burma, the Hkamti, and into Assam, the Assamese. They have been civilized for a thousand years. They had kings of their own and contributed at least one dynasty to the throne of Burma. They built walled cities. Subjugated by the Burmese kings, they had Buddhism forced on them, though they retain some of their original spirit worship. The Kachins are pure—pure?—animists. Six hundred years ago a great Burmese monk adapted the Burmese script to Shan needs and they developed a literature of their own. The Kachins have only the English script given them fifty years ago by Baptist missionaries.

Shan women are the most beautiful in Burma. With charming figures, they have lovely light skins and, when healthy, bright rosy cheeks. Chit Sein, one of our nurses, is so gorgeous that the Americans called her "Miss Burma, 1942."

The Karens were in Burma before the Burmese. They are mountain people. Burmese kings subjugated all but those in the Karenni States, and have treated them like scum ever since. They were very religious, with a mythology very close to that of the Jews. When Judson returned from his first furlough in America, he brought with him a group of new missionaries including my two great-grandfathers. Some of these missionaries, including Great-grandfather Vinton, soon turned to the Karens as being much more receptive to Christianity than the Burmese. The missionaries adapted Burmese letters, giving the Karens the most perfect tonal script of any far eastern language. So many hundreds of thousands of Karens have been converted to Christianity since, that Christianity has become their national religion. They have their own Home Mission and Foreign Mission societies. Karen women are by nature kind and gentle, and they constitute the bulk of the nurses in Burma as well as the bulk of children's "nannies." They are completely loyal to the British.

With all these varieties in training, the proper way to maintain discipline was a very serious problem requiring real thought. The ordinary Kachin enjoys being bossed by a man with a loud voice, reinforced by an occasional slap and a couple of kicks. Shans resent even the loud voice, and if you get angry with a Karen girl she becomes positively ill. The only way we could influence them at all was to treat them with respect and affection; affection even when an occasional nurse did not deserve affection, and respect even when it was pretty difficult to respect many, especially in those first days when they were so dirty. A white man or woman "respect" a native girl? Why, in the Buddhist scale, a woman is the next form of life below a male dog! Astonished at being treated with respect they tried all the harder to deserve respect. Receiving affection, they became worthy of affection.

After Dr. Ba Saw, my Karen assistant, had been with me six months, I called him to the office one day and told him how much I admired his manner with the nurses and patients and how pleased I was with the improvement in his surgery and medicine since he had been with me.

"Doctor," he said, very seriously disturbed, "if you praise me like that you will make me go to the dogs."

"No," I replied, "flattery of a person who is unworthy of praise will, it is true, spoil him; but a man who deserves the praise becomes more humble, just as you have become, and tries harder to give satisfaction."

And the nurses did try. Bathed and bathed and bathed—until they were as clean and sweet a group of girls as you could find in any country. On the march out of Burma behind General Stilwell, all we Americans could do when we reached camp was to spread out our blankets and drop down. The nurses, on the other hand, looked for water, bathed, washed out their own and our clothes, dressed our sore feet, and then helped Tun Shein serve up our food.

First, bathing all day long. Then they tried a bit of powder to take the shine off their faces. One of the girls got up her courage and bought some rouge. They decided that was fine. Then someone appeared with a lipstick and overdid the business badly. Some of the others bought one and showed her how ladies of taste did those things. When American women appeared at the Loiwing airplane factory with their nails painted in the most extraordinary colors, the nurses voted against it—until they found some mild, pink fingernail polish. Where do they get this taste? From their jungle ancestors? God knows.

Teaching them nursing is not very simple. Only a few of them have very quick minds. But in all the years only one girl failed her government examination. The process consists in not allowing them to fail. If an occasional probationer simply has no brain, we let her go early. The rest, no matter how stupid they are originally, are taught and taught until they finally understand, no matter how many extra hours the old man has to spend teaching them. Those later years we began to understand their difficulties. Western medicine is completely beyond the comprehension of these girls. Unlike Americans they do not grow up in an atmosphere where modern medical facts and ideas are overheard daily and seen in articles in the press. Medical terms are never heard. Any medical ideas they have acquired during their youth are all wrong, the vaporizings of native quacks. The courses taught them on government schedule, they cannot grasp in the way necessary to satisfy you.

But with three and four years under you, living in hospital, seeing thousands of cases, they pick up so much new vocabulary as to amount almost to a new language. Now, during their last year, we teach seniors—very, very rapidly—their course over again as if they were brand new probationers. This time they really comprehend.

One day, as they were doing their ward work together, Captain Webb was teasing Kyang Tswi by giving her some quiz questions.

"What do you know, if anything, about placenta previa?" he asked.

"Well," answered Kyang Tswi, "there are three kinds of placenta previa, central, marginal, and partial . . ." and forthwith gave him a fifteen-minute harangue on the subject. She hadn't had a peep at a textbook for eight months.

If nothing else made for good discipline, the fact that they knew, from years of observation, that we were determined to succeed in making good nurses out of them certainly made them co-operate.

Their adaptability is remarkable. When we reached India after the Battle of Burma, I brought Lieng Sing, our Chinese college boy from Singapore and Rangoon, and five nurses with me to Calcutta to purchase new equipment for the crowd. On the train we had to have lunch in the dining car under the stare of British officers. I led them in in fear and trembling. The array of silverware at such a meal is awe-inspiring; I had often had trouble myself being sure just which implement to use. But the only error that appeared was committed by the girl who had grown up in Rangoon. The rest, Kachin, Karen, Shan, from the wild jungles, did everything perfectly. I couldn't understand it till I saw they were watching me out of the corners of their eyes.

We went to a movie. Unconsciously Koi crossed her legs, bringing her foot within the range of vision of a certain officer in front of her. He thought this would be easy, grasped her foot and began climbing slowly up her leg. Koi tried gently to release her foot. He held tight. She tried again, using more strength, but without success. And then—she kicked him!

On our way home we had to hurry so I wouldn't miss my train. Koi and Hla Sein walked ahead, then came Esther and Lieng Sing, while Little Bawk, Big Bawk, and I brought up the rear. A soldier who looked like a Gurkha saw the first two girls and asked them if they were Burmese. They walked on. He fell in step and did his best to start an acquaintance. They continued to chat unconcernedly together. He gave up and turned back, coming face to face with Esther.

"Why, Esther, what are you doing in India? When did you last see your folks?"

Esther, recognizing an old Bhamo schoolmate, stopped to talk. Lieng Sing walked on out of earshot, stopped and waited for Esther to finish her conversation before escorting her home. The Bawks and I walked on by, convinced that these "uncivilized," "jungle" girls could take care of themselves even in one of the largest and most wicked cities of the world, in a country completely foreign to themselves. Where did they learn these things? God knows.

We had orders to push on from Assam to "somewhere in India," and we traveled by troop train. There were four nurses in a compartment. At three in the morning, as we were drawing into a station, a soldier climbed from his compartment through their open window. The nurse in the nearest berth screamed as he stepped in on her, and the other three girls joined her in throwing the soldier out of the window while the train was still moving! We never heard what happened to the soldier.

One thing I learned from sore experience. You could not hope to handle these nurses, no matter of what race, in groups. No argument, no matter how sound, is ever effective with them as long as they are permitted to gang up on you. Singly, and handled with affection and respect, they see the point of your argument at once, and respond. Handled as individuals and with respect and affection, we can get twelve and fourteen hours of very efficient work per day out of these girls, and they sing and smile and joke as they work. And work they will until they get tuberculosis or drop from simple overfatigue. But let them gang up, even with only one other person, and you can't argue with them at all. This has been proved numberless times. In a gang they give each other courage to resist the "old man," as they used to call me. All we ever needed to do was to separate the different members of the gang, give them jobs in different places, call them in and explain the situation to them one by one, and the affair was over. It takes courage to do wrong, and you get that courage artificially through some fellow worker who wants to do the same wrong thing.

In a hospital it is as important as in any army that orders be obeyed. Our orders were obeyed—or else! But there is much more co-operation if the reason for the order is explained, when it is not in itself apparent. Also, it is much easier to lead than to drive. That is where human beings differ from horses. In no Indian or Burmese hospital do the nurses do any dirty work. There are special castes to do individual jobs. It makes the hospital bulky with lazy personnel. It is costly. It makes it hard for the patient to get real service, unless he has plenty of money for "backsheesh." We were determined that any nurses we trained should be willing to do anything needed, no matter how foul. All I had to do was do the dirty job myself. Lose face? A big man cannot lose face. It is the petty person who has to fret about losing face. I can open up the manhole in our sewer system and clean it out with my bare hands in front of a crowd and not lose face thereby. In fact, the crowd will turn in and help me clean it out so they won't lose face by doing nothing when the old man is busy.

The first order any nurse received when she entered training was that she must be gentle. Any lack of gentleness in doing dressings or giving nursing treatment of any sort is punished drastically. If nurses don't care what happens to their patients when they first enter training they soon throw it off. Once a patient with cerebral malaria walked out of the ward, while the nurse's back was turned, and disappeared. We searched all over the neighborhood without success. Twenty-four hours later a party of soldiers discovered him lying in a marsh, half under water. They brought him back to the ward, and his temperature went steadily up till, at dawn, it reached 107° and he died. When the night-duty nurses came off, two of them were sobbing.

"What are you crying about now?" I asked.

"We tried so hard to keep that patient of yours alive, and all the time he was dying the other patients stood around and made fun of him. Nobody cared about his dying except us!"

When the night girls took over, one night, they found Thelma had written this on the night-order sheet: "Please take care of these particular patients [bed numbers of serious cases followed]. They are all my honeys, so do all you can for them."

We had some strange doctors working with the unit.

Another nurse came to me, her cheeks wet with tears. "Daddy, Doctor Blank won't give me any orders for Bed No. X. He says the patient is going to die and wants me to let him die—and I don't want to let him die."

"O.K., see what digitalin and a Namkham intravenous glucose will do for him."

The patient recovered.

Nursing Chinese patients is about as difficult a job as a nurse can possibly be asked to handle. They simply won't take their medicine. Hla Sein solved the problem. I was walking by her ward when I heard her singing at the top of her voice. I thought she must be mad so I peeped in the door. She had her bottle of quinine solution in one hand and her dram glass in the other. All the malaria patients were lying at attention. She stepped up to one after another, sang him a verse until he started to laugh, and when he had his mouth wide open poured in the bitter stuff. Her patients acted as though it was Jove's nectar she was feeding them.

The girls are so tiny. About five feet tall, they weigh from eighty to a hundred and ten pounds. One of them had such small feet that when she bought shoes she had to buy them in children's sizes. But you should see them heave their patients around, move them from stretcher to operating table and back again. They stood the long, hard tramp out of Burma better than the Americans, and got through into India in much better physical condition.

The United States Army speaks of these girls of ours as Seagrave's Burmese nurses. The nurses are not Burmese. Only Than Shwe is Burmese. But I don't mind. The other girls were born Karen, Shan, Kachin, Taungthu, and so forth, but we wouldn't tolerate their remaining Taungthu, Kachin, Shan, and Karen. We wouldn't tolerate any race differentiation. They had to be bigger than their race or we had no further use for them. At first Kachin would clique with Kachin and Shan with Shan. The old man didn't approve. He fought them tooth and nail. The head nurses would report errors of conduct of girls of other races, not of their own. The old man would disgrace himself by getting downright angry. An occasional Karen would start chumming with a Shan, a Kachin with a Taungthu. The old man would praise them from the pulpit on Sunday when it was his turn to preach. Now race has nothing to do with any of them. They are much bigger than their race. Little Bawk and Chit Sein, Kachin and Shan. When Bawk goes off on sick leave Chit Sein mopes around and gets sick herself. The Shan girl can't live without the Kachin. Koi and Saw Yin, Shan and Karen. Roi Tsai and Lu Lu, Kachin and Karen. Lu Lu thought I didn't approve of her friendship with Roi Tsai, and for months she couldn't work, until the matter was straightened out. Kyang Tswi and Esther, Kachin and Karen. United by a wholehearted decision that our fellow worker Paul Geren was a present-day incarnation of God, they couldn't be separated. If their regard for him were based on sex they would be jealous of each other. No matter what others may think, it isn't a case of sex at all; in their minds he just gets mixed up with their ideas of God—I don't blame them—and it brings them together.

At the boardinghouse where we stayed in Calcutta we met two very respected friends of mine, Dr. and Mrs. Jury, two of the finest old Burma missionaries you could hope to see. I told them that the five nurses were Kachin, Shan, and Karen, and invited them to see if they could tell which was which. If anyone could tell them apart, they should have been able; but they missed every one.

They are bigger than race, bigger than nationalists. What price a solution of this horrible world's difficulties! If Germans were bigger than Germans. If English and Americans and Russians were bigger than Russians, Americans, and English. If there were something bigger than patriotism, bigger than love of country! Would we continue to have these wars? We have no more racial strife among these nurses. We have individual strife when they have not enough work to do, but it is no longer based on race, and is therefore very short-lived.

3

Wastebasket Surgery

WITH NURSES to help, we began to take on all sorts of cases. It was to Kachins that we owed our ability to develop surgery. Having lived by the dah they were not afraid of the knife and came to have a most unbalanced admiration for my prowess with that instrument. One day in Bhamo, a Kachin with a gastric ulcer came to me to be examined. When I told him he needed an operation, he took off his shirt, pulled out his gigantic sword, put it into my hand, lay down on the floor and said, "O.K., Doctor, go ahead."

Not having an X-ray in those years, I particularly dreaded orthopedics. I used to escort the patients to the door and say, "My dear fellow, you need an operation, all right, but I don't know how to do it. You'd better run along home and forget about it." And half an hour later he'd be back again.

"Doctor, I want you to operate on me."

"But I don't know how, I tell you; I am afraid you will die."

"That doesn't matter, I won't blame you if I die."

"No, I rather guess you won't. All right, if you don't mind dying I'll do my best to satisfy you!"

I opened my first pus abdomen and put in a rubber-tube drain. When I did the first dressing, the drain had disappeared. I probed around in the man's belly but couldn't find it.

"What are you looking for, Doctor?" asked the patient.

"I'm looking for that rubber tube I stuck in you. It's lost."

"Oh, that thing. Well it was hurting me so I pulled it out and threw it away."

In those days we were so poor I couldn't afford to lose that tube. I couldn't find it in the ward, but on the verandah I was delighted to come across a baby using it for a pacifier.

When I took the dressings off my first hernia case to remove the stitches, I found the patient had anticipated me and had scratched them all out with his fingernails, and the wound was wide open. I began to be profane.

"Doctor, it itched. I had to scratch, didn't I?"

Judson College in the University of Rangoon wanted me to address the student body. I told them that all my appendix cases in those first years had died. In one of the front pews was a young professor who seemed to be very interested in my talk. He sat on the edge of the seat just drinking in my words. At the close he came up and pumped my arm up and down.

"Doctor, that was a wonderful talk. You have done me a great deal of good and given me a lot of comfort; I am to have my appendix out tomorrow."

I like to be a comfort to people!

No appendix case came to me those first years unless the appendix had been ruptured at least a month, and one patient had ruptured his three months before I saw him. Sulfanilamide had not appeared.

Personally, I always wished I could specialize in gynecology. But how can you limit yourself to specializing in any one thing in a country like that? Still we had plenty of gynecological cases to keep life interesting. The medical colleges in Burma and India are alike in that very little gynecology can be studied by male medical students, and the status of gynecological operative work is poor. Women will come to a medical missionary much sooner than to government men. Kachin tendencies toward gonorrhea would keep us supplied when other cases petered out.

Next to gynecology, I would like to be an obstetrician. And what a chance I had to be an obstetrician! No woman, much less her husband, would call me for a normal delivery, in those first days. But when everything went wrong, even the husband would call me. We had a marvelous variety of abnormal obstetrics. When the matter got beyond my depth, I had, as usual, to appeal to Tiny. Tiny took my course in midwifery and started pulling babies. A good teacher is one who can teach his pupils to become better than he is. That's how I know what a good teacher I am. I taught Tiny how to give a chloroform anesthetic, and she now can give a much better one than I can, keep the patient under for four hours without a symptom of chloroform poisoning. I taught her obstetrics, and now she can slip her long, slender fingers up into the fundus, rotate and deliver, when my fist would rupture the uterus at the first try. I always got a laugh when she went to work on a child that wouldn't breathe. The sweat poured from her face. Her temper became brittle. She panted like an exhausted runner, and panted life into the child long after I would have given it up for lost.

The only obstetrical instrument the natives have is the sharp hook. They tear the baby apart with it, rupture the uterus and even rip out half the vagina. But they get the baby out, which to them is the essential point, even if the mother and baby both die. The mother would lose face if she died with the baby still in her.

They carried in a woman with pain down below the appendix region. "She has an extrauterine pregnancy and will have to be operated on at once," I told her employer.

"Nonsense," said he, "who ever heard of a baby growing anywhere else than in the uterus?"

"Well, this one is, and I am going to operate right away."

"Not if I can help it. You have to send for her husband and operate after he gives his permission."

"He lives so far away it will take him two days to get here, and by that time there won't be any woman left to operate on," I said, and started to scrub up.

The employer, with a grim face, insisted on remaining in the operating room so as to have the goods on me if I had missed my diagnosis—remained until, on incising the peritoneum, a couple of pints of clotted blood burst forth, and then he had himself carried out by the nurses quite content, and convinced that babies were sometimes indiscreet in their choice of residence.

My first mastoid case was a charming little Kachin schoolgirl. I had never done a mastoid, but I had an old dry skull in the hospital. I pulled it out and did a mastoid operation on it, and when nothing happened to that patient I operated on the little girl, and she did well. We had many other mastoids. One came to us in a dying condition, the pus having burst through the skin, and he had a large Betzold abscess in the neck—and his ear canal and his mastoid were full of maggots. I opened the abscess, but his condition was so poor I didn't dare to do anything else. I just put him to bed and told the nurses to compel him to eat. But, like all men who are ill, he was very hard to feed. He didn't want eggs or milk or toast or anything else that was good for him. All he was willing to eat was rotten fish and a sour pickle! The nurses had been trained never to waste a cent of hospital money, and they couldn't see the sense of pushing good food down a man who was going to die anyway. So I went out, bought the rotten fish and the sour pickle the fellow wanted, fed it to him myself, and he got well.

My first gastrectomy for cancer of the stomach did well until the patient went home, and then he sent back word that I was a rotten doctor; he couldn't stow away the gigantic amounts of rice that Shans eat twice a day without getting terrible pains. It took two months to persuade him he would have no pains if he would eat smaller amounts several times a day.

Stone in the bladder is very common. My largest weighed sixteen rupees. It had been in the patient's bladder twelve years, ten of which he had spent incapacitated for work.

There was a lot of plastic surgery forced on us. There was a Chinese who had most literally "lost face," a bear having disposed of most of it including one eye, the nose, and the upper lip. A bit of skin was left on the forehead which I used as a pedicle flap to line his new nose. Then I took cartilage from one of his ribs, grafted it in for a support, and finished off his new nose with a caterpillar graft from his chest. It was rather a flat nose, but what better for a Chinese?

Dr. Hoag of Detroit told his Bible class about this case. When he had finished speaking, one of the deacons called out, "Pastor, that is not the first time something 'nosey' has been made out of a rib!"

A woman came in one day with the worst infection of lice I had ever seen. Her hair had millions of them in permanent occupation. They had bitten her on the forehead and nose until she itched so badly she had scratched the front of her head full of sores. Flies had laid their eggs and now her sores were full of maggots. They had eaten into her nose until the cartilaginous part was separating itself from the bone. After we had excised the worst areas and rid her of the maggots, the front of her head had no scalp left. We left pedicles in both temporal regions, moved the scalp from the top of her head forward, grafted skin from her leg on the newly denuded area, so that when she got well she could comb her hair up over the bald spot and hide it very effectively. She came back to me last year with an attack of malaria. This time she had no lice.

I even tried my hand at dentistry, and once I filled one of my own teeth. I had a wisdom tooth that was giving me a lot of trouble and there was no chance to go to Rangoon. So I got out my dental machine and began to grind. I was rather clever at that part of it. I did just like the dentists in the States. You know how they do it. I ground around until I found a place that hurt, and then I ground there a little extra! Then I mixed up the amalgam and pressed the filling home. But somehow, down in the bottom of that cavity I had left a bit of cotton so that when I did finally get down to civilization the whole tooth had to come out. But I filled the tooth anyway.

One of the missionaries in Lower Burma, Dr. Condict, used to pull hundreds of teeth every day. He was a doctor of divinity and not of dentistry. I could not understand why a preacher should pull so many thousands of teeth until I finally got the solution. You put one thumb in the patient's mouth and push down hard on his tongue. You fasten a tooth forceps on one of his large molars. Now you have got him where you want him. He can't talk back and he can't get away and you can preach to him all day long!

And always there were goiters. One was so large it looked like a ham. I had the reputation of being the goiter specialist of Burma. And how I hate goiter surgery. Those huge adenomata would seem to be fed by twenty-five jugular veins, and the walls of so many were so very fragile. I used to be nauseated for every operation. But they would keep referring those confounded cases to me from Rangoon and Monywa, Bassein and Yenangyaung. All our Lower Burma cases were exophthalmic, none of our Shan States cases was. I have never even read of abscessed goiters as large as many we saw. Abscessed adenomata. They seemed unusually common. In most of the cases an emergency incision to remove pus would stop the dyspnea and we could take out the tumor at our leisure. One patient was choking to death as he was carried in. In one case I did not suspect abscess and removed the abscessed tumor intact without the patient turning a hair.

But how can you specialize in anything in a country like that? You cannot do what you want to do and you cannot avoid doing things that you don't want to do. Still I did specialize, and on something new! Wastebasket surgery. Surgery with wastebasket instruments. Orthopedic surgery without an X-ray. Urological surgery without a cystoscope. Surgery without any actual cautery except a stray soldering iron. Surgery without electricity. Medicine without a laboratory, and without medicines, often. Hospitalization without a real hospital or any adequate equipment.

I used to be bitter about it, but now I am rather glad that I had to use wastebasket instruments for so many years, for I have seen what would have happened to me if I had had real tools. I had a Chinese carpenter working for me who had wonderful tools. He had the best saw that money could buy. The result was that when I asked him for a two-foot board he never handed me one from a pile of two-foot boards. He pulled out his saw and sawed off two feet from a fourteen-foot board every time. That is what happens to you when you have good tools. I, on the other hand, have become a very conservative surgeon!

The five most common disease entities in the Shan States are, in sequence, malaria, goiter, amebic dysentery, gonorrhea, and syphilis. Goiter we used to treat with iodine in one form or another if it was of the smooth type, and surgery if it was adenomatous. I had a lot to learn about the other four diseases. With malaria and dysentery I was my own guinea pig, for a doctor in the Shan States cannot possibly avoid those diseases, but I have consistently refused to allow myself to become a guinea pig for gonorrhea and syphilis.

From Assam, across the Chin and Naga Hills, the Northern Shan States and Southern Yünnan, stretch valleys of what the Rockefeller Foundation Malaria Commission men describe as the most perniciously relapsing type of malignant malaria they have encountered anywhere in the world. In the valleys from, say, fifteen hundred to three thousand feet above sea level, the malaria is 97 per cent malignant tertian, 2½ per cent benign tertian, and ½ of 1 per cent quartan. That had been my statement before they came to work in the valleys of Southern Yünnan, and their reports confirmed it. Higher or lower the percentages change quickly in favor of the benign tertian. The malignancy is borne out in Chinese history, and Chinese who knew their history dreaded to enter or pass through those valleys. Chinese came in swarms to Burma every November, when the malaria disappeared, and, having found work and made their pile, rushed back to China and its mountains before malaria returned with the rains in May. It was only with the Sino-Japanese War that Chinese came into Burma and remained there during the rains. Shans have resistance to malaria, acquired by the survival of the fittest. Kachins need no immunity, for they live in the mountaintops above malignant malaria levels. The Chinese have no resistance to malaria at all. Before they came to stay, we had very rarely a patient with algid or cerebral malaria or with blackwater fever. After the Chinese came, we had hundreds of cases, and, with the increased virulence of the plasmodium as it passed through the nonresistant bodies of the Chinese, these especially malignant forms of the disease became more common among the Shans and Kachins.

Some of these cerebral malaria cases were unconscious for six weeks before they threw it off. One patient had a mania for breaking windows. After he had broken every single windowpane in his room he felt satisfied and settled down to get well. After an attack of cerebral malaria the English government officers were required to take two years' sick leave before returning to duty. I had a nurse from Lower Burma who was quite superstitious. When she was ready to start north for training she consulted a Buddhist monk who was a reputed soothsayer. "I see your footprints going to Namkham," he said, "but I see none returning." The nurse translated that to mean that she was going to die in Namkham. She got malaria.

We began treatment at once which, with any other case, would have cured her. But she developed cerebral symptoms, and her mania was that she was going to die; and die she did, forthwith.

Of all the forms of malignant malaria, the algid is the worst. The patient with an overwhelming infection of plasmodia is icy to the touch. I have never cured one. I thought I was going to cure one once because large injections of intravenous glucose seemed to have started a reaction, but he died anyway. Chinese are very fond of this type.

Blackwater fever seems to occur only in special circumstances: patients with a special type of kidney, with very slightly or not at all enlarged spleens. It usually occurs in a person who has had chronic malaria for a long time; but I have seen blackwater fever occur in patients with their first attack of malaria. The mortality in the books is very high, but with us it has been very low. This was due to early diagnosis. There is something—what is it, a smell?—about a blackwater fever case. When you see, or smell, that something, a guaiac test is made at once on the urine. If there is no urine available, you assume that it is blackwater fever, for there is marked oliguria in blackwater fever. You immediately treat the case as blackwater fever with atabrine and neosalvarsan and avoid quinine as you would the plague. If you start treatment for blackwater fever before the urine has become black, percentages of cure are high, but if you don't suspect the disease before the urine is black, you cure very few.

As a missionary I was a most unorthodox pain in the neck. As a doctor also I was decidedly unorthodox. A good doctor frequently is the one who gets his diagnosis, no matter what has happened to the patient in the meantime. In a country where 97 per cent of the fevers are malaria, and malignant malaria at that, and where 99 per cent of the dysenteries are amebic, a good doctor will give no quinine or atabrine to the fever case or emetine to the dysentery unless and until the laboratory turns in a positive report for plasmodium and/or amebae. The fact that only one out of ten laboratory men in the country is capable of seeing malaria parasites and amebae makes no difference. If the parasites are not seen, the malaria patient is treated with aspirin and the amebic dysentery with saline cathartics. If the patient dies he is being most unco-operative. Even when the report from the laboratory is positive, treatment has been delayed for anything from twenty-four to seventy-two hours. I would personally rather treat the patient according to his smell and get him well.

During the past ten years the orthodox treatment of malaria has varied a good deal. As each treatment came out, it was, by hypothesis, perfect. You wrote out the order on the chart and said good-by to the patient, sometimes forever! You never adapted your treatment to the special case. If your patient died, it was of course his own fault. He was trying to be nasty. Any doctor who used quinine during the atabrine epidemic was just being old-fashioned. Our routine treatment had to be based on the fact that atabrine was either not procurable at all, or cost too much. But the most important point in our routine treatment is that it must not be routine. You feel your way along with the individual case and use quinine, atabrine, and especially that most divine drug, neosalvarsan, as the patient has need. Neosalvarsan has as many uses, almost, as bamboo. It will cure syphilis. Intravenously injected and unassisted it will cure a good many malarias and blackwater fevers. It is the best stimulant of the bone marrow ever produced for tropical anemias. Put it into the rectum and it will even cure amebic dysentery. It brings down the temperature of relapsing fever in twenty-four hours. But no matter what drug you may use, you cannot cure malaria in a white man without putting him to bed. That is why I never cure myself of malaria even with my own treatment. I can't catch myself still long enough to tie my hands and legs and put myself to bed. If you put your patient to bed you can cure him in about three days by giving him one intravenous injection of five grains of quinine once a day without other drugs, providing you make no mistake in the time you give the injection.

Atabrine, according to its backers, will never need to be supervised. But even the original German atabrine will cause an occasional psychosis of the manic-depressive type, and with the English "atabrines" these psychoses are common.

The malaria belt mentioned above must also be the fatherland of all the amebae. There is very little bacillary dysentery indeed. You can ignore figures to the contrary. It is customary in the hospitals of the East to call all dysenteries bacillary when the laboratory technician turns in a negative report for amebae. But as above said, the number of laboratory men in Burma who can see an ameba, even when present, can be counted on the fingers of your hands. It was not until "Big Brother" Chesley joined us that an "ameba negative" report from the lab meant a thing to me. If Chesley cannot see an ameba, the ameba simply does not exist.

If, in a strange jungle village, you want to know where the village latrine is, you only need to pick up a stick and the pigs will lead you there. Every stream and every well is full of amebae.

The medical examiner of the Mission Board in New York once said, "If Seagrave were a good doctor, he would not allow himself to get infected with malaria and dysentery." That is quite correct. If I had been a good doctor, missionary doctor, I would have climbed under the mosquito net at 6:00 P.M. every night and stayed there and I would have boiled all my drinking water myself. I certainly would not have let my cook "boil" it for me, nor would I ever have answered those numberless emergency calls at night to villages near and far. I would have let the crazy fools go ahead and die unassisted.

With these two diseases the most common everywhere, the nurses became very proficient with the hypodermic and intravenous syringes, much to the distress of the medical profession in Burma, who wanted these money-making procedures in their own hands. When nurses needed practice, they practiced on me. I had a government official visiting me one day. As we left the offices and started down the stairs, the nurse came up with my emetine. I rolled up my sleeves and she stuck it in.

"Good Lord! You don't let a nurse give you a hypodermic, do you?" I certainly do. I would rather any one of our nurses gave me an intravenous quinine than any doctor. Tiny and our son, John, went to Rangoon alone once, and John developed dysentery; so she took him to a doctor there. The doctor put the syringe together, broke off the neck of the emetine ampoule, sucked up the solution and wiped the needle on his thumb.

On Tiny's insistence he condescended to put the needle into alcohol a second. Then Tiny wiped John's arm with alcohol to make sure it would be done, but the doctor wiped off the alcohol with his bare hand and plunged the needle in before Tiny could object. Our first-year girls can do better than that.

Not long ago a new doctor who was working with us gave an order for the intravenous nurse to prepare a solution of glucose for intravenous injection to one of our patients. The girl took the apparatus over to the ward. The doctor tried, and he tried, and he tried, and could not get the needle in.

"Hold everything," he said, "and I'll go over and call Captain Grindlay."

Just then I happened in on my rounds. The nurse told me about the trouble. She didn't think the doctor wanted her to give the injection, he might be prejudiced against nurses.

"O.K., I'll have a try," I said, and ruined a couple more veins. "Here take this thing away from me and put it in yourself," I said.

There was only one vein available, about half the size of those we doctors had been playing with. The nurse took the needle, bent over and got it in the first time. The same thing has happened three other times.

There is not much tuberculosis among Shans. They live in comparatively bright and open houses under better circumstances than the other tribes. Kachins have less-open houses, full of smoke, and they sleep with their heads buried in blankets. Still, as long as they remain where they belong, in the mountaintops, tuberculosis is not too common. It is when they come down into the plains that they get tuberculosis readily. The Chinese have the largest proportion of tuberculosis. Yunnanese live in mud-brick houses with practically no air and they are very unsanitary. For their tuberculosis their only treatment is opium. Opium will stop the cough temporarily, and sometimes permanently!

The most expensive department of our hospital was the pediatrics department. Milk costs much more for one baby per day than rice and vegetables would cost for three adults. But there were a lot of babies whose mothers had died soon after birth, and the babies would die too if we did not take them in. There were a few abandoned babies also, usually twins. Orientals detest twins, and I know of several instances where newborn twins were left to die unfed. The Siamese also do not like them, so that the twins there developed a new variety, Siamese twins, where they stuck together for safety!

The year we reached Burma, the road that later became the Burma portion of the famous Burma Road had just been completed from Lashio to Namkham. It was just a mud road and was only usable six months of the year, and not always then. The bridges were all of bamboo and had to be replaced after every rainy season. Bamboo makes quite nice bridges. You break through them very frequently, but they very seldom collapse en masse under you. I had that happen only once. Usually you jack yourself out of the hole, throw some bamboos in and take off again. During the first year we had no car. The second year we got a second-hand Harley-Davidson motorcycle with a sidecar. It simply could not manage those awful hills even without the sidecar. Just then the government announced compulsory physical exams for all schoolchildren in Burma, the examiner to be paid fifteen cents for every pupil.

I examined so many thousands during my vacations that we managed to buy a Model T. Still most of our traveling had to be done on foot or on tiny native ponies. On a good many trips I could cover double distance; I would ride fifteen miles, leave the horse, and walk another fifteen before dark. The first time I did this I arrived in Wurraboom, halfway to Bhamo, at night, without food or bedding. The local teacher's wife, one of the most attractive Kachin women I have ever met, saw me and brought over some lovely clean blankets and sheets, killed the fatted chicken, and served me up a nice dinner with her one-year-old daughter strapped on her back. That daughter was Myi Tung Bawk, later known as M. T. Bawk, or "Big Bawk." Sixteen years later, her mother having in the meanwhile died of tuberculosis, Big Bawk came to us for training.

That same year, the wife of the most attractive Kachin man I have ever met had a daughter born by the breech. They called her Bawk, too: Maru Bawk, alias "Little Bawk." When she was seventeen, she also entered the nursing school. Bawk is the given name, or rather number. Big Bawk was number-two girl of the Myi Tung family, and Little Bawk was number-two girl of the Maru family. I used to see Big Bawk occasionally on my trips to Bhamo. I saw Little Bawk all the time. She went to school across the street and used to play around with Ruth Sword. They had been playing with my eldest son on the morning of the day he was drowned.

A couple of years later a Shan family moved down from China and settled in our Christian village. They had a skinny little daughter named Koi: "the last one." I can always get a rise out of Koi, who is now the head nurse of our unit, by asking her how her father and mother knew she was going to be the last one!

She did all her school work in our school. She has an astonishing brain. I asked her to let me look at her notes on one of my lectures once. No one knows better than myself how difficult it is to lecture in a foreign language without messing up idioms and failing to connote correctly one's real meaning. In her notes Koi had not only taken down every word I had said, but, at full speed, had changed to correct Burmese idioms and had changed a word here and there so as to get the proper connotation that I had desired. When we abandoned all our possessions in the jungle for the trek out of Burma, Koi abandoned even her last blanket, for fear she would not be able to keep up with General Stilwell, but she carted that notebook along.

When Koi comes to talk to me she can do it in either Burmese or Shan, and sometimes she even does it in English. I can never be sure just what language she is going to use. When we were at our busiest behind the Chinese Army in the Toungoo battle, her report consisted of two words which could have been either Burmese or Shan, though with meanings hundreds of miles apart. A glint came in my eye.

"Koi," I said, "what language are you speaking to me in? Shan?"

She stopped just one second to think what her word would mean if it were Shan, and then she picked up a broom and chased me out of the operating room!

Her own name gives her a lot of trouble, and the rest of us a lot of laughs. The Americans always call her "Hkoi," which, in Shan, is a very dirty word. Finally I took pity on her and told the Americans to call her Goi, which is neither Shan nor Burmese.

For twenty years our hospital had to fight to keep out of the wastebasket. The American Baptist Foreign Mission did not believe in any more large hospitals than they could possibly avoid. In Burma they believed in schools and had a number of them everywhere. For the rest they wanted the work to be evangelistic. Not only did they not encourage you to develop a large hospital practice but they encouraged you not to. One very able doctor, son of a Burma missionary, would have been in Burma had he not been told that he must promise not to develop a large hospital practice. He could have a dispensary or two, but that was all. My hospital appropriation from mission funds when I had thirty in-patients at a time was six hundred dollars. When I had two hundred in-patients it was twelve hundred dollars a year. We received also a government grant which was one thousand dollars a year from the thirty-bed stage, and was not raised until we were well over the hundred mark.

But I lived among those people and saw their misery. The nearest hospitals that ever did any surgery were at Bhamo, sixty miles west, Mandalay and Maymyo, three hundred miles southwest with jungle paths in between, Lashio, a hundred and twenty miles south, and Kunming, about six hundred miles northeast. I could understand no mission work that cared not to alleviate in a really practical way the ghastly physical misery of the people. The Student Volunteer Group for Foreign Missions had the motto, "The Evangelization of the World in This Generation." Even if you have hundreds of thousands of missionaries you can't really evangelize except by consistent work for at least three generations. The Americans aren't thoroughly evangelized yet after two thousand years. If they were, they couldn't stand the pain of the world. All in all, with my eccentric ideas of mission work, I was a thorn in the side of the Burma mission for years.

If evangelistic missionaries suffered half as much at failure to "cure" a man's "soul" as a doctor does when he can't cure the man's body, we might get somewhere. The old-time missionaries really did. They spoke the native languages like the natives. Their people's joys were their joys, and their sorrows theirs also. If the missionaries were going to have some fun they took their people along to share that fun with them. Nowadays it is the rare missionary that can speak the native languages intelligibly. When he has put in the correct number of hours of work he goes home and has his fun with other white people.

I used to be sensitive to the very general low opinion of Americans for missionaries. But how can we blame ordinary Americans for their low opinion when the pastors of the churches that send out those missionaries have a still lower opinion of them? I had been making a speech in the large Baptist Church at Ann Arbor, Michigan. The pastor liked my talk so well he felt like doing me a favor, and took me for a ride around the city in his huge Cadillac.

"Listen," he said, as we were returning, "is it true that not only are you a missionary, but also the son of a missionary?"

"Yes," I said, "and my grandfather and two great-grandfathers were also missionaries." He gazed at me in awe.

"Then how does it happen you are not an imbecile?"

In Namkham we played baseball and went on picnics with the nurses. They went with us when we took a joy ride in the car. Tiny had them over to an occasional meal and tea party.

They would come and play Monopoly and Chinese Checkers at the house. We went through their hardships with them and they went through ours with us. We were with them when they were well and took care of them when they were sick. We figuratively spanked them when they were naughty—and made them like it.

The only way we could make financial ends meet was with our fees. These would have been enormous if the hospital had been located in a city, but Namkham is just a country town with only a few wealthy people, and they are both miserly and very, very nationalistic. That is, they would pay a hundred rupees to a Shan quack, call me only when that quack had given them up for lost, and pay me five rupees—or at the outside ten.

Mr. Read, an Australian friend of mine for whom I had the most astonishing admiration, came to visit me. He loved to ride my ponies, but I couldn't arrange to ride with him myself. One night, just as he was going to bed, an obstetrics call came in from the top of the six-thousand-foot mountain behind the hospital. We went together on our two bigger ponies, and a couple of nurses trailed us on their smaller ones. We reached the village just before dawn and had a very difficult forceps delivery. While I was scrubbing up afterward he asked me how much of a fee I expected? "Well," I said, "I don't expect any. We never charge for a labor case, for I have too soft a heart for a woman in labor. But if they pay anything, it will be one rupee." Nothing happened till we were ready to mount, when a woman came running out and put into my hand just that amount: one rupee—thirty cents. But with those tiny fees, tens of thousands of them, we kept out of debt. Chinese coolies paid us nothing. Rich Chinese paid us almost enough for themselves and for the Chinese coolies. Kachins made us tiny token payments, and the Shans averaged just about what it cost to treat them.

4

We Build a Hospital

DURING OUR first five and a half years in Burma, Dr. Harper died. His church at Detroit, desiring to build a lasting memorial to him, gave us twenty thousand dollars to build a hundred-bed hospital. Tiny and I had the plans all ready. The plans called for an expenditure of forty thousand dollars. It was up to me to find the other twenty thousand in Burma. We located just enough money to make up the amount lost in exchange transferring the money from Detroit to Burma. The Mission Property Committee in Rangoon, however, was in those days quite imaginative, and they felt I could get all but one wing of the hospital with the funds at my disposal, providing I built it myself. To a man of my temperament, that was like a red rag to a bull.

We decided to make the hospital out of cobblestone, unlimited amounts being available in the river beds within two miles of the hospital site. I telegraphed to my father to buy us a ton-and-a-half truck in Rangoon, ship it loaded to Mandalay by steamer, where Tiny and I would pick it up. On our way down in the Chev, we heard disconcerting rumors that trucks were not allowed to use the Mandalay-Maymyo road; but the truck was on the steamer, and my father had thoroughly loaded it to the skies, so that we had to stop every few miles as we drove along and pick up a couple of chairs or a box that had been knocked off by the branches of the trees. When we got to the foot of the mountain, there, by the side of the road, was a sign stating that trucks with a load capacity of more than half a ton were forbidden to use the road. And here I was with a ton-and-a-half truck, and was it loaded! There was nothing for it but to do what any other good missionary would have done. I turned the truck off the side of the road into the jungle and waited till it was almost dark, and then I started up that hill as fast as I could go with my foot right on the floor of the car!

Halfway up the mountain a horn sounded behind me. A huge car wanted to get past. And to the radiator of that car was tied an English flag. The only man in Burma permitted to fly the Union Jack on his car is the governor of Burma, and there was the governor himself. Was my face red? It was so red it made the governor think I was one of those hard-drinking British Army sergeants driving an Army truck! At any rate the governor said nothing, and we got our truck out beyond Maymyo onto the dirt roads of the Northern Shan States. Those Shan States roads are made of red clay that becomes very slippery indeed when it rains. And of course it rained. It always rains when I have to travel. And how that truck could skid! Tiny was following behind me in the Chev, until she saw me turn end for end several times, and then she insisted on going first. If her husband was going to do those foolish things, she thought she could stand it better if she didn't have to look on. So she went first, I came along behind, and in the first twenty-four hours we covered twenty-five miles. But we got that truck to Namkham.

Then we began to haul stone. We hired a few coolies to

gather the stone, and then after the hospital work was done the nurses would pile on board and we would go out, throw the stones on, and haul back several loads. I asked my Chinese carpenter if he could estimate how much stone we would need. He could. He took the plans and a pencil and in a few minutes said we would need so many tons of stone. Later I discovered that if we had hauled as much stone as that Chinese carpenter told me to haul, the hospital would have been solid throughout like the pyramids!

On furlough in America I had picked up an old broken theodolite that Tiny's father had thrown away years and years before. My father and I took the theodolite, surveyed the hospital site, which was on the top of a hundred-foot hill by the side of the Bhamo branch of the Burma Road, leveled it off, and dug the foundation pits. Now we were all ready to build, but I had not the slightest idea how to begin. In my medical course in Johns Hopkins they had not taught me how to mix dental cement, even, let alone lime and sand mortar. But there was a missionary named Weeks in Moulmein who had put up a lot of fine buildings. I telegraphed him inviting him to spend his summer vacation in Namkham. He accepted, but could spare only one week. On the afternoon of the day he arrived for his "vacation" we started putting in the foundations, and by the time he left, a week later, we had one corner of the hospital built up to the tops of the windows of the lower story. Now I understood how to fasten those rocks together. His vacation had been such a success that I invited other knowledgeful missionaries to spend their vacations in Namkham. What a summer that was! At our meals together we ate and laughed so loudly they could hear us at the hospital a couple of blocks away.

Hundreds of tons of building material had to be brought in from Lashio, a hundred and thirty miles away. Tiny and I used to do this job together.

We started from Namkham at dawn and covered a hundred and thirty miles into Lashio by three in the afternoon, threw on a load of stuff, and started right back. When I became so sleepy that I couldn't drive, Tiny took the wheel. Once, after midnight, she was driving. I was sound asleep in the back of the truck with a half dozen barrels of cement. Suddenly she stopped the truck, so suddenly that the cement barrels began tumbling all about me, and screamed, "There is a tiger in the middle of the road. Wake up and shoot him." It all fitted in so well with a lovely nightmare I was enjoying that it took me some time to wake up; by which time the tiger had disappeared.

Another day at noon, we stopped just before hitting a giant leopard warming himself in the middle of the road. The leopard got up lazily and slipped over the side of the road into some bushes. I reached for my .32 rifle, got up on the hood, jerked down the lever to throw a cartridge from the magazine into the chamber, waited for the leopard to reappear. He never turned up, which was good for me because someone had unloaded the gun and stolen all the cartridges!

Aside from three good Chinese carpenters for the woodwork and, later, a fine Indian chap to do the plastering, most of our work was done by Shan and Kachin coolies, and a great deal of it by voluntary free labor. We chose half a dozen of the most intelligent and taught them to be expert masons for cobblestone work. The roof was completed just as the rains were breaking. Then we put in the electricity and plumbing. Mr. Smith, professor of physics in Rangoon, put in my Pelton wheel-dynamo outfit, but I had to do the plumbing myself. I was determined to have modern plumbing even if I had no hospital. All the piping was ordered in Rangoon, cut to what I thought were the right lengths, with both ends threaded. As long as the pipe was correct in length, it was quite easy. But when it was too long, I had trouble. I could cut the pipe to the right length, but I could not afford a set of dies to cut the threads on the end of the new pipe, so I had to pull out my hack saw and make the threads. By dint of sawing threads and fastening things together, the plumbing was all in and everything worked splendidly; but before long the whole system was stopped up from top to bottom. You see, the patients would throw not only paper but gauze dressings, sticks and even stones into the toilets. So I had to take the plumbing apart, clean it, and put it together again.

Not having to pay out half our funds to contractors, we not only completed the entire building according to the plans, but had a much more firmly constructed building, since we had used tons and tons more cement than the specifications called for.

But we had no money left for beds. All I could do was saw up the lumber from the scaffolding and use it for beds. Termite-ridden, it furnished the most wonderful hide-outs. Passing through a ward one day I saw a nurse down on her knees with a crochet hook in her hand jabbing at one of the beds. I stood by and counted. She got fifteen out of each crack!

WE BUILD A HOSPITAL

When we moved into the new hospital the nurses used the old wooden building for a home.

The new building filled up rapidly, until it was running to capacity. But we were not satisfied. We were not reaching the countless sick in the jungles who were too ill to travel. We felt we ought to have branch hospitals and dispensaries out in the wilds where we could place graduate nurses. The girls had had an overwhelming experience in the wards with the common diseases of the country so that they knew almost as much about them as I did myself, and, after all, it was those diseases they would be sent to treat. Anything unusual that they did not understand, they could send in to me. We opened three hospitals in our second period of service, one thirty miles west, one forty miles east, and one a hundred miles, as the crow flies, to the east of the Salween River. The girls were all graduate midwives as well as nurses, and the good they did was immeasurable. I had given no special obstetrical or surgical instruments to one of the girls as I felt she might not be too clever in their use. But one day she was called twenty miles away for an obstetrics case. When she arrived at the house the baby had been dead three days, wedged tight in the pelvis in the transverse position, its body decomposing very rapidly. The nurse asked for a scissors, and the family produced a rough Chinese bazaar product. With that scissors the nurse disarticulated the child's shoulder, removed the viscera, delivered the child, and the mother actually lived. Another of the nurses, faced with a similar transverse presentation but with the child still living, propped her obstetrics notebook up on the floor, scrubbed, made the husband pour chloroform, and delivered a live baby.

In the last year of our second term of service, an insignificant-appearing road was built for automobiles, running north from our Lashio-Namkham road to Chefang, in China, a total distance of about thirty miles. The Lashio-Namkham road was also continued over an enormous suspension bridge to Bhamo, the head of shipping on the Irrawaddy. These roads ran right through our hospital's sphere of influence. We hoped the road would continue north to Chefang and Mangshi, but didn't suppose it ever would.

PART TWO
BURMA ROAD

5

Mudholes and Precipices

1937—We came back from America with an X-ray and a lot of brand new surgical instruments. I hoped I was done with my specialization in wastebasket surgery.

Namkham was growing by leaps and bounds. Japan and China were having an "incident." China was pushing a road through from Kunming to our border, working feverishly at both ends and in the middle as well. Already our road had reached Mangshi. I hoped an "incident" would occur that would give me an excuse to travel up by car as far as the road was completed. It occurred. A telegram came in from Teng-yueh saying that a China Inland Mission lady at Longling, twenty miles north of Mangshi, was ill with pneumonia and wanted me to come and take care of her. She had previously been a patient of mine in Namkham, and Tiny and I had both been very fond of her; but I didn't need that inducement. Two nurses and I started off in our second-hand Buick.

In many places the road was only six inches wider than the car, with tremendous precipices dropping away from the side of the road. Occasionally there were huge overhanging boulders, and we had to put down the roof and fold over the windshield. Beyond Mangshi no bridges had been built. So we had to leave the car. We drove into the grounds around the Mangshi palace, and my friend, the sawbwa, was luckily at home. It was late so he put us up for the night and, the next morning, started us off on three of the smallest native ponies it has ever been my ill luck to ride.

We took an occasional short cut, but our mule path was along the route followed by the new motor road. Even on that short stretch of road there must have been ten thousand coolies at work. The hillsides were black with them: Chinese, Shans, Kachins. Huge goiters hampered their work. Dozens were lying by the road shaking with fever. Hundreds had sore eyes. A few, totally blind, were nevertheless dragging bamboo sleds on which others had dumped earth. In the rockiest parts coolies were tediously drilling holes in the hard limestone cliffs in which crude gunpowder could be packed for blasting. There was no dynamite. Every few minutes there was an outbreak of yelling and screaming and the coolies rushed aside as a muffled explosion shook the valley. Boulders bounded down the hillsides, often narrowly missing us. If a cooly failed to run at the warning, it was just too bad; but the work went on. Where the limestone was softer, hundreds of coolies picked at it with pickaxes, chipping off an inch or two at a time. Ants on a hillside! But ants work together, and what they can't accomplish!

The banian is a sacred tree to the Buddhist Shans. In the deep jungles, miles away, were huge trees of stronger wood that would have made much better bridges, but there was no time to spare. Banian wood is good for nothing. But these trees had been planted right along the roads, near the streams, to give shade and comfort to travelers; the branches are gigantic. Shans resented destruction of the sacred trees, but the road had to go through. Hundreds of these banian trees were being chopped down; bridges were being made.

MUDHOLES AND PRECIPICES

As we climbed up out of Mangshi we left behind the Shan States of China. Now we are entering Chinese China. Graves, graves everywhere! Sacred ancestors! Nothing had ever been permitted to disturb those cemeteries during the centuries; but the road must go through! The Japs were pressing in. There was still the railroad from Indo-China to Kunming, but the generalissimo was looking ahead. This road must go through! Cemeteries got in the way. They cut right through them, disinterring the bones of the sacred ancestors. China was looking backward over her shoulder no longer. She was actually looking ahead in a big way that Americans could have been proud of; but Americans were imitating the ancient Chinese in those years. They were not only selling scrap iron; but they were shipping droves of the best American mechanics to Japan to help her start airplane factories.

The road went through Kachin country, with its sacred groves of trees dedicated to the *nats*—groves so sacred to those spirits that Kachins never dared enter them. If the British had been building the road, they would have avoided trespassing at all hazards. I mean hazards! They would have had sharp turns to right and to left, blind corners, deep cuts. But China was awake at last. Japan was pushing in and the road must go through. *Nat* altars and shrines were chopped down. There was something bigger than *nats* in the offing!

But to me, the most extraordinary thing about "the Road," as I saw it that day, was not the number of coolies toiling with pick and shovel and crowbar. I had seen that before. It was not the lack of reverence for banian trees, cemeteries, and *nat* altars. I had felt impatience at these sacred things, too. The extraordinary thing to me was the marvelous surveying job that had been done—the wonderful grading of that road. They were steep grades, as steep as a road should ever have, but they were steady! There was a reason for the steepness of each. The work had been done, not by some amateur who had been given the job because he couldn't be used by the government elsewhere, but by a man who understood surveying. I couldn't believe my eyes. Surely, the Chinese had just accidentally made the grading perfect!

Amazed, and very deeply impressed with the new road, we pulled into Longling Town and, after much effort, discovered the home of the sick missionary. She had right lobar pneumonia and was very ill. But, as usual, I had the breaks. One of the nurses, tired as she was, went on duty while the other got a few hours of sleep. For no reason at all, as far as I was concerned, the patient within four hours had a favorable crisis. In twenty-four hours she was so far along the road to recovery that there was no point in our staying further. When her companion missionary thanked me for my marvelous cure, however, I remained silent. If she thought my arrival had helped the patient, so much the better. There is no point in opening your mouth when you have nothing to say!

We returned to Namkham the second morning. Two months later the Burma Road was completed into Longling, and Tiny and I and three missionary guests drove all the way there to visit our pneumonia patient. Driving there in the morning and returning that same night, we reached Namkham about two the next morning. The head nurse heard the car and came to meet us under the big banian. Some Palongs had come to call me for a transverse presentation over on the far side of our seven-thousand-foot ridge. I could get within ten miles of the village by using the car for the first fifty miles. Three nurses and a couple of men went along. We sang at the top of our voices, hoping thereby to keep me from falling asleep as I drove. Just before dawn we parked the car in a small village and began the ten-mile climb. I had fallen asleep riding ponies. I had fallen asleep driving cars, much to the car's detriment. But I had never fallen asleep while I was walking. This was my first experience. But the whole trip was useless. The woman had delivered her own baby. It was one of those very rare cases of spontaneous birth of a transverse presentation. We slept an hour and then went home.

Then came graduation time—the most hectic of the year: nurses being nursed through their preparation for the government examinations, then being distributed to their several stations for work. The government examinations in Lashio and the breaking of the monsoon occur simultaneously every year during the first two weeks of May.

On our way to Lashio we found government coolies throwing earth on the graveled road, to a depth of nine and ten inches to raise the road level. Sixty miles of this would be pretty ghastly for travel purposes if it should rain before our return, and this was likely, as two of our nurses had to be taken to our hospital east of the Salween and installed in their work there before I could start back.

The examinations went off well. On the afternoon of the last day we returned as far as Hsenwi Town, left the two nurses who were to join our Namkham staff and, with a broken center bolt in one spring, pushed on to the Salween. Arriving on the great river's bank at midnight, we tried to get a little much-needed sleep under adverse circumstances. The back seat being full of luggage, the two nurses curled up semierect in the front seat, and I took up a precarious position on the running board. The mosquitoes were ghastly. Not far away there was a tiger who seemed most provoked about something. Every few minutes he let forth a monstrous roar, and the nurses would jump as if they had been shot. Personally, the nurses worried me more than the tiger; but my real nightmare was snakes. All in all I was glad to see daylight. We boiled coffee and then crossed the Salween in dugout canoes.

From the far bank we traveled on ponies furnished by the sawbwa of Kokang. One more night on the way and we reached our hospital. When we first began the work in Kokang the hospital was a grass shack, but, the work developing rapidly in importance, the sawbwa had, during my absence in America, built us a new hospital of sun-baked brick with a tile roof. That night I slept in a tiny tent furnished by the sawbwa, and I had barely climbed into bed before the rain came down in sheets, through the canvas, soaking me to the skin. Now I was in for it. I had to start back and start at once, or I would never be able to drive the Buick into Namkham for the rains. The *myosa* furnished me two fresh ponies, and, riding them alternately at a rapid pace, I reached the Kunlong ferry at about four. My speed was increased by the fact that when we came to steep descents, the ponies just set their four feet and slid. Occasionally, if the slope was so uneven that there was danger of their falling with me, I dismounted and did the sliding under my own steam, erect, prostrate, or prone, as luck would demand.

On the west bank of the Salween I met a British captain who was as anxious as I to get back to civilization. He had an

MUDHOLES AND PRECIPICES

Indian soldier and a cook. I offered him a ride and he accepted. We started right off, luckily passing several places where more than half the road had already been washed away after only twenty-four hours' rain. The Buick just managed to squeeze by. As soon as we began to climb I put on four chains, every two or three miles having to stop and repair them with wire. First one and then another of the chains disappeared in the mud, and I replaced them with spares. On the steeper grades the three men pushed. The cook was worth nothing, but the British officer and his orderly were worth four normal men. The last five miles to the top of the Salween-Irrawaddy divide are so steep that you have to use low gear to ascend even in dry weather, and the rain was still pouring! Only the two rear wheels had chains now. The officer and his two men rode not at all on this five-mile stretch. They would push me to a start and then trudge along after me while the Buick struggled along, skidding this way and that until suddenly it slipped to the edge of the precipice and I was forced to stop and wait for them to catch up and give me another start. At last we reached the bungalow a half mile from the top. The road from there was reputed to be graveled. Sure that he could hop a truck there next day, the officer elected to stop and get some sleep. It was then two in the morning. I decided to go on alone. A few yards short of the top my right rear tire blew out. It was still pouring rain. The batteries of my flashlight were so worn out that I could not release the much battered chains. Praying this time in only two languages—I forgot to sing—I climbed into the back seat and slept until dawn.

Putting on my spare wheel I decided to go through Hsenwi to Lashio and buy a new set of chains before picking up the nurses and returning to Namkham. It was a good thing I did for from Kutkai on we were ploughing through deep mud—the embryonic Burma portion of the Burma Road. The hundred and ten miles from Lashio to Muse required eighteen hours. Again at two o'clock in the morning, "zero hour" for me, we started across the Muse plain, when suddenly the two front wheels plunged over the bank of a three-foot deep and eight-foot wide river that had appeared from nowhere. This time I quit; but the nurses walked back, awoke some villagers who dug away the bank under the car, sloped down both banks of the new stream enabling us to get across. At Selan we slept the two hours that remained before dawn and then began the last twelve miles home.

6

We Build a Nurses' Home

THAT YEAR the hospital was filled to overflowing. We placed mats on the floors between the old wooden beds and iron beds that I had had made in Rangoon. The nursing school had grown till there was not sufficient room for all the nurses in the old hospital building. With great days in the offing it would be the worst thing for the government if we had to shut down part of our hospital and decrease the number of nurses on account of lack of funds. Days were coming when every hospital bed and every trained nurse would be needed. I wrote to the commissioner of the Federated Shan States, Mr. P. C. Fogarty, whom I had never met, and put the case as clearly as I could. I requested a grant of five thousand dollars for a clinic for women and children, and asked that our annual grant of one thousand dollars for hospital expenses be doubled.

Ten days later Mr. Fogarty appeared unexpectedly at Namkham. When I met him I asked if he would like to look over the hospital; but no, he must talk to me in my office first. There, his face grim, he drew out my letter. I had made some astonishing demands, he told me. Surely I didn't think that, without taking the matter up with the Defense Department at Rangoon, so large a grant as this could possibly be made. The Department would insist on very convincing facts being presented to support my case. I told him I realized all those details and was prepared to furnish any facts he required. After securing various statistics from our books, he finally consented to go on a tour of the hospital. He was astounded at the amount of surgery, the extent of pediatric work, the large number of cases of venereal disease of all sorts being treated in the same wards as the other patients. But nothing can describe his amazement as he went through the women's ward and saw women, with all manner of diseases, being treated on the floor as well as on the beds.

"Why don't you have more iron beds?" he asked.

"No money, sir," I replied.

"How much do they cost?"

"About twelve rupees for the welded iron in Rangoon. We rivet the pieces together ourselves in Namkham."

"Would three hundred rupees help you out?"

"Yes, sir."

He walked on to the row of smaller rooms intended for one patient. There were four to six women patients on the floor of each.

"I'll send you five hundred rupees."

A week later we got a check for seven hundred and fifty! Mr. Fogarty took up the question of building grants with the Defense Department. Things like that take time. We kept getting more and more crowded. Then, one day stopping in Kutkai on our way back from an urgent trip to Lashio in the Buick, we learned that that very morning the two chiefs of the Defense Department had gone through to Namkham, with the idea of looking over our hospital for a couple of hours before returning for a short trip up the Burma Road. They had an hour's start on us. Tiny and I jumped into the car. There were too many things at stake. If we could catch up with them and give them a personally escorted tour of the hospital they might become convinced of the importance of the work and help us. Otherwise we were certain we would fail to get any grant at all. An hour after leaving Kutkai, the rubber-hose connection on the water system sprung a leak. We had to keep our eyes open for water and fill up, at first, every ten miles, then every five, and finally every single mile, waiting each time for the overheated engine to cool down before adding water. It was one of the slowest trips we ever made from Kutkai to Namkham.

Ten miles out from Namkham, as we were filling the radiator, a car approached us; two gentlemen descended and introduced themselves as the Defense Department secretaries. They expressed their polite regrets that we had not been in Namkham and stood chatting about the hospital, the Burma Road, and the possibilities of the road ever being completed. They went on. Tiny and I looked hopelessly at each other. Our luck hadn't held this time.

But two months later, approval was given for a grant toward the nurses' home, payable at once, and one for the women's clinic building the following year. Close on the arrival of this notification came a personal letter from Mr. Arthur K. Potter, one of the two secretaries. A ten thousand rupee personal check dropped out. The money, said Mr. Potter, was a much-too-small effort on his part to help us in the development of our program of medical work in the Northern Shan States. There were no "strings" tied to the gift. It was to be used in any way calculated to be of most permanent value. We deposited the money in the bank as a buffer fund to save the hospital from any debt liable to occur if we pursued our policies of medical development forcefully. Tremendously encouraged and emboldened by the availability of this fund we went ahead, drawing on it when in trouble, and repaying funds into it as we received occasional windfalls from grateful patients. But word leaked out among the Kachins that Mr. Potter's gift had amounted to a hundred thousand rupees, and thereafter they paid even less price in hospital fees than before.

So in the rainy season of 1938, Tiny and I sat down and drew up plans for a two-story nurses' home. She made suggestions from a woman's, and I from a structural, point of view. As we were drawing the plans, we had in the hospital a patient from the royal family of Mangshi State. Representatives of both Mangshi and Chefang were continually visiting this patient, so Tiny and I used every opportunity, in and out of season, to describe our program to them, emphasizing our difficulties in putting up the nurses' building. We even gave them practical demonstrations. With a great deal of effort I repaired our old ton-and-a-half truck until it could run—sometimes—and converted our Chev touring car into an ugly half-ton truck. Day by day they saw nurses jump on board after the day's work and help haul stone. They were so astonished that they even volunteered to help load and unload. Luckily for us the two cars broke down several times when these people were helping us and, members of royal families though they were, they had to walk home. Soon after they left the hospital, a rumor filtered down that the sawbwa of Mangshi would like to lend us two new three-ton trucks to haul stone as his contribution to the hospital work. Rumor though it was, I promptly hired the Shan who had helped drive my truck when we were building the main hospital, and we started north over the Burma Road that night. The rainy season was just over, and there was plenty of mud to plough through.

The sawbwa was very gracious. Dinner was just being served and he wanted us to join him. As we were disposing of a fifteen-course Chinese meal I told him of the rumor and of our very great need for the assistance he was ready to give.

"But you have no drivers," he objected.

"Yes, I have, and they are both here, ready to start in the morning."

That was so typically American that it floored him completely.

"All right," he said. "The two trucks will be ready in the morning." He seemed to like Americans, for in the morning it was three trucks instead of two, and the sawbwa furnished his own driver for the third truck. He went the Americans one better!

Nine tons at a time instead of a ton and a half! We had to haul rapidly, for when the country really dried out after the rains, the sawbwa would need the trucks to fulfill his responsibilities in the construction of the Burma Road. When the Shan driver finished a day's work, Tiny took his truck and we continued to haul.

Knowing that with the completion of the nurses' home we would begin the construction of the women's building, we took time by the forelock and began leveling the site of the latter. Tons of earth had to be removed. Trained in wastebasket surgery, we felt that that waste earth should be put where it would do some good. Where could we put it? Our only remaining dream was a decent little stone bungalow for us to live in, where we could be properly screened from the mosquitoes that constantly made havoc of our work. We had the site already picked out on the little hill beyond the hospital. We could use the waste earth as a fill for a future road connecting the hospital with the doctor's residence. Wouldn't it make things quicker all around if I hauled the earth there in the truck whenever there was no stone ready? I tried it out, loaded on three tons of earth and backed down the incline that we had begun years ago, with the same purpose, when we were leveling the site of the main hospital. Just as I reached the predetermined point, I braked suddenly. The right rear wheel broke through into a two-foot deep termites' nest, and the loaded truck turned over one complete roll and landed "on its feet" in a bunch of bamboos. I love bamboos! If it had not been for them I would have rolled over fifteen more times.

I was rather dazed. That was *one* experience I had never had before! While I was sitting there, feeling more or less battered, a bunch of nurses who had heard the terrible crash rushed out of the hospital with the cadaver stretcher to pick up the old man's dead body. When they saw him sitting there in the driver's seat, still alive, they flung down the stretcher and went back to their respective jobs. Tiny heard a rumor that her husband had been up to mischief again and came running down to see whether he was still alive. He was. Tiny ran back home again, and I sat on, feeling more or less neglected, and ached, and ached.

Finally my Lahu mechanic turned up. He was most solicitous, and his sympathy stirred me to action.

"Get all the schoolboys and all our coolies and a big rope," I directed, "and pull me out of this."

When they were quite ready I started the engine, and with the men and the nurses, who had by this time begun to realize that the old man was in a bad way, pulling simultaneously, I drove back up onto the road. I was happy again, for the truck had not been hurt at all, except for one small dent in the fender, which we straightened forthwith.

I hauled no more earth for the fill. I let the coolies do it in their little bamboo baskets.

Finally we were ready to build.

On the site we had chosen for the nurses' home were two mat-walled houses on stilts, the bottoms of the posts resting on cut-stone blocks. We had to get them out of the way and still have them available for use for private patients who were always complaining that we had not enough private rooms. Some of us jacked up the house and put long wooden runners under the posts, connecting them to each other. Others cut down trees of appropriate girth and sawed them in four-foot-long rollers. Every rope in both the Shan and Kachin compounds was commandeered and fastened to the cottage at strategic points. The Shan and Kachin schoolboys turned out for a field day. One pull, and a rope broke! The house did not budge! We had no windlass, and the pulls were, of necessity, jerky. I rigged up a block and tackle and we tried again. This time the house went so far as to shudder. The yelling of the schoolchildren had caused half the town of Namkham to turn out for the show. Someone told me there was a Public Works Department rope in the government bungalow, and someone else said my friend, the Chinese contractor in town, had another. We got them both and tried again. Now the house was convulsed, but still wouldn't move forward. As usual, I had to give in and send for the nurses. They crowded up to the far side of the house, and as the males pulled, the females pushed, and the house plunged forward to the ends of the runners. Then we inserted new rollers and, plunging this way and that, we slid the houses around until they finally and very accidentally happened to fall into their right places, with an error of not more than two inches. That was close enough for me. The discrepancy couldn't be seen unless one were looking for trouble, and if anybody had as mean a mind as that, there were plenty of other errors elsewhere that I could add to his collection! That day we were grateful for the numerous times the nurses had had to push cars and trucks through mud, in training for the day they would have to push houses.

The first wall of the nurses' home was about four feet above the ground in November, 1938. I was setting a window in place with a plumb bob, when from nowhere appeared the handsomest man I ever met. He offered me a Chesterfield. His name was Dan Gourley and he was, he said, advance agent for an American airplane manufacturing company that had been bombed out of Hangchow and Hankow and had decided to set up their factory in Kunming. While settling in Kunming, Japan had begun to bomb that city also, so they had determined to find that spot in China, farthest from Japan, which still had possibilities for easy transportation. On the map, the Namkham valley seemed the most promising. He had been referred to me as the man best acquainted with the valley. Would I be willing to help him locate some spot where nature facilitated the building of runways above the level of the paddy fields?

Great Scott! an airplane factory in the Namkham valley!

He did not look like the confounded liar he seemed to be from the context of his speech.

"The company sent me from Haiphong to Rangoon by plane," he said. "The manager of the factory, Mr. Hunter, is trying to come through from Kunming by car over the Burma Road. I want, if possible, to have a satisfactory site picked out for the factory before he arrives. I would appreciate your help."

By this time my eyes began to focus again.

"Yes, I can help you," I said. "There is a perfect low plateau the other side of the river, on Chinese soil. I delivered a baby in the village there just last week. It is a natural landing field." I threw down the unromantic plumb bob. "Come over to the office. I have an inch-to-the-mile map there, and I can show you just where it is."

I spread out the map and showed him my choice, as well as two other plateaus, much smaller, but closer to the Burma border. Then I took him to the hospital verandah and pointed out the actual spots in the distance.

The next morning, armed with the map and an English-speaking Shan guide whom I furnished, Mr. Gourley set out to explore. He returned delighted.

"Your first suggestion is a perfect spot," said he, "but it is too far from that little spur of the Burma Road. I have selected the two other sites. They are within a quarter mile of the border and we will have no trouble transporting our supplies."

Mr. Gourley returned to Rangoon. We went on building the nurses' home, not quite sure why Gourley had tried to excite us.

Then, one day, a station wagon, the first I had ever seen, drew up under the banian tree. A thick-set, muscular man stepped out. It was Mr. "Chuck" Hunter, manager of the Central Aircraft Manufacturing Company. He had come down the Burma Road from Kunming as far as the Salween River and then, one day's journey by car from his goal, had had to turn back to Kunming and come to Burma by air. There were Chinese engineers with him. After paying his compliments, he went across the river to Pang Kham, the English bungalow nearest the chosen site at Loiwing, and set up headquarters in a grass shack.

Though their headquarters were so close to us, they were busy and we were busy and we did not see much of each other.

Ever since the first year in Namkham, Tiny had had a vegetable garden near our house where she had experimented with seed procured from all over India and Burma, finding varieties of American and English vegetables that would grow in our climate and determining the seasons when each variety did best. As she succeeded in her work she extended the area under cultivation until we were well supplied with the most delicious corn, tomatoes, head lettuce, celery, carrots, and sweet potatoes that it had ever been our good fortune to eat. They were at least as good as similar vegetables purchasable in America. Now, her period of experimentation over, she ploughed up several acres of farm land owned by the mission and began to grow vegetables for the nurses and even for the hospital. Some of the new vegetables, like carrots, the nurses had to acquire a taste for; others they recognized at once as having a much fuller and more delicious flavor than their own home-grown foods. Tiny had even started a pineapple garden in which she produced fruit from imported Hawaiian plants several times as juicy, sweet, and tender as the local natives could produce. Seldom a day went by when the chief gardener did not carry several bushels of assorted vegetables and fruits down to the hospital kitchens. Now with homesick Americans in the valley Tiny began to pick baskets of "first-fruits" and take them over to Loiwing. The airplane company reciprocated by lending us an occasional truck overnight to haul the tons of manure that grateful patients presented to us in the near-by villages. The word *awza* in Burmese means either "manure" or "prestige." Ai Lun, who married E Hla, didn't know the latter English word and so, when called on to make a speech at the wedding dinner Tiny gave them, really succeeded beyond all expectation.

"It takes a lot of manure to change the son of poor people into a medical-college student," he said, "and Doctor Seagrave furnished the manure."

I will never hear the last of that one!

7

Journey to Kunming

A TELEGRAM came from Rangoon. Several important Baptist Mission secretaries had been attending a "World's Alliance" meeting in South India. They wanted to get into West China for some more meetings, and had heard there was a new road from Burma to Kunming. They wished to go over that new road. Would I drive them to Kunming? I certainly would! I had wanted an excuse to go over that road to Kunming myself. Besides we had a brand new Dodge as the result of the Potter Fund, since the Buick was ruined.

The two secretaries arrived one evening, and we started the next morning. Tiny and John and I rode in the front, the secretaries and their baggage behind. The Bhamo branch of the Burma Road to the border was the worst section of the whole road. Before we got to the border we had bashed in the bottom of the petrol tank, but luckily it didn't leak. We had to carry enough petrol to get us to Kunming. After we had reached the border, the road began to get better. The British had not been able to believe that the Chinese would really keep their promise, and so had delayed carrying out theirs. Later the British section was the better.

The first night we slept with my friend, the sawbwa of Mangshi. He introduced us to the central government's officials, who visaed our passports and gave us a card with Chinese writing on it which was worth more than our passports.

The next morning we pushed on to Longling and waited hours on customs. We had to make a deposit of the price value of the car to guarantee that we would not sell it in Kunming. Thanks to the Chinese writing on the card, the Dodge was "valued" at about a third of its real worth, since that was all the money I had!

We pushed on, hoping to make Paoshan before nightfall. That gorgeous Salween divide! Up, up, up out of Longling, and then you can see, way over the other side of the Salween, a snaky road curving, in most dramatic fashion, up a gigantic mountain. It takes hours to get to the road, over there, where it reaches the top of that mountain. We started down a series of ghastly precipices, the road getting narrower and narrower. Then we passed the fifty-mile mark on our speedometer, and it was Tiny's turn to drive. Tiny is the only driver who can drive me without my getting sick; but this time I had to close my eyes and swallow and swallow! One of the secretaries offered to drive. I refused with thanks. It was bad enough with Tiny, and I knew what a wonderful driver Tiny was, from long experience. I was taking no chance on strange drivers.

The beauty of that gorge: fearful, terrifying beauty! All along its course, the Salween is fierce and cold. In no part that I have seen is it as beautiful as along the Burma Road. We saw it at its best. There was no other traffic. We owned the Burma Road that day—we and the ragged Chinese coolies who threw their baskets of gravel on the road and patted it into a smooth surface with their hands. Along the road were rollers, cut from huge blocks of stone, and hauled either by coolies or by a single water buffalo. I shall never forget those coolies of the Burma Road, men and women. Men with nothing on but a pair of ragged pants full of holes so large that the trousers did not hide their nakedness. And they smoothed the road with their hands! Little loving pats! We were glad we had taken John along that day. The first little white boy these Chinese coolies had ever seen! The women coolies oh-ed and ah-ed over John. Undoubtedly their long, hard day's work was made easier for them that day. They had something new to talk about.

And so to the suspension bridge across the Salween. I had seen the huge iron sections of that bridge carried up over the Burma Road—before it was a car road at all. All the passengers dismounted while I drove over. Could that flimsy structure that sagged under the weight of a single man hold our Dodge? It not only could hold the Dodge, but it held many a four-ton truck loaded illegally heavily in the days that were to come. Country of romance! The Burma Road has become romantic to the American of the street during the last two years. I was traveling through country that had been romantic to me for fifteen years! Many of our patients had come from this country.

Tiny had had enough of that drive down to the river. I drove up the other side, a much easier task than hers had been. Paoshan was endless, miles away, yet we had to stop every few minutes while the two secretaries took pictures. At least, one of them took pictures with a camera; the other took pictures with his eyes, disappearing suddenly so that we could never tell where he was. Closer to Paoshan we came upon a couple of old-time Chinese, high-arched bridges which the low-slung Dodge could not negotiate without special care, blocking of wheels with stones, etc. About dark, we reached Paoshan. What a relief! With much difficulty we located the house of the China Inland Mission where we hoped to spend the night. They had heard of me from my old pneumonia patient and made us welcome, cooking us some eggs and Chinese ham for dinner, though we were almost too tired to eat. I slept in the Dodge that night.

From Paoshan the road has to descend again to cross a river almost as low as the Salween—the Mekong. Not so fierce in its beauty, the Mekong River is probably the more beautiful. At least you can see more beauty at one time. Descending, we passed our first groups of surveyors and engineers at work, many of whom had been trained in America. The road and its steady grades was not just an accident after all! The trail reaches the Mekong and then follows along the bank for miles before crossing on another apparently frail suspension bridge. Now comes drama! The car climbs out of the Mekong along one tributary after another, each turn opening up new vistas of entirely different scenery. The grade becomes steeper and steeper, until, the radiator of the car boiling madly, the top is reached—a pass two thousand feet higher than those on the great transcontinental roads that cross the Rockies.

We knew of no mission station along this day's route and had a definite repugnance for the idea of sleeping in the old Chinese inn of that day. A corner of the road seemed much more romantic for a place to sleep. Both of the secretaries were so long-legged that they chose to spread their bedrolls out on the ground. Marion curled up on the front seat, I on the back, and John just fitted in between us on the floor. Everything was simply grand, until Tiny let her knee fall on the horn button, bringing everyone to attention. Surely the Japs were upon us!

There is no end to amazement as the car keeps rolling to the east. The Salween and the Mekong gorges have not exhausted the scenic possibilities. No wonder we froze that night! Climbing still higher from our night camp, thick frost and new-formed ice crunched under our wheels. Here and there a little flurry of snow, and then, against a clear blue sky, the snow-capped peaks behind Talifu. Wild mountain torrents pouring into the Red River. Our first vision of Chinese Army recruits marching east to join the forces in action against the Japanese. The heavenly blue of the great lake at Tali. An hour strolling through a huge Chinese bazaar. Tibetans on the streets. Then night in a warehouse of the Southwest Transportation Company.

On from Tali the road is an older one, built before the Japanese "incident." There are other cars traveling here. Care must be taken to avoid collision around sharp corners. Much more open spaces. Densely cultivated valleys. More frequent towns. Salt factories. Coolies with heavy blocks of salt on shoulder harness trudging up and down the road. A coffin with some distinguished dead being carried home by coolies to be buried with his fathers. A last night in a brand new inn of the variety being built by the Southwest Transportation Company for travelers on the Road, and then, after a last climb, the lake of Kunming spreads out, with fabled Kunming itself beyond.

We found a French hotel, left our things there, and made a hurried trip around town. I paid a pilgrimage to the C.M.S. (Church Missionary Society) hospital, the nearest mission hospital to us in Namkham; to the bazaar for food for the return trip and for gasoline. Tiny, John, and I must start back before dawn.

Not having to stop every few minutes for pictures to be taken, we made the return trip in three days.

A letter appeared in the post one morning—an application from a young Karen doctor named Ba Saw. After graduating from the medical school of Rangoon University he had developed tuberculosis and had been refused a government position. Months at Taunggyi, in the Southern Shan States, had improved his condition very greatly. If I could arrange to take him on as an interne he would, he said, be glad to work without pay. He was the son of Karen missionaries to the Chins of the wild mountains of West Burma. I was fed up with all my previous assistant doctors, whether Kachin, Indian, or Karen. Since they had each passed the Rangoon University examinations, sometimes on the third or fourth try, they knew it all and were not willing to learn more. Give them a chance to operate and they were too proud to study up on the operation the night before, no matter what happened to the patient! Not knowing much myself, after passing my examinations the first time at Johns Hopkins and zealously studying every book I could find for sixteen years, I was apt to be a bit impatient at their "complete" knowledge. But I couldn't do all the routine work myself.

Ba Saw came. His right lung was collapsed with a pleural effusion. I ordered him to work no longer than a maximum of four hours a day. It was the only order I gave him that he ever disobeyed. With only one lung he was forever on the job. No matter what nurses you put on his side in a baseball game he would lead them to victory over my side three games out of every four. Whether he was to do the operation himself or not, he would get out his and my books on operative surgery and study up the next day's operation. A man of completely charming personality. A man whom both men and women love. A perfect Christian, he didn't have a trace of hypocrisy anywhere in his make-up. No fancy phrases and slogans. No prudery. Incapable of exhibiting anger, though capable of deep indignation at the mean things of this world.

I have taught Ba Saw a lot. He has taught me a lot also and continues to teach me.

I gave him ten dollars a month spending money from the start. Six months later I had to argue with him for a long time before he would let me raise him to twenty dollars. A few days before Christmas he came to the office and shamefacedly asked for a loan of a hundred rupees. Every cent went into Christmas presents for nurses and schoolteachers. A year with us, and inevitably romance sprang up between Ba Saw, the most charming Karen male I had ever met, and head nurse Bella, about the sweetest Karen girl you could hope to find! Tiny and I were delighted. In 1941 they had a lovely wedding. As long as I live, may they both remain on our staff!

Construction had begun at the airplane factory seven miles across the plain. Their trucks began to haul supplies up from Bhamo. One night nurses came running for me. One of the Americans at the factory had just been brought in in an Indian truck. His truck and trailer had crashed down a mountainside. The cab had been crushed completely, and he had remained in the valley for hours until the Indian happened along and picked him up. He had recovered from a mild concussion when I saw him and his delight at falling into the hands of an American doctor was pitiful! Tiny came and helped me tuck him into bed. An American woman tucking him in! Unbelievable! He broke down and sobbed. Later I saw the curve where his truck had dropped. He was lucky to get off with only a concussion and a deep gash in his thigh.

8

The Plague

Food trucks passing from Bhamo to Namkham in five hours when heretofore such articles had taken five days on mules . . . A tremendous fire breaks out in the Bhamo bazaar and destroys half the native town . . . Rats leave the burning houses and have a difficult time finding sufficient food . . . Trucks loaded with food are standing ready to start for Namkham in the morning and the rats leap aboard . . . A month later rats are dying in Namkham by the hundreds . . . Householders pick them up by the tails where they drop on the floor and throw them out into the garden, and the bubonic plague comes to Namkham for the first time in eighty years. Virgin country! I telegraphed for enough plague vaccines for our entire staff and wondered when the first case would appear.

Almost immediately I was called. The patient had been ill since the night before. By the time I reached the house he was dead. He had died so rapidly after the onset that there was no sign of disease on his face. Two rather large ecchymoses on his body were all the signs of plague I could find. The next day another patient was dead in the adjacent house, and in two days three in this second house had died. All of them were cases of septicemic plague. I telegraphed the civil surgeon in Lashio and the assistant superintendent in Kutkai. I sent our staff through the town urging people to be vaccinated and personally urged vaccination on the lord mayor. Aside from the Chinese community, led by a very intelligent Chinese friend of mine, everyone refused vaccine. We telegraphed for vaccine for the Chinese. Plague cases appeared all over. Rats began to drop dead from the ceiling. Down the street rats would run and fall over dead in front of you. Rats dropped on a group of nurses delivering a labor case in the town. Lashio had done nothing. I telegraphed the superintendent in Lashio himself, asking for a free supply of vaccine from the government, as I could not afford giving free injections by the thousands when each one cost me ten cents. The civil surgeon complained to the superintendent that Seagrave was just having hysterics. Plague was endemic everywhere and not epidemic, and there was nothing to get excited about. Under compulsion from the superintendent, permission was granted for me to order all the vaccine I wanted, bills to be sent to the government. Shans refused to be injected, though by now cases were taking forty-eight hours to die, and they died with terminal plague pneumonia. I wired Lashio again and under pressure from the superintendent, the sawbwa issued an order ordering everyone in the plains to be vaccinated. Then true bubonic plague appeared.

We set a time favorable to the lord mayor and, with a corps of nurses to assist, we started inoculations in a big way. The lord mayor submitted first, but the germs were already in him and in two days he developed bubonic plague and died. We injected more than half of the people in town. Many of those ordered for vaccination refused to appear. The plague began to search out their homes and many of those who had refused vaccination died. Where all but one in a house had been vaccinated, the one unvaccinated person acquired the disease and died.

But occasionally a person who had been vaccinated acquired the disease, and a small per cent even of those died. The nurses and I were constantly exposed to the disease, using every treatment in the books—and out of them, for that matter—to try to save lives. I decided to use a second injection of 3 c.c. of the vaccine on our staff. My luck never holds, when it comes to trying to avoid work. After each injection, an obstetrics call would come in and I would have to foot it all over the valley, febrile reaction and all.

Plague began to appear in near-by villages. With the local police to help, we went out to give injections in those villages. The first day was completely wasted. Villagers had heard that we were coming and had evacuated. Not one person was at home. The second time this happened, I telegraphed the assistant superintendent for Kachin troops to help us. The Shans are scared to death of the Kachins. The acting mayor sent for me and begged me not to put this indignity upon him. He would guarantee that his own police would enforce our orders. We tried again with little success. Then the assistant superintendent himself arrived. He was disgusted that I had been put to so much inconvenience. The villagers must come to me. He sent out Kachin troops and arrested the headman and elders of each village where I had had trouble and threw them into jail. Our troubles were over.

Village by village they presented themselves in the bazaar at appointed times. By now the total number of deaths had reached such a number that the civil surgeon had to admit we were starting a major epidemic. The League of Nations' public health chief for China came in and demanded immediate action against a disease which, if allowed to cross the border, would by itself compel China to cease her resistance against Japan. Telegrams flew to Geneva and London.

The civil surgeon visited us to see if we knew how to do the inoculations. He sat, grim, on a seat in the bazaar and saw nurses—nurses!—giving the inoculations. At a distance, try as he might, he could see nothing wrong with their technique. But nurses could not possibly be free from mistake. A dear old Shan lady of sixty presented her arm and a nurse slipped in the needle.

"How much vaccine did you inject?" he asked the nurse, gruffly.

"Two c.c., sir," she replied. Correct! Disgusted, he stamped out to see if he could locate something else to complain about.

That afternoon he walked into my office. He had heard that I buried my Potter's Field cases so close to the surface of the ground that the dogs unearthed and devoured the bodies. I told him I would investigate and make a report that evening.

The head nurse and I walked over to our Potter's Field. Four or five graves had been broken into and the bones scattered about, but each of these burials was in a Chinese coffin. Bodies buried by me are never in a coffin. These cases had been buried by relatives. Furthermore, the coffins had not been broken into until termites had eaten through the lid of the coffin, which meant that by the time the local pariahs scattered the bones about, there was not more than an odor of meat left on the bones.

I turned in my report. The only thing he could think of was smallpox vaccinations.

"I shall have to report to the government in Rangoon," he said, "that you have charged fees for smallpox vaccinations. This is illegal."

"The government did not furnish me free vaccine," I said. "I charged just sufficient to recover the costs of the vaccine paid for by myself."

"Well, I shall have to prosecute your nurses for performing vaccinations without having taken a special three months' government course in the subject."

"No, they have had only a three years' course in subjects bearing on vaccination, and are only skilled enough in such subjects as to make government officers glad to have them assist at major operations performed on their own bodies. Furthermore," I said, "I also have performed many vaccinations without the special three months' course; so, when you prosecute the nurses, you will also please prosecute me."

Threats of prosecution were still being made more than three years later after Japanese troops had entered Burma.

That year we gave some ten thousand inoculations of plague vaccine, and as soon as the number of people injected reached 60 per cent of the population, the epidemic stopped.

But we were having real trouble ourselves now. Nurse Nang Leng and I had been trying out various injections on a pregnant plague patient. Our legs were being bitten as we injected. Three days later Nang Leng had a bubo in her groin. I made a smear from the gland which proved positive. The airplane factory had a small stock of plague antitoxin and on our urgent plea for help, sent us over a few c.c. I gave Nang Leng 10 c.c. and then started off on an obstetrics case twenty miles away. On my way there I had a peculiar pain in my right armpit. On the return trip I kept feeling that aching spot, and discovered that I had a bubo myself! I told Tiny about it and she insisted on giving me an injection of the serum. Then I came down with a huge chill and the most gorgeous headache I ever enjoyed in my life. Rats had been dying in our house, and one had died in the bookshelf behind the chair in my office. Every single child under ten that had contracted plague in the town had died, even though the child had previously been vaccinated. Tiny and I fought over the matter tooth and nail. She didn't want to leave me and I didn't want our two boys to get the disease and die. I won the argument finally; Tiny turned me over to the head nurse and took the boys out to our school in Muse for the period of quarantine, preparatory to taking them down to Maymyo and safety.

Thanks to the 6 c.c. of vaccine I had received, I was an entirely uncomplicated case. I had far more trouble with the serum reaction that followed a week later. I even went so far as to faint for the first and only time in my life.

Altogether ten of our hospital staff got the disease, but, thanks to double dosage of vaccine, all of us recovered.

The American engineers had now come and settled in Loiwing in grass shacks. Many had brought their wives. Thousands of workmen and coolies were at work under American supervision putting up one building after another and installing machine tools. A very attractive Chinese surgeon, Dr. Horace Yu, graduate of Northwestern Medical School, had come. With the help of engineers he had drawn up plans for a factory hospital, and the building was going up rapidly. Dr. Yu's very charming and beautiful wife, an American-born Chinese girl trained as a nurse in Peiping Union Medical College, joined him. Mrs. Yu and her little daughter lived in our home for several weeks. Until their hospital was completed, the factory sent all patients needing hospitalization over to us. Our financial situation, for the first time, eased off a little. Honest Americans in the valley, people who speak your own tongue! On our first visit to the grass shack, which they dignified by the title "Club," there was a chap named Al Anderson, an airplane engineer, who viewed with distress the intrusion of missionaries into the sacred precincts of the club. So, perhaps, did many of the others; but being Americans they all made us welcome. Later, when they discovered what scandalous missionaries we were, they changed their ideas of missions in general. Al himself adopted our car and every bit of machinery our hospital possessed, kept them in perfect repair, and, when any mechanism gave out completely, replaced it with a new machine ordered out from America. He soon became the Big Brother of all the nurses, for whom he was quite willing to take on all comers, ten rounds each.

After I had recovered from the plague I received a formal invitation from Messrs Hunter and Walsh, factory manager and general manager, to dinner. I knew something was up, and made up my mind to refuse. But that dinner was far too delicious. Tiny was still away with the boys and it had been a long time since I had had anything fit to eat. By the time the meal was over I had practically no resistance left! Their idea was for me to stop being a missionary and come over to run their hospital on a generous salary. I had helped order their hospital and surgical equipment and knew there were no "wastebaskets" in the list. I would be practicing medicine and surgery in the way every doctor dreams of doing. But—I liked my stupid idea of missionary work, and I had become badly spoiled by the fun of always having more work on hand than I could ever possibly do. Namkham was my brain child. Even if the American Baptist Mission sent out another missionary, or two, or three, to take my place at Namkham, it would be like divorcing an only son.

I had my alternative suggestion ready: Their job—director of the hospital—was nothing like a full-time job, and if I had no work to employ me other than holding down a chair in the grand new club building, I would soon go mad. I would spend three days a week at Loiwing and assume full responsibility for the work of the hospital, make emergency trips at any time if an American needed special work done. In the other two-thirds of my time I would continue my work at Namkham. They should pay me only a part of the salary suggested and, by mission rule, this money would be used for the Namkham hospital work. I would be able to build the little stone doctor's house Tiny and I had always wanted, and other dreams for Namkham could be realized. Both men objected, but it was a case of accept my offer or have no American doctor for their Americans, so they finally agreed.

When Tiny found out about my contract, she was furious! She wanted me to live to hoary old age, and I wanted to live fast and most furiously, no matter how soon I went on to my reward—or punishment! The only occasions when Tiny's resentment decreased were when the Americans threw a party. Tiny had had itching feet from the first time she heard a foxtrot, but her husband, the only eligible male in Namkham, was too clumsy to learn how to dance. But Leckell and Stoker had taken prizes for dancing in the States, and several of the others should have had them too.

And so thrice-weekly trips to Loiwing began, fourteen miles each way by motor road. I soon discovered that aside from my American patients, most of my work was to keep the hospital staff from resigning singly or en masse. All the Chinese engineers and workmen were from East China. Refugees driven out by Japan, all had lost their homes, and many their families. There was a very tender and delicate mental balance. The slightest suspicion of insult and the balance was lost and feuds developed. Doctors, authorized to grant leave with or without pay from factory duties, were the chief scapegoats. Dr. Yu, who refused to be intimidated into granting leave with pay to well persons, soon became their pet abomination. Doctors who preferred to distribute leaves lavishly to a smattering of gangsters, and thereby live in peace and comfort, soon became abominations to their director and had to leave. Not one week went by that I did not have to spend many hours of argument with some member of our staff. Even the medical chief demanded that a nurse be discharged, and when I refused to dismiss her for a first offense he lost so much face that the president of the company had to give him an expenses-paid trip to study in the Calcutta School of Tropical Medicine to restore his dignity. Finally, to keep some semblance of order, we had to have Chinese Army sentries patrol the halls of the hospital.

The factory was now turning out training planes.

On the first anniversary of the breaking of ground for the factory buildings, the company threw a great party. Mr. W. D. Pawley, the president, made a speech in which he called to their attention the extraordinary growth of the factory from

THE PLAGUE

grass shacks to a thriving modern plant in the incredibly short period of twelve months.

"You have seen wonderful changes in this past year," said Mr. Pawley. "I can promise you that during the year now starting you will see just as vast changes at Loiwing."

Mr. Pawley was a much better prophet than he thought. There was a vast change those next twelve months, but not quite of the variety he had planned; and the year after, the change was still more astonishing!

Soon after our nurses' home was completed in 1938, Tiny went out on an obstetrics call. It was a normal case in which a long, long wait was inevitable before the baby could be born. Tiny went into session with her pencil and a piece of paper, and came home with a gorgeous floor plan for the women's and children's clinic. It was such a divine inspiration that all we had to do was work out the dimensions and blueprint it. We built it that first eight months of 1939 before the plague put us temporarily out of commission. When the latter was over and my Loiwing work was running smoothly—all but the weekly resignations—Tiny and I both went into a huddle to put our dream house on paper. Putting dreams on paper is not too easy a job, but in a few weeks we succeeded beyond our wildest expectations and produced such a good plan that the factory engineer could only add one artistic touch to give it perfection—complete drawings for a fireplace, a small-scale model of the grand fireplace in the Loiwing Club's drawing room. Stone hauling was again the insurmountable obstacle. The factory had plenty of trucks but they were in use all the day long. Finally, the Americans found a solution. After work on Saturday, they would drive over three trucks and haul stone for us till dawn Sunday morning, if the nurses, our few coolies, and I would load the stone. Meanwhile, Bill Cummings and his family had moved to Namkham on a mission plus government agricultural project for the Kachins. Bill is just as crazy a missionary as I am and just as continually up to mischief of some sort. You can tell how crazy he is very easily—he named his youngest son Gordon Seagrave Cummings! This scheme of hauling stone all Saturday night was so insane that it appealed to him as much as it did to me. Tiny and Hazel sobbed in each other's arms, and then took turns producing us some marvelous midnight suppers!

Mr. Fogarty, the commissioner, was not idle. He had more "ants in his pants" than I had in mine. During the dry season of 1940 he had widened and paved the entire Lashio to Kyuhkok (at the border) section of the Burma Road. But he still connived with me to develop the medical services of the Northern Shan States; and that year we opened three more jungle dispensaries: one on the Burma Road, halfway from the border to Kutkai, one thirty miles east of Kutkai, and one forty miles southwest of Namkham in the state of Momeik. The nurses in charge traveled two weeks of each month through an area thirty to forty miles in diameter visiting their patients. During that first year they took no in-patients. Then, as their work proved most satisfactory, we put two nurses at each point and they began to receive in-patients as well. Our first jungle hospital at Mongpaw became a very thriving institution, and the local chiefs joined me in putting up a lovely cobblestone building there for twenty patients. Kokang was now a three-nurse institution.

The Burma Road and the Loiwing airplane factory shared

first honors for importance in Chungking. Nothing rivaled malaria as the possible cause of failure of these two projects. The United States sent out malaria experts to study our peculiar variety and to institute effective methods of prevention. They made their headquarters at Chefang and spent much time at Loiwing. Even our hospital was not beneath the dignity of their help. Our laboratory had become quite worth while, but we were not satisfied. They offered to give a special six weeks' course in malaria to our two best laboratory nurses which would not cost us a thing. E Hla and Hara came back from Chefang most efficient in their work, and they have given a two months' course to each pupil-nurse since.

Then the rains of 1940 broke. From that time on I have not had a moment's peace, and I hope I never will.

Plague broke out this time in Muse, at the upper end of the valley. One of the Loiwing workmen spent a night in Muse, picked up the disease, and, after a very short illness, died in Loiwing.

Then began the Loiwing rat hunts. Extraordinary things! Chinese workmen surrounded each house that had a floor near the ground with a barricade of galvanized roofing. Coolies pried up the floor boards one by one, and then the fifteen or twenty men in each enclosure, Americans and Chinese, went mad. Clubs in their hands they struck wildly at each rat as it ran out into the open. As they were killed they were thrown into a five-gallon can. Five gallons of dead rats—a hundred and fifty to two hundred of the rodents—was a normal catch from each house.

The Loiwing hospital staff, doctors and nurses, were quite busy enough with malaria, dysentery, and typhoid, so I brought over Namkham nurses, and we injected 40 per cent of the personnel with 3 c.c. of vaccine and the remaining 60 per cent with a total of 5 c.c. When the factory personnel had completed their injections we vaccinated in the surrounding villages. We continued to kill rats, getting positive smears from their spleens and bone marrow till the end of the rains, but not another case of plague appeared at the factory.

9

Malaria and Airplanes

WHEN THE nurses moved from the old hospital building into the new nurses' home we shifted all venereal and dirty patients to the old hospital, giving us much more space for cleaner cases. The women's clinic had lovely wards, and single rooms for private patients, while many of our other wealthier patients preferred rooms in the little cottages, for there they could keep their friends with them. Now our new house was being completed rapidly, when, with the beginning of our second plague epidemic, rats began to die in our old home. This was too much. I didn't want to ship Tiny and the children out of Namkham again, to be away for months! Though the new house still needed a great deal more work, we decided to move in and keep away from the plague. From then on our workmen wasted no time. Tiny was in the house and kept them on the move. After the epidemic Ba Saw moved up to our old house and had decent quarters at last.

Lashio had a new civil surgeon, Captain (now Lieutenant Colonel) Lindsay. I began the same compulsory vaccination of the entire Burma side of the valley that had proved so effective in limiting the disease the year before, and sent nurses out in teams. Captain Lindsay wrote me a long letter from Lashio saying that since I was performing compulsory vaccinations he would be unable to assume any responsibility in the matter of the plague epidemic as he did not believe in compulsory vaccination, which was a variety of fascism. Furthermore, he was convinced that the best way to cure these stupid villagers of their horror of vaccination was to vaccinate those who were willing, and let the people die off who refused protection. This was, to me, an entirely new concept. I could never persuade myself that it was correct, and in any case I could not forget the Burma Road and the fight of China against Japan. But Captain Lindsay was the best civil surgeon Lashio ever had; far too big a man for Lashio, and as fine a man as you could hope to see in the Indian Medical Service. If as big a man as that had an idea, there must be something to it. God knows I wanted nothing to continue the feud that somehow had developed between me and the Burma Public Health Service. But it was too late. I had crossed the Rubicon, and I had to finish the job. We gave fifteen thousand injections that rainy season. There were few deaths. No plague went up into China along the Burma Road, and by 1941 plague ceased to be epidemic in our valley. In 1941 I refused to have anything to do with plague vaccinations except in our mission.

That rainy season of 1940 would have ruined my disposition entirely, had it not been for an occasional happy incident. The road from Namkham to Loiwing was terrible, and the trip horribly monotonous. Once in a while things happened to make life interesting. I left Loiwing one afternoon just as the sun was going down. Passing along by the American golf course, at just that time of day when a driver is not quite sure whether to turn on his headlamps or not, I saw a leopard step to the side of the road and stand still to watch me pass. I was in a sedan with a splinterproof glass window which I could close rapidly, so I drew up abreast of the leopard and stopped. He could not have been more than fifteen feet away from me. I had no gun or I could have shot him easily. I don't know why I stopped except that I had been so very, very bored. For several minutes the leopard and I looked each other over with mutual interest, then he slipped forward into a bush where I could see so little of him that I was not quite sure of his plans. I decided that the place had become the sort it would be good to get away from, so I started off. But my lights wouldn't come on. I drove about seventy-five yards, stopped the car, and replaced the fuse. Now the starter refused to work. Expecting teeth to crunch into my shoulder any time, I got out and pushed the car forward till it reached a descent in the road; and then I jumped in and went on. My psychology is all wrong. The thought of a harmless snake fills me with horror; but a tiger or leopard is so beautiful a sight that it fills me with artistic delight!

Two hundred Chinese troops had been sent to do guard duty at the factory. They were quartered in small bamboo barracks. Coming from nonmalarious parts of China they were not protected by a single trace of natural immunity. The wards of the hospital were so crowded with the factory workers that there was seldom room for sick soldiers. The chief physician and one of the internes paid regular visits to the various barracks, distributing medicines; but the cases of malaria that developed could not be cured without actual hospitalization. Blackwater fever in soldiers came to be common, and by the time the patient reached an occasional free bed in the ward his urine was really black. Algid cases were carried in, their bodies icy, with up to 10 per cent of their red blood cells occupied by malignant tertian parasites. The mortality for malaria was higher among the soldiers than was that for plague in the valley this second year of the plague epidemic. Personally, as I visited the barracks, I was appalled. I appealed to Mr. Hunter for permission to use the bamboo isolation hospital which the factory had built to house plague patients that never appeared, and urged him to rush construction of more buildings. As the Loiwing staff was too busy to deal with the new wards, I brought over a team of nurses from Namkham.

Then I borrowed a truck to gather in the sick soldiers. Mr. Hunter, thinking I had made much ado about nothing, came along in his station wagon to see for himself. At the first barracks I asked the captain to "fall in" the men so that I could select those for hospital care. They most literally fell in, stumbling, heaving about like drunken men, dragging out companion soldiers slightly sicker than themselves. Mr. Hunter picked up in his arms one erratic patient whose legs could not quite get him into line and deposited him in the truck. Then he leaned himself against the side of the truck a minute, wiped his eyes and blew his nose loudly.

"Doc," he said, "I never saw anything so pitiful in my life. How can a man be as sick as that and live?"

Loaded with malaria cases, we drove to the foot of the hill leading up to the "plague" hospital. Some interested Americans turned in and each carried a sick soldier up the hill. It was late, so we treated them wholesale, while the truck went on to the other barracks for more malaria casualties. The nurses were given a little twelve by ten grass shack to live in. It had been built for use as a morgue for plague cases! Al Anderson brought in three camp cots, all he could find, and two nurses slept on each when they were off duty. One of the girls was that goofy

Burmese child, Mercy. About four feet eight in height and seventy-five pounds in weight, her sense of humor was positively gigantic. The soldiers' isolation ward promptly became known as the "Mercy Hospital," and Americans in need of laughs continually went to Mercy for treatment. The management was so worried lest the girls wouldn't have enough to eat while doing this special work for them that the main hospital kitchen sent up Chinese food, the club sent down American food, Al kept bringing in special desserts, and the girls had smuggled in their own special dishes of "rotten" fish and "rotten" beans. At the end of each two weeks we had to bring the nurses back to Namkham for treatment and send out a new group!

I have never seen blood so full of malaria parasites. For several days we lost patients daily; then the value of the treatment began to become apparent. The high proportion of blackwater fever, cerebral malaria, and the algid type decreased and the uncomplicated variety became the rule. To celebrate the improvement in health of the Chinese soldiers, the club threw a party, and three of the nurses put on a series of Burmese dances that brought down the house. It is not surprising that Namkham nurses have developed an extraordinary idea of what constitutes an American. All the Americans they met were hard workers, whether their immediate task was the sort usually done by coolies or an office job requiring brain work of a high type. Every American treated them with great gentleness and amazing respect. So when, a few months ago, a couple of men were detailed to work with Esther in the operating room, and stood or sat around all day watching her as she rushed about her preparations for the morrow's long list of operations, occasionally making sneering remarks which she was not supposed to understand, she was naturally much perplexed.

"Daddy," she said that evening, "didn't you tell me those men are Americans? Are you sure they are, really?"

With Loiwing and war news continually filling my mind, it was only natural that I should dream of planes bombing the factory. The dream was very realistic. Again in October, 1940, I dreamed the same dream. It was my day to go to Loiwing, but I had had some very major operations to do that morning in our own hospital and as I was so tired I lay down for a short nap before going over. This time the dream was so realistic that I could even hear the drone of the engines. Suddenly I heard Tiny screaming for me from the bathroom where she was in the midst of her bath.

"Gordon, Gordon, wake up! Those are Japanese bombers!" I took one look at the flock of "swans," discovered it was no dream, and yelled to the two boys to run to the valley where we had arranged for them to hide. Leaving Tiny to dress frantically, I ran over to the hospital. Nurses were already evacuating the patients according to our prearranged plan, and I passed several who were carrying male patients on their shoulders out into the woods. E Hla and the operating-room nurses were loading the Dodge with all our surgical instruments and baskets of sterile goods. On the far side of the hospital a Burmese was staggering along with his wife in his arms. I had just finished a major abdominal operation on her that morning. The husband was shaking with fright and his wife was fast sliding out of his arms, so I snatched her from him and carried her into a nullah. Running back I found a little five-foot nurse with a huge insane Kachin woman on her back. She was determined that if the Japanese were saving a bomb for us, as we expected, they should at least not hurt a crazy woman! We were just depositing our patient in safety when the bombers circled back over us. They had saved a bomb, but it missed us by a mile, and nearly massacred a Palong picnic party.

The bombers had passed over neutral Burma, both on their way to Loiwing and on their return.

The Dodge now loaded and volunteer cars coming to help, I started on with a team of nurses, Tiny coming along a few minutes later with another team. Four carloads, in all, went. I touched an occasional high spot in the road on my way, reaching Loiwing about half an hour after the bombing; but somehow or other Tiny, in spite of her late start, arrived at the hospital simultaneously. Dr. Yu and the first-aid men he had trained had already carried most of the casualties in. The operating staff was distracted; but with one Chinese nurse and Low Wang, the Chinese orderly who is still with me, to help, our nurses lit primus stoves and boiled instruments. The power mains had been destroyed and we had no electricity. We were just ready to begin operating when some fool turned in a false alarm. All the factory nurses ran, so I told our nurses to hide out, too. When nothing appeared and we came back, we began operating. Dr. Yu took the amputation and other orthopedic cases on one table, with Tiny to give his anesthesias, and I took the abdominal cases on the other while E Hla put them to sleep. We both worked fast. The internes selected cases and had them waiting in the doorway of the operating room. As I finished one major abdominal case and the nurses lifted him onto the stretcher, I moved over to the patient nearest the entrance. He moaned to me in Chinese, "Take me next, please take me next." He was covered with a blanket so I could not see just how badly he was hurt. I wheeled him toward my table, but the head factory nurse jerked him back and insisted I take another patient who, she said, needed operation more urgently. Thinking she knew her job, I took her patient, finding it to be a simple flesh wound. Then I went again to the other man, drew back the blanket and found one leg almost completely severed at the thigh with no tourniquet in evidence. Disgusted that favoritism should come into play during a time like this, I hurried to control hemorrhage; but the patient died. If I had operated on him first, as I intended, I could very probably have saved his life.

It is extraordinary what a ghastly wound can be caused by an insignificant bit of shell.

Not nearly so many casualties would have occurred if the Chinese had thrown themselves flat on the ground. Instead of lying down, however, everyone had started to run. The total number of killed was never accurately known. An entire family was buried alive in a hole they had dug to cache their personal possessions. Some children never found their parents again. One woman lost her husband and three children and went mad for several months.

A patient reached my table who had an apparently simple wound of the right hip below the crest of the ilium. There was no sign of abdominal involvement that I could describe verbally, but I opened the abdomen just for the fun of it, and there was a two-inch rip in the small intestine. This was one of the pitifully few abdominal cases that lived.

A woman, eight months pregnant, had a tiny puncture in the left flank, from which oozed a little blood. Sure the shell fragment must have passed into the uterus, I opened the abdomen which contained a lot of blood and amniotic fluid. Tying off the ovarian artery that had been injured, I delivered the baby by Caesarian section. Across the dorsum of the baby's right foot the shell had made a wound, the scar of which that child will carry till the day he dies. Both mother and child did well.

And so on, case after case: splenectomies, removal of several feet of lacerated intestine, amputations of the leg and arm. A shell fragment had penetrated the skull of a little lad just John's size and build. Dissatisfied with some of the first-aid work, I became very impatient that all my calls for one of the physicians were unavailing. Where had that man disappeared to? Dr. Yu and Tiny were working heroically at the other table, saving lives by the dozens, yet losing patients just as I was, because the inexperienced internes could not decide correctly which cases were most urgent. Had the head of the Department of Internal Medicine been killed by a bomb?

Night was coming on and we were not half done. No electricity. Americans were trying to buy Storm King gasoline lamps across the valley and to borrow those the mission owned; but they had not returned. What light could we use? I remembered two packages of candles in the drawer of the desk in my office and sent a nurse for them. Entry to my office was possible either through the door of my secretary's room or through that of the office shared by Dr. Yu and another physician. Both doors were locked. The nurse looked for the orderly who kept the keys. He was nowhere to be seen. She tried the door again.

Surely there was someone in that room? She knocked and knocked and nothing happened, yet that soft noise, like a child crying, persisted. Then the orderly appeared with the keys and opened the door. In the office, his head bowed on his arms, sobbing, was the physician we had been looking for.

Some people just cannot take it. Others, like these crazy nurses of ours from Namkham, just haven't sense enough to be scared when the bombs drop. The doctor, with his long legs, had disappeared rapidly over the Burma border soon after he sighted the planes. He went so fast and so far it had taken him hours to get back again, and even then he could do nothing but sob while Chinese died all around him.

Candles kept us going, with the aid of an occasional flashlight, till the Storm King lamps appeared. Americans had driven thirty-eight miles to Muse to buy them. At eleven o'clock the physician, who had come on the job reluctantly after being caught sobbing, insisted there were no other cases that needed operation before morning. The Americans dragged us up to the club for coffee and sandwiches. They treated our Namkham nurses as if they, too, were pure-blooded Americans. After an hour of relaxation—divine relaxation—we went back to check on our patients. Two of those who "did not need operation" had died while we were resting. All the factory nurses had gone home. All the casualties, whether operated on or not, needed an injection of morphine, so three of our nurses volunteered to go on night duty, tired as they were. It was high time I changed my blood-drenched clothes. Dr. Yu could offer me a shirt, but nothing else. When I reappeared from my office, dressed in that shirt—and nothing else—those crazy nurses burst into raucous laughter! Al Anderson took pity on me and lent me some pants.

In the hall, one of the staffmen grabbed my arm and begged me to look at his son who "didn't need an operation." A shell fragment had struck him in the leg causing a compound fracture of both tibia and fibula. We splinted his leg carefully, put him on his daddy's lap in the back of the Dodge, and when we reached Namkham debrided the wound, placed the bones in position, healthy fragments and all, and applied plaster. From then on the father did his best to make me take off the foul-smelling cast. Sensibly, he did not remove it himself. When I took it off, a couple of months later, the wound was well and the bones had grown together in perfect position.

At eight on the morning following the bombing, I started again for Loiwing to help operate on the "less seriously injured." While tanking up in town, several trucks came by. They were full of casualties. Dr. Yu, who was aboard one of the trucks, explained that they had decided to move all their hospital patients over to us in Namkham so that they would have no responsibility for carrying them to safety if bombers returned. That suited me; it would make my work much easier! What did not suit me was the horrible groaning of a man on the floor of one of the trucks. He was one of those cases that had not needed operation! All that was wrong was a compound fracture of the thigh. He had on no splint. One of the three nurses that had volunteered to go on night duty was on his truck. "At each bump," she explained, "the poor fellow screamed with pain." Twenty-four hours later, in spite of everything we could do, he died of gas gangrene.

And so, for days, we were operating on bomb casualties, removing arms and legs and using the "Spanish treatment" where we could. Tiny was fascinated by a woman who had lost her arm near the shoulder, but whose baby was untouched. Impervious to pain, she lay with the baby in the crook of her remaining arm, smiling and smiling! Times without number I caught Tiny standing in the doorway gazing in awe at that woman and her child!

Then came the days of paralysis. Chinese staffmen, workmen, and coolies disappeared from Loiwing and took up residence in little villages on both sides of the border—where they should always have been living from the first days of the factory, instead of all bunched up in a small, prominently visible area waiting to be bombed! The Americans who had begun the factory in grass-shack homes, took up residence in grass shacks, "somewhere in Burma." "From Grass Shack to Grass Shack"—what a book, if one of those Americans would only write it! President Pawley's prophecy was certainly fulfilled after that single bombing. Instead of working by day, the factory—such personnel as could be found—worked at night hauling off machine tools to the Burma side and hiding the generalissimo's private amphibian plane which had been flown in for repairs, and other machinery, over miles and miles of the Chinese side of the border. For our part we were paralyzed for fear we would not be in Namkham, near enough to help them, if another raid occurred. We did not dare push our outside work.

Our hospital had never been full, judging by present standards! Now there wasn't one spare inch available. The shock of the bomb raid made many of the pregnant Chinese women go into labor early. Our maternity building was jammed with women outdoing each other. Now I learned the true use of a husband when the wife is in labor. No matter how hard a certain woman tried, her baby postponed its arrival. It was getting to be a nuisance. Finally the husband insisted on being admitted to the delivery room. Every time his wife had a pain he let out a terrific grunt! She duplicated it. At the next pain, the husband's grunt was more extraordinary—so was his wife's. The third pain came on; the husband's grunt was one long wail of anguish. The wife took a deep breath, made an awful face, and—out came Mr. Baby!

For months the factory hospital remained closed and patients were sent to us. Our plant had again to be adapted to take care of them. With funds furnished by them, the old hospital and the small cottages were fitted with running-water toilets. Septic tanks were built. Fearful that their precious hospital equipment would be destroyed if the bombers returned, they sent most of it over to us either for our temporary use or to be stored. Our attic was floored, and supplies not susceptible to heat were stored there. On their hospital staff I selected two who could work with me in perfect harmony and who could not lose face if I smiled at them: Dr. Tu and Low Wang. George N. Tu had been born in San Francisco, received his medical education at the Imperial University in Tokio, and was working up a nice practice in East China when the "incident" began. Since then he had come diagonally across China, a couple of hops ahead of the Japs whom he detested. He was by no means a surgeon by nature like Ba Saw, nor could I ever instill the spirit of SURGERY into him. But as an internist he was very fair. He worked with the medical branch of the unit behind the Chinese Sixth Army, and when that army broke before the Japanese he hurriedly married Head Nurse Nang Leng and rushed off with her to Kunming.

Low Wang was the Loiwing operating-room orderly. He fell in love with me long before the bombing, insisted on staying at Namkham after the factory hospital closed up, was with the surgical unit behind the Fifth Army from the battle of Toungoo on, walked out happily into Assam, and is with us still. He is the author of the famous remark made as we reached the top of a range in the Naga Hills, "No, I am not tired. My knees have just gone soft." About as large as one of our nurses, he works as long as they and does his best to see that they never have to do any of the dirty work in the operating room. Unable to read a word in any language, he comes to every service and "reads" every hymn and every scripture passage. He plays baseball with terrific energy but can never be in the right place when the ball arrives there. When he came over to Namkham he could not speak a word of Burmese, but now he is very voluble in that language and often acts as my interpreter. He has only one "fault." He treats every Chinese cooly or private as if he were a major general!

Our effort to fit the Loiwing nursing staff into our work was disastrous; and that experience still colors our attitude toward mixing in with other units. It never turns out right. All the dirty work comes down on the Namkham girls who never refuse a job, no matter how nasty, and all the little plums go to the other group.

After months had passed, the factory personnel decided that the Japanese were never coming again and consented to go back to work. The hospital reopened. Tiny and I took a deep breath and decided that since we were no longer tied down to the Loiwing job, we would go ahead with some more dreams for Namkham. Taking John to school in Taunggyi and leaving Sterling for a few weeks with his grandmother, Tiny went with me on our first protracted jungle trip together, visiting our most distant hospitals at Kokang and Momeik. It was grand. We were surprised ourselves at how good the work done by these hospitals had turned out to be.

10

Medical Officer on the Burma Road

Mr. Fogarty came to us in perplexity. He was not satisfied with the medical facilities on the Burma Road. Venereal disease was being brought in by the drivers of the Lend-Lease trucks which were moving by the thousands along the road. Diseases not known before in Burma were being brought in from China, and there was always the chance that plague would be carried up into China. So many of the truck drivers were unskilled that trucks were being smashed up daily. The morbidity caused by malaria among the road coolies was so great that the Lashio branch could not be kept in condition, nor could the surfacing of the Bhamo branch proceed rapidly. Would I please make a suggestion?

It was a foregone conclusion that he could win any argument with me. He and I were alike in more ways than one. Both of us were experts in getting other people to do things for us—only one plan did he ever have for me that I refused to consider. I didn't need to consider it. Tiny turned thumbs down on his idea—to ask me to give up Namkham and be chief medical officer of the Federated Shan States! To me he only expressed his regrets. But now he was asking my help in a matter about which I cared more than he did, and Tiny and I had plenty of suggestions ready.

"We want to have two more hospitals on the Burma Road

besides that one at Nampaka; one at Muse and one at Mong Yu. We want them to have mat walls, thatch roofs, and dirt floors, till we prove them valuable; ten beds in each; salary for the necessary nurse in charge to be paid by the government; and a grant made to cover costs of medicine if you desire us to give free treatment."

"But you can't supervise them satisfactorily," he said, "and they are so far apart they will be of no assistance in preventing malaria among the road coolies."

"That brings us to our next suggestion," I replied. "If the government will buy us a half-ton ambulance and make a grant to cover the cost of necessary petrol, we will make trips twice weekly to Mong Yu and back, dispense to the sick of the villages en route, give preventive doses of cinchona to the coolies, supervise the work of the nurses in each of the hospitals, and bring back to Namkham all those patients whom the nurses are unable to treat satisfactorily."

"It all sounds good, but I do not believe you will ever have much success in roadside dispensing! However, the ambulance will pay for itself even if it only makes possible your supervision of those Burma Road hospitals. You may buy the ambulance, provided you will do one more thing: build a twenty-bed stone hospital where the road crosses the border at Kyuhkok."

"But," I objected, "there is a government hospital at Kyuhkok now, and I don't want to get into trouble again with Captain Lindsay."

"You won't. That hospital is for the soldiers at the frontier post which is being moved back this side of Kyuhkok, and the hospital there will cease to exist in a few months."

"All right, I'll build the hospital and staff it with three nurses." He had gone me one better, as usual, but I had to have that ambulance.

I made the first trip with the ambulance. Two nurses went along each time to make my work easier, give them a change from their monotonous routine, and act as interpreters. We had to travel the first thirty miles on the unpaved Bhamo branch, through Muse, till we reached the main paved road a few miles from the border. Between Namkham and Muse the coolies were almost all Shan. From Muse to the paved road at the "105th mile" were two hundred Indian coolies whom the Burma Oil Company had lent to the government, desiring to haul their oil to China from Bhamo. Beyond 105 the work was done by gangs of Chinese and Kachins. We never had much success in giving preventive doses of quinine to the first group of Shan coolies, probably because I didn't want to waste time arguing with them. They had natural immunity, anyway. At Muse we stopped at our new hospital, examined and prescribed for the patients, and ate the delicious breakfasts cooked by head nurse Saw Yin, who is now top nurse of our medical unit. From Muse to 105 we never had trouble. The nurses and I walked up to each Indian, opened our jaws wide—at which their mouths opened wide also, in sympathy—and popped in two tablets of cinchona before the cooly could recover from his surprise. These men were continually constipated. I shall never forget their exhibition of good breeding when we gave them their Mag. Sulph. They tipped their heads back and filled their mouths with the solution without letting the bottle touch their lips, and then passed it on to the next man.

Beyond 105 the Chinese and Kachins were already acquainted with me, and instead of having difficulty in persuading them to take their medicine, we had difficulty in preventing them from running off with our entire supply! At "91" there was a bazaar village—one of the favorite night stops of the Lend-Lease truck drivers. There were always lots of drivers there, and many villagers came down from surrounding hills with groceries to sell. This was always our longest stop. The uncle of one of our Shan nurses had a tea shop. He spoke Shan, Kachin, Chinese, Burmese, and some Hindustani, and was a power in the community, so his shop became the waiting room for patients from distant villages.

Stopping again and again, as we came to gangs of coolies at work, we pushed on to Nampaka, instilled pep into the Kachin nurse there who needed that article more than any other we ever had, treated her patients and finished the trip in the evening at the Mong Yu hospital, sixty miles from Namkham. The Kachin nurse here always had dinner ready, determined that we should like her food better than that furnished by the Karen nurse at Muse in the morning.

After dinner we returned to Namkham, picking up stretcher cases at the different hospitals or at the villages along the road. If the day's work had gone well we could reach Namkham at 10:30 P. M. If there had been unusual numbers of patients—well, we had the night before us!

Tiny made the second trip each week. We used to vie with each other to see who would have the most interesting tales to tell after we got back. On my trips I had to see many special cases which she had picked out to refer to me, and that always made my trip longer. It was Tiny who worked up the village dispensing service. By the time she had finished arguing and smiling, smiling and arguing, the most reluctant villager was willing to take any medicine, or undergo any operation. The rest of us were satisfied with whatever patients happened to appear for treatment. Tiny made a great many more want to come for treatment.

Certain that the day would come when one or the other of us would be too ill or too busy to make the ambulance trips on the appointed days, we decided to train nurse drivers. Two of our head nurses, Htulum and Nang Leng, had driver's licenses. Htulum had learned in Maymyo, where she had spent years as a nurse after completing her training with us. Nang Leng had driven around our valley. Neither had driven on the "Burma Road," and driving on that road is one of the most dangerous things one can hope to do. There were blind corners and steep precipices everywhere; unskilled drivers, and, above all, drivers who were driving trucks which they did not own and which cost their transportation companies nothing: Lend-Lease trucks. They were drivers who could earn a pretty penny by putting the gears in neutral, turning off the electricity, coasting down every hill, and then selling in China, at a fat profit, any gasoline thus saved, seldom getting hurt even when their trucks fell over precipices. I actually saw the crushed ruin of a truck that had rolled over many times as it fell down a three-hundred-foot cliff. The driver had a half dozen bruises and a cut lip! They were men who cared nothing about what happened to the other fellow into whom they crashed. Htulum was careful but couldn't see well at night. Nang Leng was scatter-brained. It used to take me forty-five minutes to go from Namkham to Loiwing. Nang Leng made it once in twenty-five, and as a result her future husband, Dr. Tu, bragged about what a wonderful nurse she was!

Those were the girls Tiny and I had to train. How much easier it is to do things yourself than to teach other people to do them! Tiny and I could drive the ambulance trip ourselves and come home healthily tired. We could let the nurses drive it—and reach Namkham again in a coma! But always throughout my foolish life, there has been that inner something or other that compelled me to teach people how to do things, no matter how eccentric or unorthodox—a sense of some great event ahead that would need every talent I could develop in all who came under my influence. That strange urge was behind every decision of policy in our medical work, in our nurses' training; behind acceptance of duties for which I was myself poorly trained: an urge to learn first, how to do the thing myself, and then to find someone whom I could teach to do it for me. I never knew what it was all about! Now I have a feeling that the last nine months showed me why I have been so obsessed all these years.

We taught them. First we let them drive only in the valley. Then we let them drive the straight stretches of the Burma Road. When they finally made up their minds to try to drive, as we drove we let them experiment with the worst sections in the daytime. When they graduated with honors they were permitted to drive at night also. Then the time did arrive when neither Tiny nor I could make the ambulance trip. Htulum did it alone. We couldn't sleep, that night, until we heard the ambulance return safely. Until the unit started off to work with the Chinese armies, neither of the girls had had a crash. The only accident occurred to the old man himself, when he was treating a group of coolies by the side of the road and a truck crashed into the parked ambulance.

The rainy season of 1941 arrived soon after the ambulance service started. Burma Oil Company trucks soon had ploughed deep ruts in the road to Muse; the ruts filled with rain, and a part of the road was little better than a morass. The B.O.C. drivers were always kind to us and frequently hauled us out of our troubles. As tough as the drivers of the other transportation companies, they had been in the habit of thumbing their noses at us until the day that one of them, starting out from Bhamo, ruptured a gastric ulcer. How that man drove his truck fifty miles with an acute abdomen, I can never think; but he was determined to come to us for treatment rather than turn back to the Bhamo hospital. While he was recovering from his operation, the other drivers stopped in to see him and soon became acquainted with us. From then on, the sight of our ambulance flag caused them to extend every courtesy to us or the nurse-drivers.

Tiny came home one night with a tall story. Just as she left Namkham she passed a man on a bicycle. He passed her a few miles out again as she was trying to get out of a mudhole. Zigzagging back and forth, she finally reached Muse, twenty miles away, a half mile ahead of the bicyclist. Could I beat that one?

The very next week I started out and passed a man on foot who was leading a mule. Five hours later the man reached Muse just ahead of me. Tiny was sure I was lying!

Tiny was so provoked at the number of times I got back way after midnight! But I couldn't help it. I had a perfect genius for getting stuck in the mud. There were always cases saved up for the doctor because of difficult diagnosis. Besides, I always carried my gun, and there were so many things to shoot after midnight. Tiny has never carried her shotgun since the day she shot a partridge through the windshield and knocked her teeth loose with the recoil of the gun! But during the rainy season, almost no trip after midnight ended without our seeing one of the small yellow panthers that raise havoc around the villages. During the cold weather we saw many foxes, but during the rains there are these huge wildcats. I never shot foxes, little cute things! But I shot five panthers, much to the delight of the Karen nurses who ate them for dinner.

Nang Leng was with me one night when I had forgotten the gun. Suddenly she grabbed my arm.

"*Kya, kya!* Tiger, tiger!"

I stopped the ambulance.

"*Behma le.*"

"Don't you see him sitting there under those bamboos beside us? He walked out from behind the pile of gravel!"

Sure enough, there he was, sitting like a huge pussycat with his front legs drawn up close to his body.

"*Thake hla de, naw,*" I said. "He is perfectly beautiful, isn't he?"

Nang Leng agreed. We were both having the time of our lives. Just then one of the patients spotted the tiger through the ambulance window and started screaming; so reluctantly I drove on.

Nang Leng returned from her first trip alone in the ambulance. She had taken my Lahu boy with her, and they, with the help of some patients, killed a huge python that they had found trying to climb a very steep bank. They had killed him with small, short clubs. Nang Leng had put a guard on duty on arrival at Namkham to make sure no one would steal the python's gall bladder before I saw the snake in the morning. She was wise, for a Karen patient was doing his best to get by the guard as I came on duty. Nang Leng eventually stole the gall bladder herself, and sold it for a hundred rupees to native quacks for use in their medicine. The Karen nurses ate the rest of the python, and we got the skin, or rather the Japs did.

During the first month of the rains of 1941 coolies gathered tons of gravel for the hospital at Kyuhkok. It was to be a stucco building. I tried to haul the gravel in the ambulance, but only small amounts could be carried for fear of breaking the springs. Loiwing again permitted us to borrow a truck each Saturday evening, after work, and keep it till dawn the following Monday. At first the trucks were old ones, some without brakes, some with no headlamps, some with very faulty engines. It was not much fun driving. But after midnight we had the Burma Road to ourselves, and this offset the other dangers. Our masons were by this time very skilled. There was little supervising to do, and Tiny did this on her ambulance trips. Later, as part of their program to help the A.V.G. (Flying Tigers) which was training in Burma, they bought a lot of new trucks, and my work became much easier. The hospital was completed the first week of December, 1941.

Not one trip but the ambulance brought home patients, filled to capacity—the ambulance, not the patients! The patients were completely emptied before they got to Namkham! More than half the cases were surgical. A fourth were complicated malarias, while the rest were a smattering of pneumonias and other medical complaints. Mr. Fogarty was greatly impressed. The Chinese were building a Burma-Yünnan railroad, and the United States had sent out a malaria commission to help them avoid that havoc-causing disease. But they were working on the Chinese side of the line. Trucks were hauling building materials for the railway from Lashio, east from Hsenwi, across the Salween at Kunlong—where we turned north to our hospital at Kokang—and fifteen miles beyond Kunlong to the border. The road coolies on this route were Chinese, and malaria had completely incapacitated them for their job. Mr. Fogarty said that if we would build two new hospitals on this road, at Namsarawp and Kunlong, and extend our ambulance work to Kunlong and the border, the government would buy us a new ton-and-a-half ambulance to make it possible. All he had to do was tell us about the way those Chinese coolies were dying and we bit!

While the new ambulance was being built we started the longer weekly trip—a hundred and fifty miles each way—with the first ambulance. This trip took two days instead of one. The Kunlong road was much more difficult than the Burma Road. I did not dare let either of the two nurses drive it alone, expert as they had become. Only Tiny and I could manage it. Most of the Kunlong road was so narrow that cars could not pass each other except at rare intervals. If one met a car or truck in a narrow spot there was nothing to do but back up hundreds of yards and let it by. Although graveled since my historic trip five years before in the Buick, the graveling was as yet poorly done. The road was horribly bumpy, and the drivers did not know Joseph. They would not make way for me at all. But no matter how provoked I would get at those drivers, I could laugh it off as I read the names they had given to some of the trucks. One was labeled, *Ky'ma lin lah be* ("my husband has come"). Another gloried in the name, *Apyo lin Gyi* ("husband of all virgins"). On the top of still another was written "Mae West."

Knowing the coolies were Chinese, I took Ohn Khin along on the first trip; she was a granddaughter of the sawbwa of Mong Mow. Her Shan father had married a Kachin, and she had known how to speak Chinese since childhood. Without stopping to dispense on the way, we passed along the road at night, reaching Kunlong shortly before twelve o'clock. On the way back the next evening we stopped at each cooly camp. The Chinese did not know us yet and we had to argue with them to persuade them that we were trying to be of help. One camp said they had no sick. From the way they talked, Ohn Khin was sure they were lying; so she persisted. They at last admitted that one of their number was sick, so she took her flashlight and hunted around the jungle. She located him, finally, lying naked in the jungle, barely conscious, his body wet with black urine, which, owing to his incontinence, he had voided on himself. She turned back and demanded that the other coolies produce the clothes they had stolen from him when they threw him out to die. They brought out a pair of ragged trousers. "Now carry him to the ambulance," she ordered. They refused. "All right, then, I'll carry him there myself," said she. Shamed, they put the man on a stretcher and carried him to us. We stowed him away, covered him with blankets, and gave him a dose of atabrine and an ounce of glucose. Arriving at the hospital in Namkham at dawn, we administered a pint of glucose solution intravenously and gave repeated intravenous injections of atabrine. Three weeks later we took him back to his camp well. I gave him ten rupees to spend, saying he must tell others what had happened to him.

The Chinese on the Kunlong road finally became acquainted with us. We had loads of fun with them. The new ambulance, when it came, had medicine shelves above the windshield from which we could reach the drugs without having to go outside. The coolies crowded up to the windows and got their cinchona tablets, and whatever other special medicines they asked for, if we were convinced they really needed them. Nurses dispensed out of one window and I out of the other. Soon we discovered patients were getting too, too clever. Having received all they were entitled to from me, they slipped around and, pretending to be someone else, tried to draw rations from the nurses as well. We always glanced back at the men as we pulled out. Invariably they were gathered in little groups comparing notes to see who had managed to get the largest number of pills of various sorts.

Then the assistant superintendent of Kutkai wired me to join him at Namsarawp, where we could choose a satisfactory site for the new hospital we were to build of mat and thatch. It was the eve of the seventh of December, 1941. I expected that, as usual, we would push on and spend the night up in the mountains sleeping in the ambulance, so I was carrying no mosquito net. Mr. Barton insisted, however, that I stay the night with him in the Namsarawp plain, as he had other business to attend to and wished to travel on to Kunlong in the ambulance next day. Never in my whole life have I been so miserably chewed by mosquitoes! It was hot, but I covered my body and head with my blanket, leaving only a small air hole. The mosquitoes chewed my nose. Sweating from the blanket, it was only natural to kick it off the minute I fell asleep, and swarm after swarm of mosquitoes had their blood meal. A glorious feeling greeted the appearance of dawn, with its resultant freedom from my tormentors. After choosing a delightful site above the bazaar, beside the homes of some friendly Shans, we drove on to Kunlong, dispensing to everyone as we went. Mr. Barton enjoyed it as much as we did. Heretofore rather skeptical about missionaries, he began to unbend slowly and even went into a contest with me to see who could produce the most interesting songs. He won on variety of music, producing a couple of sonatas à la tra-la-la. I on my part could rattle the leaves and startle the coolies at least a furlong farther than his voice could carry. When our voices gave out and we started telling our favorite stories, it was a draw. The nurses in the rear of the ambulance sat in astonishment through the whole concert, gazing in awe at the Englishman and the American who had suddenly gone mad.

Sleeping again near Kunlong, we were met, as we reached the new motorboat ferry installed for the Yünnan-Burma Railway, by a Chinese official who told us about the attack on Pearl Harbor—a garbled version, because he located the attack at Singapore! So at this time we did not realize that America had been attacked.

"Let's hurry the selection of the site for the Kunlong hospital as much as we can, Mr. Barton," I urged. "I want to get back to our own radio and listen in on this thing; if Japan has cut loose, Burma is in for it."

Hurrying back much faster than the road warranted, I met

the Namkham-Lashio bus. The driver waved me to stop, and Dr. Tu, who had hospital business to do for us in Lashio, stepped out.

"Mrs. Seagrave is critically ill with malaria," he said. "She has been delirious and Dr. Ba Saw is very worried."

We stopped for no more patients! At Namkham, Tiny was conscious again, but very weak. Dr. Ba Saw had done a wonderful job giving her various intravenous and intramuscular injections, using the right drugs, as her condition demanded from time to time, and pulling her out of the cerebral malaria attack with the utmost skill. Tiny's favorite nurses had been on with her continually without thought of rest for themselves. She remained critically ill for many days, but the cerebral symptoms, at least, did not return. About the time she was able to be up again, the malaria parasites injected into me by the mosquitoes at Namsarawp that night had multiplied to sufficient numbers to put me in bed for a day. Since then Tiny and I have had relapse after relapse of malaria, neither one being able to afford time to cure it completely by staying in bed.

PART THREE
BATTLE OF BURMA

II

The Beginning

THE NEWS on the radio was not so good. Sooner or later they would be in Burma, and then where would our hospital be? We felt around to find out what the government officers had planned to do to us. Mr. Fogarty's idea was to have me send our entire third-year class of pupil nurses to Taunggyi to work in the British Army's base hospital there. That did not suit me, for the girls would be little better than ayahs there, allowed to do none of the things they had been trained to do. Mr. Porter, in Lashio, did not want us to do anything. He was convinced the Japs would never succeed in entering Burma in force. Mr. Stevenson, in Kutkai, sure the Japs would enter Burma by the Burma Road, was going to use us as a base hospital for British troops, pushing us back from valley to valley if things didn't go well. Yes, and how were we going to move around when we had only two ambulances, and how would we be good for anything if we were dispersed over the entire map? Yet we must do something, because every year for the last ten years I had promised the government that they could count on us in any military emergency. Our problem was not whether or not we wanted to serve, but how we could serve efficiently and really help the country. I hated "eyewash."

Then Bill and I took our ladies over to a dance at Loiwing. I asked "Chuck" Hunter if he could figure out some way in which our hospital could become mobile so that we could move swiftly to the scene of action when hostilities started.

"Listen, Doc, why don't you go down to Rangoon and persuade them to give you some Lend-Lease trucks. The authorities would rather have them given to Americans who they know will not misuse them. They have given us some to help in our work with the A.V.G."

On our way home, Tiny, Hazel, and Bill Cummings and I talked it over. The idea seemed pretty good to us, but there was the difficulty of getting enough drivers. It was Christmas, and I had to go to Rangoon in any case to take delivery of the new ambulance, and Bill consented to go along with me in the Oldsmobile which the factory had presented to us. Tiny was still too weak to drive long distances.

Cooped up in the car for three days on end were two of the craziest missionaries the A.B.M. ever produced in Burma. We saw no scenery the whole trip, for our tongues were moving so rapidly that we persistently interrupted each other. Starting out from Namkham with only a hazy idea, continuous argument caused the pieces of the puzzle to fall into place and the picture gradually to come into focus. Realizing the difficulties we would encounter, we thought out solutions for each one, so that by the time we reached Rangoon, with the blessing of the new Shan States commissioner upon us, we had detailed plans ready to present. While we were traveling down, Rangoon was bombed twice, the first attack being a massacre. Nothing could persuade the natives, when the bombers appeared, that they were not looking at another Hollywood film; so they gathered in the streets to see the free show, making perfect targets for bombs and machine guns. The hospitals were full to overflowing, and the nursing staffs of the Dufferin and Ram Krishna hospitals had disappeared. I was astonished at the smallness of the bomb craters. The Japs were not using the huge demolition bombs they had used in Loiwing. In both raids bombs had dropped within a very short distance of my dying mother, so my friend Mr. Smith, of Judson College, and his wife, had taken her off to temporary peace in Prome.

Mr. Fogarty was in Rangoon, now chief liaison officer between the government and the Army. Bill and I went to his house at once to lay the project before him; but before we could say a word, he started laying his plans before us!

"Seagrave! I was just hoping I could get hold of you. I want you to start for Prome tomorrow night and open a four-hundred-bed hospital at once for bomb casualties. I will give you three days to set up, and then your first hospital train of patients will arrive. Can you do it?"

"Yes, if you can get a telegram through to Namkham asking for eight of our key nurses to be brought down to help me with the volunteer assistants I will have to secure locally; and I will be glad to do it if you will help us with this other project of ours," I told him, as I outlined the plans Bill and I had made.

"I'll take you around to Army headquarters first thing in the morning," he said. "Now I will have to hurry over to the governor's council meeting and put the Prome matter before him. Come back in the morning."

The next morning Mr. Fogarty's face was wreathed in smiles.

"It worked," he said. "The governor approved of my plan for sending you to Prome most wholeheartedly; so the Burma Medical Department immediately discovered that they had

underestimated their own ability to handle the situation and are no longer talking of evacuating all casualties to Calcutta by sea. They decided that if you could start a four-hundred-bed hospital on three days' notice, so could they; so they are getting busy at once. Now we can go around to the Army."
Fogarty moves in mysterious ways. I felt a little dismay at having been used as a red rag, and yet Fogarty would have been quite capable of tying me up in Prome for a month or six weeks if his red rag had not produced results.

I am afraid the next two days made us get just a little embarrassed. Every officer we met, from the deputy assistant director of Medical Services to the brigadier general, had heard all about us. We could only hope they hadn't heard altogether too much! I would have liked permission to censor the stories before they heard them. The director of Medical Services was the only man to criticize our plans. We should, he said, have asked for thirty three-ton trucks instead of six. Then they could call us a mobile hospital unit. With only six trucks they could dignify us with no higher title than a mobile surgical unit. We told him that the title was entirely immaterial provided they gave us a real opportunity to work—and work together as a unit composed of doctors and nurses who were used to each other's ways. Scarcity of drivers made thirty trucks impossible for us, but we could locate six missionaries, who were at a loose end because of the war, to drive the six trucks. It was specified that no member of our unit should receive pay. The government medical stores would issue anything needed that was available, but we would have to secure the trucks and necessary blankets and sheeting material from Lend-Lease. Approval of General Hutton having been obtained, it took only

THE BEGINNING

a few minutes over the telephone to secure the trucks and Lend-Lease supplies from the American officers in charge.

Early the next morning we took delivery of the trucks and other supplies and loaded up with all the gasoline we would need during the first month. The medical stores filled our requisitions in record time. Mr. Baxter, financial secretary to the government in Burma, gave us a thousand rupees of his own personal funds to cover incidental expenses liable to occur during the period essential for organizing our unit. Several missionaries were out of constructive jobs because Judson College, of the University of Rangoon, had closed down. Driving our hospital trucks seemed to them to offer possibility of real service to Burma. It certainly would prove more interesting than sitting on chairs for the duration. Paul Geren and Whittington joined us then, and for one of the trucks we secured Mr. Tun Shein, a Karen who had had years of service with MacGregor's, one of the companies handling the teak of Burma. A college graduate, elephant catcher, a little bit of everything that we needed so badly, he took the job first as a lark, then later became just as vitally a part of our work as Bill and myself. Tun Shein could hear the squawk of a hen laying an egg five miles away, and come back with both the hen and the egg! Speaking Burmese, Hindustani, and English as well as his own Karen, and understanding the psychology of each race, he was a perfect liaison as well as supply officer! He is more important now to this unit than I am. There are plenty of other doctors, but only one Tun Shein. As long as he is with us we won't starve, nor will we get into conflict with Burmese or Indians.

That day in Rangoon great pressure was put on us by the mission and by the American consul general to get all American women and children out of the country. Now what were we to do? Rangoon Port was almost out of commission as the result of only two bomb raids. How much longer could it remain open? Indians, maltreated by the Burmese for years, were streaming out of town by the tens of thousands on their long trek for India. Most of them were on foot, their possessions strapped on their backs. Many were driving their cattle and goats along with them, hoping to have something, when they arrived in India, with which to begin their lives anew. Some had large pushcarts and wheelbarrows, trishaws—bicycles with sidecars—and anything that would roll. A few had "salvaged" some brand new truck chassis on which huge packing cases were bolted. Yes, the Indians were definitely leaving, and Indians are essential for Rangoon docks. Bill and I had a major problem on our hands. What sort of advice should we give Tiny and Hazel? Each of us had two small sons in Namkham. Hazel was not very well, and Tiny had been very ill for a long while. If Tiny were well she would be of immense service with our unit either at the front or keeping the Namkham hospital open while we were away. If she regained her strength, she might stand the trip to Myitkyina if we had a chance to fly out from there, but from Myitkyina to India on foot would be beyond her in any case. If the Japs gave our friends in Loiwing time enough, they might fly her and the boys out from Loiwing at the last minute. There were too many ifs. If Tiny remained ill (and I had tried so long to restore her to health without success) I would never be free for continued action at the front.

The day after our return, January 2, we put the matter up to them. May I never have to go through another day like that!

THE BEGINNING

Finally the two mothers decided they had better go over to India and take no chance with the children. Twenty-four mad hours were spent packing the most essential things, and then Tiny started off in the Oldsmobile, one of the trucks accompanying her to pick up supplies for the unit that we had been unable to bring on the first trip. She reached Rangoon just in time for a week of continuous night bombing. The A.V.G. had shot so many Jap bombers out of the sky that the Japs did not dare come in the daytime. Night after night Tiny had to grab up the children and run for the slit trenches and stay there till dawn while bombs dropped all around. All the missionaries were keyed up and their tempers very brittle. After what seemed like seven years instead of seven days, the three obtained passage on a steamer for Calcutta. The letter Tiny wrote from there on her arrival was the last to reach me till July. Someone told me later that he thought she had sailed from Bombay, but it was not till I reached India that I knew she had safely reached our home in Ohio.

January was a busy month for Bill and me. We had to arrange our trucks for immediate departure when the Army authorities ordered it, while I still had all my regular hospital work to do and ambulance trips to make, and Bill had to wind up some important phases of his agricultural work. We had a driver for each truck, but we should have had a dozen spare drivers trained, and ready, to take over when occasion demanded. That meant nurses again. Several of the nurses had shown great interest and natural ability in car driving. I took them in rotation on each ambulance trip, and they learned very rapidly. Tiny had already taught Dr. Ba Saw the rudiments, so he learned his remaining lessons quickly. Bill outlined a miniature "Burma Road" on our football ground and made the more promising nurses drive those huge trucks back and forth on that road. Soon they reached the point where we could let them practice on our valley road, with one of us ready to pull on the hand brake or snatch the wheel out of their hands in an emergency. Coming back from the long ambulance trip to Kunlong, always at night, there was no danger of smashing into other cars, so I took my life—and theirs—into my hands, and let them drive the ambulance. Theodore, my secretary, took lessons and did very well indeed.

Now we had our equipment all ready and planned a practice mobilization. Every nurse had her place in the trucks assigned to her, and the position of each truck in convoy was announced. Key nurses had lists of last-minute things which they were to load on the trucks after the signal was given. Each boy who had volunteered to go with us was told what he must do. I allowed them fifteen minutes after the gong had sounded to be ready to start. On this practice the trucks were to go down the main hospital road, around the hospital hill, and come back up the private road leading to our house. I slipped up on only one thing. I forgot to assign a driver for Bill's truck; and Bill was out of town. The gong rang out; everything was chaos for a few moments; then I led off the convoy with my truck. As I went around the corner of the hill I looked back over my shoulder. All the other trucks were taking their assigned place in convoy. Who on earth was driving Bill's truck? It was swerving from the ditch on the right to the precipice on the left in very accurate imitation of the way a snake travels. Lord! What if the girls in that truck were to be killed on a practice trip! The mountain hid them from view, and I drove

THE BEGINNING

around and up the narrow road to my house—a road just a few inches wider than these huge trucks and so steep that I had to go into compound low. Back at the hospital again I watched the other trucks and the big ambulance pull up. Htulum and her ambulance rolled into position in great style. Ba Saw and the Americans were like old-timers. Finally Bill's truck arrived —driver Theodore, of all people! I was speechless! Theodore had heard me telling the nurses a hundred times that they must be ready in any emergency. He felt that this applied to him! It was a dress rehearsal; Bill, one of the principals, was absent and a driver was necessary. Even if he got killed in the process he was determined he would not be found wanting!

While we were still gasping with relief that Theodore and the nurses had not been killed, a friend came running up from Namkham to say that all the bazaar people and shopkeepers, hearing we were starting for the front, had evacuated the town! It was days before they discovered it was a false alarm and returned.

I do not think we could have gotten through those weeks, after Tiny and Hazel left, if it had not been for our Sunday evening song services. We had had them for years, teaching the nurses to sing accurately and in harmony. Some of their voices were very, very sweet, and all of them could carry a tune. They enjoyed the services as much as we did, calling for hymn after hymn until our throats were all worn out. These last four weeks one sang with a lump in one's throat. Tiny was not at the piano, and the boys were not turning somersaults on the floor. But still we were all one big family, loving each other and going through the same period of hope that soon we would be doing something of vital importance to this country of ours. The effect on our morale was so extraordinary that we kept up these weekly sings all through the Battle of Burma and after.

A division of the Chinese Sixth Army was reported to have arrived in Kengtung State. Two other divisions were due to come through into Burma by way of the Burma Road. Somehow we knew the Army in Burma intended to assign us to the Chinese Army. We were the only hospital in Burma that had Chinese-speaking nurses, and we were the only non-British hospital available for military use. It was known that the Sixth Army had no medical-school graduates to do their surgery. But I had begged headquarters not to tie me up with medical work for an idle army. Namkham, the work we had developed in the Northern Shan States, the Burma Road hospitals—all seemed well worth maintaining until there were actual battle casualties that needed treatment. Then a peculiar order was telegraphed in. We were to start immediately for Wanting and report to the liaison officer there for duty. What Wanting did they mean? Surely not the Wanting at the border, forty miles away from Namkham and a hundred yards from our Kyuhkok hospital? It must be the Kengtung State Wanting. I sent Bill to Lashio to find out. Yes, it was our Wanting. We stayed put. We were already in Wanting. Army Headquarters in Rangoon had not looked closely enough at the map. A few days later, the British liaison officer assigned to the Chinese Sixth Army came in to see us. It would be two weeks before the Army would cross the border on the way to the Southern Shan States. He would let us know the actual date on which the first convoy was traveling and we could follow it down to Takaw, where the Kengtung road crosses the Salween. We kept the trucks loaded, continued training the nurses who were learning to drive, and for the third time gave them their course in first aid. Our ambulances made their scheduled trips. When we could stand this "mark time" business no longer, Bill and I would climb into the Oldsmobile and go over to Loiwing and meet some of the A.V.G., and listen to their stories. One young A.V.G. had had such a struggle getting into his shirt one morning that he was a minute late getting off the ground, and his pals had taken off without him. As he gained altitude he discovered a formation of Japanese bombers above him. He was so afraid of being killed that he pointed his nose straight up and ploughed through the Jap formation, bringing down three planes as he went. I became intensely curious as to what my reaction would be if I got into danger. Would I cut and run, or would I plough right through the danger like this A.V.G. boy?

The liaison officer reappeared. The first regiment of Chinese, he said, would start on Wednesday. It would be better for us to start on Thursday so that there would be no difficulty getting mixed up with the Chinese convoy on the road. So, on Thursday, we started off under a barrage of pouts and tears from the nurses, whom we had decided to leave behind to keep up the Namkham hospital work. Promises of rotation between Namkham and the front had no effect. Sein Bwint lost no time writing me a letter accusing me of persecution because I had not let her come with us. Five other nurses started a Gandhiesque non-co-operation strike because they had been left behind.

12

Lend-Lease Trucks

WE SPENT the first night in Kutkai getting used to Army life. Arriving in Lashio the next morning we drew out our first stock of rations and cooked breakfast in the jungle, ending our second day's journey in the bazaar sheds at Pangkitu. While we were eating our breakfast next day at Laikha, another liaison officer appeared, who told us we were to report at Mongnai instead of at Takaw, on an entirely different road. We got to Mongnai at sunset, and there Brigadier General Martin, chief of the British Liaison Mission to the Chinese Army, met us. He informed us that our orders were more extensive than we had originally been given to understand. Our unit was to serve not just one division but the entire Chinese Sixth Army in the Southern Shan States and Karenni, over a front extending from Kengtung State, three hundred miles east of Loilem, through Mong Pan State a hundred and fifty miles south, and into Loikaw, capital of Karenni, a hundred and fifty miles southwest. Since the main roads to these three stations met in Loilem, a delightfully situated town, General Martin advised us to set up our base hospital there. We pushed back to Loilem that night. What kind of men did these British think we were anyway, giving us a job of that size? After refusing us the dignity of the title of Mobile Hospital Unit they were ordering us to be a whole confounded medical corps! It was well known

LEND-LEASE TRUCKS

that the Chinese Medical Corps consisted only of a few men trained in first aid, and of companies of stretcher bearers. We would somehow or other have to do all the hospitalization for the entire Army. General Martin promised me a free hand in adding to our personnel any volunteer doctors I could secure, providing they worked without pay, but said I was to ask for no British medical officer to be assigned to us. My job was so large that a commission as lieutenant colonel was offered me.

I declined with thanks. They could make me an honorary lieutenant colonel—Kentucky variety—but I was taking no chances of losing my American citizenship!

We selected a lovely pine-covered hill east of Loilem, and the government secured contractors to put up a lot of bamboo and thatch wards under the pines. With as big a job as this before us we knew there would be endless miles of travel to and from the small advance hospitals that we would have to develop; so Bill set off at once for Rangoon with five drivers, two of them nurses, to attempt to secure a half-dozen jeeps. I, for my part, went off to Mong Pan to get in touch with the regiment of troops that had just arrived there and decide as to the necessity of having an advance hospital in that place to care for their needs.

The road to Mong Pan branches off from the Kengtung road at the Namsang airfield, passes southward through Mongnai, then down steep grades to Langkhu, a hot, coconut palm-covered plain. From Langkhu the road is of much more recent construction, graveled but very narrow, rising sharply up to the Mong Pan plateau. At Mong Pan one sees the first signs of Siamese influence in the pagodas and monasteries. Beyond

Mong Pan Town the British were hurriedly pushing construction of a motor road down to the Salween. The first regiment of Chinese was marching along this road as I drove up. They were just the sort of Chinese I was used to, many of them stumbling along in the grip of fever. They would certainly need one small hospital in Mong Pan Town if I could persuade the political officer or the sawbwa to construct it. No solution suggested itself to my imagination other than the development of a system of small, nurse-controlled hospitals like those we had built along the Burma Road, supervised by means of weekly trips.

Returning to Loilem, I tanked up and started early the next morning for Kengtung, where a division of the Sixth Army had been stationed for more than a month. I took along the nurses who had come from Kengtung for training, since they had not been home for four years. We crossed the Salween Ferry at Takaw in the early afternoon, only to find that the road from there on permitted only one-way traffic, and the gates would not be opened for the east-bound traffic till seven in the evening. A visit to the local British officer secured for me a pass permitting us to travel all night. The nurses cooked dinner and we set off. The road to Kengtung is steep, full of curves, and very, very narrow. To avoid going over precipices the car had frequently to push against the bank on the other side. About three in the morning I was so sleepy I stopped the car, leaned over the wheel and dropped off for an hour. The four nurses had been sound asleep in each other's arms for some time. I had promised the officer, however, that I would be off the road and out of the way of west-bound traffic by seven, so I forced myself awake, drank a pint of hot coffee from my thermos and drove on, reaching the A.B.M. compound with a leeway of half an hour. We were welcomed with open arms, given a nice bed to spread out on, and I fell asleep after extracting a promise that no one would tell Mr. Buker I was there till nine o'clock. The promise was not kept. In fifteen minutes Buker came striding in in great excitement. I pretended to be in a coma, so at last he went away and let me have my two hours' sleep.

Buker thought I was an answer to his prayers and letters, none of which—not even the prayers—had reached me. I was delighted to find that in Kengtung things were already arranged. The mission hospital had been turned over to the Chinese Army under the direction of a Chinese physician from Rangoon who wished to join our unit. The English civil surgeon was very cordial and anxious to help us in every way. Buker took me around to headquarters, introducing me to two generals who seemed very fine types and most intelligent. With the aid of an interpreter I explained the orders that had been given me and agreed, on their advice, to open a front-line hospital at Mong Hpayak near the Siam border, from which serious cases could be transferred to the base hospital by ambulance. I arranged to leave our nurses in Kengtung and promised to send back others to open the Mong Hpayak hospital the following week. Then, at noon, I started back. I was lucky enough to get about five hours' sleep that night.

I had done all I could for the few days during which hospital construction was going on, and I knew that my first week away from Namkham would be very difficult for Ba Saw and E Hla; but I had forgotten to warn General Martin that, until there was actual battle, I would be making frequent trips back to Namkham. Taunggyi was only sixty miles west. I decided to see the general, outline the plans I had formulated, and get his approval. Running around the streets in Taunggyi were Bill, Htulum, Koi, Paul Geren, Whittington, and Tun Shein with their new jeeps. We had a celebration. Our work would be just possible now, whereas without the jeeps we would have been making much ado about nothing as far as medical service for the Chinese Army was concerned. Htulum and Koi had acted like old-timers, driving those jeeps up from Rangoon. They viewed with scorn their old man who was, at that time, afraid even to ride in one of the darn toys!

At Namkham it was just as I had feared. The nurses we had had to leave behind, albeit temporarily, had been just as mean as dirt because we had not taken them to the front. I pointed out to them the fact that they were very lucky in being assigned their share of the Namkham work at the beginning, before hostilities commenced, as they would not need to return to humdrum work in the middle of the excitement that would come later. They were only half convinced. Bella was now at term. Her pelvis was very narrow and she and Ba Saw were terrified at the thought of her having the baby while I was away. As Bella was not very strong and ought not to have another pregnancy soon, it would be more than they could bear if trial labor resulted in the death of the child. That evening I performed a Caesarian section, stayed with Bella for twelve hours, and then went off on the regular ambulance run for Kunlong. From Kunlong I returned to Loilem. Two more regiments of the Sixth Army had gone through to Mong Pan, and the general, whose headquarters was in that town, wished me to open our hospital there at once.

Htulum was the top nurse of our unit. It seemed only logical to put her in charge at Mong Pan with two younger girls and Lieng Sing, our Chinese college boy, to help her, Koi remaining in charge at Loilem. Htulum, being such a good driver, could keep a jeep at Mong Pan for use as an ambulance; while, if he was willing, Dr. Gurney of the English mission at Langkhu would answer emergency calls from Mong Pan when Htulum got into trouble. Loading a sufficient amount of supplies for the new hospital into a truck, we started off, Htulum trailing us in her jeep. As we passed through Langkhu we stopped and had tea with Mr. Short and Dr. Gurney. Another kindred spirit that was always looking for trouble, he already had his hospital full of Indian troops, with an occasional Chinese soldier or two who had been taken ill on the way to Mong Pan. Afraid he might be drafted some day for an office job in some out-of-the-way place far from scenes of action, he was delighted with the idea of joining our unit, and volunteered to make trips up to Mong Pan every other day to supervise Htulum's work. I am a most unfortunate chap. Short and ugly, every other male in our unit is tall and handsome, making me look and feel most awfully insignificant. Gurney was the prize of them all: a fair-haired Englishman with a lovely scar on his upper lip that looked as if it had been received in an honorable duel at Heidelberg! Sulkily I drove on to Mong Pan knowing it would be but a very short time before all our nurses fell in love with him. As a matter of fact, in two weeks they had dubbed him *achit galay*—"little pet"—or, as some of the nurses translated it, "first love." They have the name written above the door of his room at the present moment!

The sawbwa of Mong Pan built Htulum a fifty-bed hospital

of bamboo and teak-leaf thatch, above a cement floor of some unknown origin. There was a nice little nurses' home beside it. I was quite pleased with the arrangements, feeling no qualms at leaving the nurses there. I was sure they would be able to take care of themselves. One of the younger nurses was the Princess Louise, granddaughter of the sawbwa of Lawksawk—who was a very old friend of mine. Louise is unfortunate. Everyone falls in love with her, from my son John to a certain Chinese major at Mong Pan. Htulum and Lieng Sing were worried, at first, at the persistent attentions of the Chinese major, but Louise told them not to fret—she could handle him! So she took the poor man and made him teach her Mandarin until she was an expert. I lent her to my American Army colleague "somewhere in India," the other day, to act as interpreter.

"Louise is grand," said the major. "She must be one of your top nurses, isn't she?"

"No," I replied, "she is one of the youngest. We have a lot that know more than she does, good as she is." The major shook his head. He didn't believe me. But Louise is really grand. Educated in a convent in Burma, she speaks very nearly perfect English, and she has centuries of breeding behind her. A Shan princess, she is not too proud to do the most menial tasks for patients of any race; and she can keep her admirers, no matter of what race, just exactly where she wants them.

On my next trip to Mong Pan I discovered that the feeling the nurses had for Dr. Gurney was fully reciprocated. The girls had had a big laugh out of him. On his first visit he had poured sweat preparing and giving hypodermics of quinine to patient after patient.

LEND-LEASE TRUCKS

"Why not let us give those hypodermics for you," said Htulum, "while you examine the patients and write out the orders for medicines which you think they ought to have?"

"My goodness! Do you girls know how to give hypodermics?"

"Well, we don't know all about it, but we have given a few thousand and we can give intravenous injections, too, if you prefer the quinine given that way. Dr. Seagrave has supplied us with distilled water."

So Dr. Gurney confined his attentions to physical examinations, diagnosis and writing of his orders upon the sheets of toilet paper with which the nurses provided him. Wonderful thing, toilet paper! The nurses used it for almost everything except the use for which it was intended! It made wonderful emergency temperature charts and order sheets and served very well to wrap up medicines for ambulatory patients. They indented for such large supplies that the British ration stores must have felt that there was a cholera epidemic on!

When surgical cases, and a few casualties from raids into Siam, needed more than Htulum was able to give them, Dr. Gurney transferred the patients to his own hospital at Langkhu, asking if I could spare him a couple of nurses. I sent him first Pauline, and later Ohn Khin, also a princess, granddaughter of Mong Mow. Pauline and Ohn Khin still trail Dr. Gurney around everywhere and are never so happy as when near him.

Eight miles north of Loilem a missionary colleague of Dr. Gurney's, Dr. Barr-Johnston, had a small hospital. His civilian work practically at a standstill because of war rumors, he consented to take his ambulance and surgical equipment with him and assume responsibility for all our work east of the Salween in Kengtung State. That was an immense relief to us. Still we would be in a very tight spot indeed if hostilities were to break out along our whole three-hundred-mile front; so after settling our unit in the newly completed buildings near Loilem and taking a half day off to get control of a relapse of my malaria, I made another flying trip to Namkham. The morning following my arrival was spent in doing a lot of major operations Dr. Ba Saw had saved up for me. Late in the afternoon, I paid a visit to Loiwing to report on the job that had been given us, and to ask the co-operation of the company in contacting Chungking, Chengtu, and Kunming, with a view to obtaining medical officers for our unit.

For the following two weeks the work consisted of flying trips to first one and then another of our small hospitals, of which we now had six. What wards the contractors had completed in Loilem were full of Chinese soldiers—accident cases resulting from poor truck driving as the Army moved south, pneumonia caused by exposure, and the everlasting malaria. Troops were concentrated in Loilem itself. Rangoon had been evacuated, and Hla Sein, the first girl to lose her home and all her people, had a few days when her laughter and cheerful singing were silenced. Then hard work came to her rescue, and the songs and laughs burst forth once more, never to subside. The last division of the Sixth Army was moving into the Karenni States east of Toungoo, with headquarters at Loikaw. The Fifth Army, much better troops, was hurrying down, convoy after convoy traveling night and day through Mandalay to Toungoo where they were digging themselves in.

At Mong Ton, beyond the Salween and only a few miles from the Siam border, advance units of the division that had its headquarters at Mong Pan had made contact with Siamese troops. I picked three nurses, of whom the chief was Chit Sein, "Miss Burma, 1942," to open a small hospital there. Having no doctor to spare, I asked Paul Geren to go with the nurses and add to their prestige as well as protect their morale. A forty-mile walk was necessary from the end of the dirt road beyond Mong Pan. I felt positively ill as I escorted the little party to the road's end. The other two girls were Kachin and had been toughened by many years of life in the mountains, but this little Shan beauty, brought up in comfort, was in for a very, very hard trip which I was sure she could never stand. I was convinced that I was bidding them a permanent good-by. Later a nice long letter came back by messenger from Paul. Chit Sein had smiled and laughed the whole way there, standing the trip much better than he had. One day's journey from Mong Ton the Chinese had sent out a group of dignitaries to welcome them and bring them to the post in style. A tremendous Chinese banquet had been prepared in their honor. Paul, a doctor of science, was assumed to be a doctor of medicine, and all the sick officers sent for him. Being a canny man, Paul took Chit Sein with him on each visit.

"Chit Sein," said Paul in an undertone, as he made a theatrical examination of the patient, "what the dickens is the matter with this fellow?"

"He has malaria," Chit Sein replied without moving her lips.

"What do you think ought to be done for him?"

"Chinese like injections; I think we had better give him a hypodermic of quinine."

"Chit Sein," said Paul in an authoritative tone, as he put away the spare stethoscope, "this officer has a bad attack of malaria. Please give him an injection of quinine."

Under the treatment of such a handsome doctor and lovely nurse, it was impossible for the patients not to get well!

Mong Pan hospital now had a hundred beds. Htulum had become very popular not only with the Chinese Army but with the medical officers of the Indian troops that still remained there, and the latter continually sent particularly difficult cases to her for treatment.

When we were about to leave Namkham for service, Htulum had come to me.

"I have been engaged for ten years to a Kachin schoolmate of mine who was planning to study veterinary medicine," she said. "My folks did not approve of him and tried to compel me to marry other men whom they preferred; but I loved this man. We postponed our wedding until he got himself a good job and I had had enough fun nursing. He has his job now, and I am getting older. I want to marry him on the first of April but I don't want to miss out on our unit's war service. Can you give me a month's vacation beginning from the middle of March? As soon as our honeymoon is over I will return to duty and remain with the unit till the end of the war."

"O.K.," I said. "That's fair enough. I will take you back to Namkham myself on any date you set."

It was now the second week of March, so I asked Htulum if she was ready to start home.

"No," she replied, "I am having too much fun here, and I still want to make one trip to Kengtung with you the next time you go there. If you will take me back to Namkham four days before the wedding that will be quite enough."

On the eighteenth day of March, I was due to have a birthday. I hoped that, without Tiny there to remind them, the nurses would forget about it; so on the seventeenth I went to Loikaw to make preparations for opening our last branch hospital there, and purposely did not get back to Loilem till nearly midnight on the eighteenth. As the car pulled in by my shack, the strains of "Happy Birthday to You" swelled out from the throats of the entire unit—boys and girls—all of whom would have stayed up until morning if necessary. My shack was decorated inside and out with flowers "salvaged" from the town. On my table was a tremendous assortment of presents surrounding a three-tier birthday cake. My eyes were a bit damp as I opened the presents and read the little birthday messages in ungrammatical English, in Burmese, and Shan. When I had thanked them, Htulum, who had come in her jeep for the occasion, told me that there was still another present, but it was so big they could not carry it through the door of my hut and had had to park it outside. I went out to look. There it was, a palatial latrine! Over the door was written, "Happy Birthday to the Doctor from the Boys with Love." Then we all had a big laugh, went back in, and finished off that cake with extraordinary efficiency!

13

Under General Stilwell

NEXT MORNING we started for Kengtung with the large ambulance loaded with supplies for Dr. Barr-Johnston. Htulum, Esther, Hla Sein, and Roi Tsai went along to study geography. Htulum and I took turns with the driving. We got a few hours of uneasy sleep, scattered as we were on top of bundles of medicines and gauze. Barr-Johnston was at Mong Hpayak near the Siam border. Stowing away a meal of Chinese *hkow swe*, grandfather of all chop sueys, we pushed on. I really believe that trip from Kengtung to the Siam border is the most beautiful in Burma. My experience with narrow roads was rich, but this road was the narrow road to end all narrow roads! It was literally nothing but a shelf, sometimes cut out of solid rock, sometimes built up with stones from the river's bed. You had to scrape the cliff to stay on the road at times. We were in Kaw country, and the nurses soon dubbed the women "bare navels." Every Kaw woman had a pipe in her mouth and a bare, protuberant abdomen. Extraordinary! The ambulance engine was running on only half her cylinders, so we did not reach Mong Hpayak till after dark. Barr-Johnston had so many patients that he had taken over a lot of bazaar buildings and had a flourishing two-hundred-bed hospital. Before the Japs burst through, our unit was handling seven hundred and fifty beds over a three-hundred-mile front for the Chinese Sixth Army alone. The little Shan nurses were so glad to see us! I wonder where they are now? They did not connect with us on the evacuation. I hope the Japs did not get them, for they were too lovely to turn over to Japanese soldiers.

With two drivers, we made the return trip in record time. Esther and Hla Sein, singing almost continuously, kept getting back to that old Karen song of mythical origin.

KAREN SONG

With its delightful minor harmonies we sang it over and over until it became the theme song of our unit. Americans who are assigned to interview us, or work with us, often come with deep-seated prejudices against missionaries and Christian natives; but let us sing that song for them just once, without warning, and they decide our folks are pretty good after all! There is a distinct majesty about that tune.

Next morning we separated at Loilem. I had just heard that Lieutenant General Stilwell had arrived from America to take over command of the Chinese armies in Burma. Was I going to have a chance to work under an American general after all? Had there been some plan behind all my years of misery practicing wastebasket surgery, building up all that work in the Shan States, forcing myself to keep on pushing, God knows why, when all the odds were against us? Was I, perhaps, to be permitted to do some little bit that would help the America that I loved and called my own even though most of my life had been spent in a foreign country? If so, all the misery I had gone through would have been worth while, for as a result of it, I was the only American doctor in the world who had under his command a group of nurses that could speak Chinese and all the languages of Burma; nurses who had been so trained that they enjoyed nothing so much as hard work and emergencies of all sorts; nurses who fought and went on strike if they were not chosen for the hardest and most dangerous tasks; nurses who looked upon anything calling himself an American as a sort of tin god! God! Was there a real place for us in this damnable war after all?

I had not the least idea that General Stilwell would see me. What little reputation I had obtained in Burma would be completely unknown to him. If I had tried to brag about what we had accomplished in the Shan States, General Stilwell would be perfectly justified in dismissing me with a shrug. To believe that the general was a judge of men, without prejudice against missionaries in general and "Burmese" nurses in particular, was surely wishful thinking. At least so I thought as I traveled north to Maymyo, the general's headquarters, leaving Htulum to go south to her post at Mong Pan for the last week's work before her return to Namkham and her long-delayed wedding.

I was mistaken; General Stilwell would see me! His medical chief, Colonel R. P. Williams, would also like to have my ideas with regard to supplies necessary for the Chinese armies. Very, very diffidently, I asked that my surgical unit be permitted to serve the Fifth Army, which was in action at Toungoo, while the medical unit maintained the hospitals already at work with the Sixth Army. Still more diffidently I begged that our units be transferred from the control of the British Liaison Mission to the American Army. Nobody was more surprised than I when the general approved of my suggestions and promised to issue the necessary orders as soon as things could be arranged with the British. I completed the trip to Namkham, relieved that I had not been thrown out on my neck!

At Namkham everything was serene. The nurses had started to co-operate again, beginning to believe that I loved them after all! E Hla, especially, was glad to see me. Ba Saw, relieved from his Namkham duties by the arrival of a Burmese woman doctor who had worked with me previously in Namkham, was fretting for permission to return to the front. Bella was well after her operation. The baby was putting on weight. As the jeep climbed out of the valley with two more nurses, whose turn it was to go to the front, I looked back. Suddenly a feeling of homesickness came over me. I was positively nauseated. "I'll bet that is the last time I see those buildings in Namkham," I said to the nurses. They kept their mouths shut. Thank God for people who know when it is best not to say anything!

At Lashio a telegram reached me: "Htulum killed. Wire instructions." Lord! What had happened to that poor girl? Just about to be married to the man she loved for ten years, could she really have been killed? Why had I not insisted on her returning to Namkham at the time originally agreed upon between us? If she had returned then she would be alive and sewing on her trousseau! I rushed on to Loilem to find out. Htulum, returning to her post in the jeep, was traveling on a perfectly straight, loosely graveled road, when her left front tire burst, and the car turned over. Htulum's skull was crushed by the windshield and she died instantly. The nurse with her had sustained three fractured ribs but was doing well, while Moses, the orderly, had escaped with a few bruises. They buried Htulum among the beautiful pines by our hospital.

It was a sad group of girls that met us that day. Our first casualty the most competent girl of the unit! Something drastic was needed to set the girls back on their feet again. That "something" was lying on my table: orders from General Stilwell to report to General Sibert at Pyawbwe before setting up for active duty at Pyinmana. I called all the girls together.

"I don't want any heroics this time," I said. "I know there is not one of you girls that would not follow me into hell! We will need twelve nurses at Pyinmana, but our Sixth Army work has to go on. The girls who remain are going to have just as hard a task as those who go, and are going to be in just as much danger without having the thrills of Pyinmana to help them in their daily work. Paul Geren and Tun Shein are going with me, but Mr. Cummings is staying on with the Sixth Army group. Take a slip of paper and write on it where you personally feel your real place in this picture is and hand the slips in to me."

The slips returned; we counted them out. Thirteen girls asked for Pyinmana, one of them the girl with three broken ribs. The others had indicated one or the other of the Sixth Army hospitals as the spot where they felt their work would prove most valuable.

"Well, girls," I said, as we bade them good-by, "you can count on Bill and me. We won't leave you in any of your hospitals unprotected if the Japs ever break through and a retreat becomes necessary. Some of you already know and love Dr. Ted Gurney, who is top doctor now for the Sixth Army, and Ba Saw is coming back to help. Give them the satisfaction in your work that you have given me and scramble for the trenches when the Japs come over!"

Bill accompanied us as far as Kalaw where he had a summer cottage. Spending our first night draped all over his floor and the few beds, we raided his stores for everything the Japs might like to have and then, amid a burst of sobs at the thought of leaving behind the beloved "son-in-law," as the nurses called him, we hurried on down the mountain, our trucks and jeeps camouflaged with branches of trees in the most approved Chinese Army pattern. At Meiktila the British garrison gazed in unbelieving awe at a group of "Burmese" girls heading for the front instead of running away at top speed! On reporting to General Sibert we were informed that a group of British

Friends Ambulance men had volunteered to serve with our unit and would follow us down immediately to Pyinmana. General Sibert recommended that we pass the night in Pyawbwe, but I requested permission to push on at once as we all wanted to get on with our job.

It was midnight when we reached Mr. Case's agricultural school on the outskirts of Pyinmana, the F.A.U. trucks on our heels. Mr. Case was away looking for food for the Chinese Fifth Army that he was feeding, but we assumed he would approve of our using his buildings; so we set up our operating equipment while the F.A.U. boys went on to the front for their first load of patients. When the operating room was ready for action we snatched a couple of hours' sleep, waking up again at 4:00 A. M. to the sound of the returning ambulances.

We started operating at once. Those operations before dawn that morning are hazy memories. All that stands out in my mind is the trouble we had keeping plaster casts on our patients. There was a high percentage of bone injuries requiring "Spanish treatment" and we were using plaster steadily; but it was very inferior and took so long to set that the patient was awake and tearing at it while it was still soft. Nurses tied arms and legs together, but the patients tried so hard to get free that the casts were cracked and broken. While I was removing a foot of intestine from one badly injured patient, Mr. Case walked in. He was delighted that we were doing something for the Chinese, but he could not permit us to remain in the agricultural-school buildings. He had had a great deal of trouble keeping a sufficient number of boys with him to help secure food for the Army. If we remained the boys would be in terror of our drawing a Japanese attack on the buildings and they would run away. I did not tell Mr. Case that if his boys ran away from the group of girls working with me they would be the only males in the world capable of doing so! The best way Case could ensure having his staff of males remain on duty in the agricultural school, bombs and all, would be to keep our girls located there. But I was too sleepy and busy to argue. During a short lull we piled our packing cases back onto the trucks and moved over to the "Child Welfare Center" where there was one small, very inferior building. On the bottom floor were two small open porches. We chose one of the porches for the operating room and set up four operating tables. The upstairs floor was soon covered with bedrolls, while the main floor was reserved for patients. The ambulances now returned from their second trip to the front, and with a good deal of trouble, the Friends located us in our new setup. We started operating again and were soon in our stride. This was getting to be old stuff. Four of the nurses were upstairs getting a little sleep preparatory to taking over when the first group downstairs dropped from exhaustion. Two of them, with the help of Low Wang and Lieng Sing, were giving first aid to the casualties as they were brought in and deciding the order in which the patients would be sent for operation. Esther and Big Bawk each had two tables assigned to them and were pouring chloroform in a way that would have delighted Tiny, who taught them. Koi, Kyang Tswi, Ruth and Little Bawk were assisting, one at each table. The sun began to scorch us. Off came my surgeon's gown, then my rubber apron. I would rather catch a Japanese bomb than perish from heat stroke as I moved from table to table debriding devitalized tissues, putting bone fragments together, throwing powdered sulfanilamide tablets into the wounds and applying plaster casts. Sweat was still pouring, and my shirt, undershirt, and stockings came off and were thrown into a corner, leaving me in nothing but a pair of bloody shorts. It was grand to be a man! I could work in a pair of shorts without anyone's getting excited! The poor nurses were not so fortunate. Their thin little Burmese jackets plastered tight to their bodies, they had to sweat and gasp and like it! A squadron of Japanese bombers passed over us on its way to Mandalay, and I forced the girls to jump into the slit trenches in the back yard. An hour or so later the formation returned. Since the girls were convinced that all bombs had been disposed of and that the planes were returning empty, I could not persuade them to leave off operating. Just as the planes were straight above us the bombs began to scream downward.

"Lie down, you darn little fools," I yelled as the bombs burst a scant two hundred yards down the street.

Paul had dragged the spare nurses into one of the trenches and heard them praying as the explosions shook the house, "Oh, God, don't let the doctor get hurt; don't let him get hurt!"

As fire began to sweep the town we returned to our operating tables. Civilian bomb casualties were now being brought in. I simply could not locate the bullet in the thigh of one of our Chinese patients.

"Here, let me have a try," said Koi. She inserted one tiny finger in the wound, using it as a guide for a long forceps, and out came the bullet!

"Listen, woman, what are you helping me for? You take over

this table and do your own darned operations! I'm busy. Debride each case, get the bullet or shell fragment out if you can, pack the wound, and if the destruction is extensive, put on a plaster cast."

Kyang Tswi and Ruth were getting along pretty well also. All I needed to do was select uncomplicated cases for them, explore, and leave them to trim, while I kept them in view out of the corner of my eye. Little Bawk and I handled the worst cases: abdominal, chest, and head wounds. Just as we were really going to town I looked up and saw General Stilwell standing in the doorway! The room behind him was littered with the patients we had been operating on, lying on our little cotton mattresses. On the ground outside nurses were receiving patients from the trucks and giving first aid. Three Chinese casualties were standing by the wall of the operating room waiting for nurses and Friends to carry away the one who had been operated on so they could climb up on the vacant operating table and sigh thankfully as Bawk or Esther began to chloroform them. My body was covered with blood. Well, I was in for it! The general certainly wouldn't have any use for me now!

Soon after the general left, some liaison officers appeared with a few Chinese soldiers whom they had impressed to help bury the dead.

"Can't you help us get some food for these patients?" I shouted over the verandah railing. "Some of them haven't had a bite to eat for three days."

Soon a liaison officer returned with several Chinese soldiers and a lot of rice.

"Look at that white foreigner there on the verandah," he said to the soldiers. "He has taken off everything but his shorts and he is covered with blood and pus from your Chinese buddies. How about you boys taking off a few surplus clothes and feeding and otherwise helping all these casualties?"

He stood watching us. The sweat was pouring down my face, and one of the spare nurses came to wipe it off with a gauze sponge, inexpertly knocking my glasses off. Her hand swooped down and caught the glasses in the air before they crashed on the cement floor.

"Gosh, that was close," I said. "If they had broken I would have had to operate by sense of touch until we could get some more lenses from Calcutta."

The nurse stood trembling all over for some time because she had come so close to wrecking our work!

We had not had many bites to eat ourselves and had forgotten all about food, as a matter of fact, when Tun Shein asked us to knock off for a while and eat the dinner that had been ready for some hours so that the cooks could get some sleep. When we went upstairs we found the rice and curry served up on enamel plates on the floor. The town was blazing merrily. Paul assured me the flames were not coming our way, and would not do so unless the wind veered around to the west.

"O.K.," I said, "give us plenty of warning if the fire spreads this way so that we can get the patients out to safety."

The food disposed of, we went back to our operations. Two Storm King lamps and the burning town furnished us light. Tomorrow, I thought, we must locate some other place where we will not have to worry about fire. We ourselves and our precious supplies are not important. With the trucks always handy we can get away easily, but the patients are a different matter. Already we are filling the surrounding houses with them. During the first thirty-six hours we have operated on a hundred and fifty. We must find some hospital fifty or a hundred miles back that will receive our patients.

About midnight we turned in. At two there was a stamping, and the girls on night duty aroused me to receive some distinguished visitors. Colonel Chen had brought a Dr. Mei to see me. Mei, a graduate of Johns Hopkins and a surgeon of no mean repute throughout China, had been told of my telegrams to Chungking, Chengtu, and Kunming for help. He had brought a corps of his nurses with him and was planning to set up just the base hospital we needed at Pyawbwe, General Sibert's headquarters. That was grand news! I promised Dr. Mei several truckloads of patients as soon as the trucks could move in the morning. It was pretty nice, being able to send our patients back to a first-class man like Mei. All through the Burma War our chief grouse was that we could not keep our patients with us so we could follow up our own cases and check on the correctness of our surgical procedures. At least we did not have the right type of follow-up treatment. Later he did us the honor to say that after checking fracture cases with X-ray he found that he need never worry about the primary work done on the casualties cared for by our unit. And Colonel Wong informed us that 45 per cent of the cases we sent back were able to return to military duty.

The next day, as we were treating the truckloads of new casualties, Paul explored the town. There was nothing big enough for us but the lousy jail, and he advised our moving three miles closer to the front where there were some abandoned Government Agricultural Institute buildings. I drove out to have a look and was so pleased that on my return the nurses packed up, nurses and Friends loaded the trucks during the first lull, and we moved—the second time in forty-eight hours.

14

Hospitals under Fire

Pyinmana, March 30th—This is a grand place. The school building has a nice cement floor and plenty of windows. There is a laboratory with all sorts of glassware which we must carry with us if we have to move again. There are two teachers' houses. The Friends have moved into one and our group is in the other. There are a lot of huts scattered around the grounds and we can put patients into them. Today bombers passed over us twice, one formation bombing Pyinmana again. It is nice to have clean well water. Our patients had thrown bloody bandages into the other well at Pyinmana. We all got a nice bath by the well, the nurses bathing in their *longyis* (skirts) and us menfolks in our shorts. We can have water carried to our bathrooms tomorrow.

March 31st—Another big day. The F.A.U. brought in several more truckloads from Yedashe where the Chinese are making a big stand. They lost the Toungoo airfield. Magwe field has been bombed, they say, and about thirty A.V.G. planes were destroyed on the ground. I guess that leaves us without any air support. The only decent landing ground this side of Namkham seems to be Pyawbwe and the Japs are over Pyawbwe every day. While we were getting ready to operate, an American officer drove up and said he was Captain O'Hara of the Dental

Corps. General Stilwell had ordered him to come down to help us. Another one of those tall, handsome guys! What the dickens was I going to do with a dentist, especially this one! After he had watched us for a while he offered to do some of the smaller operations. Gosh, he didn't even know how to scrub up! He washed his hands just like any dentist does before he sticks his thumb in your mouth! He made a mess of a couple of simple cases and then the F.A.U. brought in another of those shattered jaws like the one that took me so long to put together in Pyinmana. While I was exploring the possibilities of the case, O'Hara took a look.

"Listen," he said, "I don't know anything about surgery, but I can put that jaw together for you."

I let him go to it with a sigh of relief. By George, that fellow certainly knew his job! By the time he had finished I had something I could really drape that face over.

Friends are the funniest Englishmen I ever met. They pick those blood-covered patients up in their arms as if they were sweet and lovely. Every Chinese seems to them to have been named "George." The Friends themselves don't seem to have any last names; they are teaching the nurses to call them "Bill" and "Eric" and "Martin." The girls get a great kick out of calling white men by their first names! Well, if the girls can get a laugh out of them it is all right by me. Today the Friends were out cooking for the patients. I wouldn't feed the slop they produced to a pig!

April 1st—An observation plane circled over us several times this morning. The Chinese have a gasoline dump fifty yards away from us, camouflaged by banian trees. I suppose the Japs were looking for it. I had to give the nurses a tongue-thrashing because they insisted on staying out to watch the planes. One squadron passed over but didn't drop any bombs on us or on Pyinmana. Captain O'Hara is still here. Today Captain Eldridge, who seems to be an Army publicity man, paid us a visit and took a lot of pictures. These nurses of ours seemed to strike him as quite picturesque. He was so astounded at the idea of nurses driving trucks and jeeps that we posed a couple of pictures for him. When we quit work, late tonight, we were so tired we had a short sing. That Karen song certainly has real harmony. I like to sing out on those low bass notes; the nurses think I am funny!

April 2nd—Captain Eldridge seemed to like that Karen tune. Must have been listening to it over at the other house when I thought he was in bed. During our rush hours today several newspapermen came in, but I was too busy to talk to them. Heard later that they had been surprised to see Esther give three anesthetics at one time, jumping from table to table. We have five tables now. The F.A.U. stole one from an abandoned hospital in town. They are going to steal me a sterilizer tomorrow—"salvage" it, I mean. Captain O'Hara doesn't seem to object quite so much to having to work with me as he did. But he doesn't like our food!

April 3rd—Another captain turned up today while I was matching the nurses for blood transfusion: Captain Grindlay trained in the Mayo Clinic after finishing Harvard. Looks just like a Mayo Clinic man, too! I will have to keep a stiff upper lip and do the best surgery I can. At least he hasn't operated on as many different parts of the body as I have! One of my cases today was a man with a bullet through his skull. I asked Grindlay if he didn't want to handle that patient, but he preferred an abdominal case. There was nothing for it but to go ahead as if O'Hara and Grindlay were not there. I used my old wastebasket trephine to remove about three square inches of shattered skull. The brains were beginning to ooze out even before I cut the dura mater. I simply could not locate the bullet, so I put in a vaseline wick and sewed a few stitches in his scalp. Bet he dies tonight! Grindlay had a patient with a piece of shrapnel in his hip just like one of those cases at Loiwing. He finally listened to me and opened the abdomen and found the intestines were ripped up just as I said.

Grindlay had a tale to tell about his trip down. Those planes that passed over us this morning were apparently headed for Mandalay, because Mandalay had been bombed and was burning madly as he came through. He had stopped at the medical stores there to ask for medicines that Colonel Williams requisitioned for me. The officer in charge said the drugs would be ready in three or four days. Grindlay said no, they would be ready right now!—and in half an hour he had them! Pyawbwe was also bombed and the whole town east of the railway was burning. Good thing General Sibert's headquarters are west of the railway! Pyinmana had its fourth bombing this afternoon. The F.A.U. went in right away and found a lot of casualties at the station. One woman had had both legs blown off and died just as Grindlay was getting her to sleep.

We stopped for a while and had dinner again on the floor. All the available furniture is being used in the operating room. Grindlay and O'Hara look disgusted when they see us eating the rice and curry with our hands. We have very little silverware, but I am eating with my hands myself as a morale measure. No oriental likes to be bombed, but if I can make these girls realize that their old man is in this thing on an equal footing with them and takes no privileges, they will keep on the way they have done, ignoring the bombings as if they liked them. Later I can start using silverware again. This responsibility for the mess of these officers weighs heavily on me. Ko Nyunt cannot possibly cook two messes. Tun Shein is helping in the kitchen as it is, like any menial. We make a special effort to give O'Hara and Grindlay silverware and a suitcase or box to sit on, but I know they are still horribly shocked. While we were eating, Little Bawk was stung by a scorpion as she put one of the operative cases to bed. Sometimes those scorpion stings are so severe that they incapacitate; but we sucked the poison out and there is as yet little swelling.

This morning, when the bombers went over, Chinese soldiers saw some *hpongyis* near the road signaling with their long robes, and hanged three of them out of hand. Just as we were sitting down to dinner they marched two more past us and a minute later we heard a crackle of rifle shots. The Burmese are so stupid. They think that if Japan conquers the country they will immediately be given independence. Their reading of the proverb is, "A bird in the bush is worth two in the hand." I doubt whether, of the Burmese themselves, more than 10 per cent are fifth columnists, and certainly 10 per cent are completely loyal. The great majority are kind and gentle and want only to be left in peace to make enough money from their rice fields to live in what to them is comfort. Certainly the Burmese we have met have been very co-operative. The

Shans and Kachins and other people of the mountains are at least 90 per cent loyal to the English whose justice they recognize fully.

There has been tremendous traffic on the road past us all day. The trucks are going down empty and coming back full. Liaison men say the Chinese are retreating from Yedashe. What worries me is that bridge across the Sittang at Pyinmana. The bombs today dropped very near it. If they should destroy it we would cease to be of any use to the Chinese Army. We had a consultation of all hands, and decided to move on tonight.

Shwemyo Cliff, April 4th—We packed up late last night. I am afraid I was not of much use. One of the darned boxes lit on my foot and took off some skin, and I was so tired from the operations that I could make only a pretense of bossing the packing. It was a pretense, all right, because Koi and Esther can do a much better job than I can. Those Friends were Herculean in their efforts. Eric can throw a hundred-and-fifty-pound case into a truck without any help. Big Bawk is almost as good as he is when she gets excited. Paul is such a handsome chap it doesn't seem possible that he could do half what he did tonight, and Tun Shein continually astonished me. I am afraid I am getting old. Had some fever yesterday.

The Shwemyo Cliff bungalow is where we are now: first place we could find north of the Sittang bridge. Got here at four o'clock this morning, so tired we just dropped down on our bedrolls and slept till nine. My brain case is still alive and, furthermore, conscious and up to mischief, although he seems a bit crazy. We unpacked and set up for work, but had to run for the nullahs every two hours as squadron after squadron passed over us. We are much too much in the public (Jap) eye here. The bungalow is right on the brow of the hill where they can't miss us, and today the planes swooped down and machine-gunned the village at the foot of the hill. Every time the planes had passed by and we returned from the nullahs, someone had to go after that brain case. Once he had run half a mile away. Why *does* he live? Hasn't even got a fever!

As soon as their trucks were unloaded this morning, the Friends went off with several loads of patients to bestow them on Dr. Mei at Pyawbwe. They came back minus one truck which the Japs had strafed. All four tires had been ripped to pieces. The drivers plopped into the ditches on each side of the road just in time.

Had to swear at those nurses today. A blistering hot wind came on and they got fed up with running for cover every time the bombers came over. Maran Lu climbed up a tamarind tree and wouldn't come down, so I dragged her down and over to cover, and darn near dislocated the poor girl's shoulder.

We all went down to the river to bathe. Grindlay is so shy he won't bathe anywhere near the girls, even in his shorts. He went off fifty yards and bathed by himself. While we were bathing, a Chinese colonel discovered us and said there were a lot of machine-gun casualties ten miles down the road. The Friends went after them, on their way passing a truck that had caught fire when the bullets struck. The driver's companion and three soldiers were sitting in their seats, burned to a crisp.

The driver himself and any other soldiers that had been aboard, not being hit by bullets, had got away. We operated on the casualties under the house. The bugs were awful!

April 5th, Sunday—Tennant, head of the F.A.U., came in from China today and had a long talk with the Friends. Chinese soldiers are shooting Burmese fifth columnists. Didn't have any casualties because the Friends can't locate the front! Bill Brough, top man of our special group of Friends, and I took the opportunity to run around in a jeep and find a more suitable place. Tatkon, a few miles nearer Pyawbwe, was our choice. It was raining as we loaded the trucks again at night, but the girls kept singing! I suppose they were happy because Tun Shein butchered a pig that Case bestowed on us. We all liked that pork curry, but Grindlay says it is "wretched slop." O'Hara is eating almost nothing. Nurses are commenting on the fact that Sunday is always our busiest day. Every Sunday is moving day!

Tatkon, April 6th—An observation plane circled over us as we got up. There was no place to hide except in a sugar-cane field, and I am scared to death of snakes. Prefer bombs any day! About a quarter of a mile away there was a government "Rural Uplift Center," the compound of which is full of beautiful banian trees under which we could hide the trucks as well as ourselves. All of us felt this was a much nicer place, so we moved again. The American officers and the Friends have taken over a little bungalow, and our unit is in the upstairs floor of the school building, which is quite nice, now that we have torn out the wooden partitions between the rooms to let the air through. Blistering hot! Ko Nyunt burned the oatmeal again this morning, much to the disgust of Grindlay and O'Hara. But what can I do! No use getting angry with Ko Nyunt who has his troubles trying to cook food without any cooking facilities whatever. I keep getting fever, so I don't care what they feed us. That night with Barton at Namsarawp in December is going to be the finish of me yet! The nurses give me so many injections that I manage to keep on working, which is the most important thing. First the English and now General Stilwell have so much faith in us that we must keep going!

In spite of our horrible food Grindlay and O'Hara seem to be getting over their antipathy for our unit. Grindlay can't understand the nurses insisting on making up his bed for him every day although they are as tired as he is. Tonight, not having been worked to death, our morale was at a low ebb, so we had a sing. Both officers stayed for it. Neither of them can sing, but they sit and listen in amazement at the wonderful harmony the girls raise. Geren has a really fine voice, but insists on singing soprano. Several of the Friends are Welshmen and are certainly an addition! They are teaching us new tunes for "Love Divine" and "Guide Me O Thou Great Jehovah." The latter is the tune the Welsh miners sing in "How Green Was My Valley." The bass in it is passionate! I hate the old tune of "Love Divine" so much that this new effort suits me down to the ground. O'Hara asked the girls to sing "There's a Church in the Valley," and from his expression, you might think he was having a glimpse of Heaven. Every time we sing the nurses call for "Diadem" and "The Spacious Firmament," that poem of Addison's sung to a tune from "The Creation."

I think the thing that astonishes our honored guests the most is the wide variety of songs the nurses sing: anything from the grand old hymns to the jazz "gospel songs."

April 7th—Tun Shein has found some Burmese coolies to dig slit trenches for us. They work in the early morning and late afternoon, disappearing during Jap bombing time. Planes have been over again and again today. The nurses pulled a new gag on me so that I wouldn't make them jump into the trenches— the sand keeps getting into their hair! Silly fools stand on the edge of the trenches in full sight waiting for me to jump in first! Unless I jump in there is no possible way to make them take cover. Darn it! Those Jap planes are interfering with my sleep. Every time they come over, a squad of nurses comes running for me. Wish they would leave me alone! Still, it was fun watching them today; they kept swooping low over the road, machine-gunning the Chinese trucks.

For some time I have noticed that O'Hara never takes shelter in the same trench that I do, no matter where it is. I figured, as a result of my inferiority complex, that it must be due to some personal objection to me, but it turned out today that he was afraid both he and I might be hit by the same bomb! He was willing to be hit by a bomb in the pursuit of his duty, but wanted me, in such a case, to be still alive and able to operate on him!

Both Grindlay and O'Hara feel no special desire to be killed in action defending Burma or India or China, though they would have no qualms at all if they were to be required to die for the United States. Somehow my mind can't see any difference, the way the world situation has developed. Maybe I am deluding myself with wishful thinking, but somehow or other I keep feeling that everything we are trying to do here is being done for America and, perhaps, the whole world. Nobody feels the insignificance of our work more than I do, but it keeps us cheerful to imagine that our work may be worth something, after all.

The Friends brought in thirty-four patients, of whom all but two were serious casualties. There were three brain cases, and I did them all. Since my first brain case is doing so well, walking all over the place, everyone thinks I am a brain surgeon! Two of these died on the table, but I still feel cocky, for the third was the worst, and he is still alive! The girls put him on the table soon after the ambulances arrived, but in addition to having a shell fragment in his brain, he had shell wounds all over him and looked so ghastly that I told the nurses to carry him out and let him die in peace while I went on operating on the other seriously injured cases that I might possibly save. When all the operations were done I was about to take off my gloves; but Ruth asked me if I wasn't going to operate on the patient they had thrown out behind the kitchen.

"Golly," I said, "is he still alive? Gosh darn it, bring him in." It took me another hour to finish him off. I don't believe he is going to die after all. Grindlay is helping the nurses give him a huge intravenous injection of glucose.

The bugs are awful. The only way I can stand it is to operate naked except for the pair of thin Shan pants that Tun Shein located for me today. The nurses obligingly scratch my back at frequent intervals. Grindlay is apparently getting over his shyness, a bit. He can stand the bugs anywhere but on his bald head. O'Hara will not go to bed as long as there is any work to do. Even if he can't find a patient to operate on he sticks around helping the nurses with their jobs. Grindlay had trouble with a neck wound today, tearing into the jugular vein as he was debriding. He packed the wound and the patient is O.K. I was away at Yamethin at the time trying to "salvage" some hospital equipment.

I have been jealous for some time of the way the girls have a nickname for everyone, or call them by their first names. They have already adopted Grindlay and call him "Uncle" quite shamelessly. O'Hara, as soon as they caught sight of his hairy chest, became "Mr. Bear." Tun Shein is "Little Uncle," Geren "Big Brother," Gurney "First Love." Bill Cummings, being the favorite of all the nurses, is known as my "son-in-law"; but they won't call me anything but "Doctor" to my face, "The Old Man" behind my back, and "Our Father and Mother" when they write me letters. This afternoon at lunch, before the casualties began to arrive, the Friends were having a lot of fun kidding the nurses, and they were certainly up to mischief! One of the Friends decided that Roi Tsai needed to be spanked and chased after her. She naturally ran to me for protection.

"That's right, run to daddy," said the Friend. Koi, ringleader in everything, began to call me "daddy," and now none of the nurses calls me anything else unless I am administering a rebuke. It makes me homesick for John and Sterling.

Moving so often we have broken all the mantles for our gasoline lamps, and only one Storm King lamp was available for the operations when the sun set. Candles help some.

Kyang Tswi is working too hard. She gets thinner every day. I suppose it is the heat. She has never done well in a hot climate since that spot of tuberculosis she had the year she came into training.

April 8th—The Friends arrived with twenty-five casualties at dawn. There were two belly cases two days old that I turned over to Grindlay. He had to remove two feet of bowel from one case, doing a beautiful anastomosis. I took time out to watch him. He sure knows his stuff! Both those cases are doing right well. So is my brain case of yesterday! He is still unconscious, but his condition is good. I shall have to send away the first brain case I did south of Pyinmana, since we have no room for him. Most of the cases today had serious shattering wounds of bone. Grindlay had one case with four compound fractures. That guy is a hound for work! The nastier the case the better he likes it. The Friends brought in another eighty cases. The older girls were all in, so I put Little Bawk on as first assistant to Grindlay when he was operating on his abdominal cases. Mean way to make a young kid like her the one and only assistant at the sort of abdominal cases he was operating on; but he seemed to like her. At dinner tonight he said she was a "natural," and the best assistant he had ever had. And he comes from the Mayo Clinic!

I have decided to send Paul back to Namkham with Kyang Tswi. She has a few tuberculosis rales in both apices. Lord, don't let that girl die! Paul can start back before dawn so as to be off the main Mandalay road before the bombers appear. It really is kind of the Japs to choose such regular bombing times. Kyang Tswi wept when I ordered her off, but promised me she would co-operate. I, for my part, assured her we would bring her back as soon as she got control of her disease.

15

Medical Major

April 9th—Paul and Kyang Tswi started off about four this morning. At four-thirty Bill Brough and Brian Jones, who had left last night with two trucks to bring in casualties, came back with one truck. There were twenty patients crowded in on the straw. Bill had quite a tale to tell. At the usual first-aid post they had few patients. The Chinese officer said that there were a large number of serious cases farther on, so Bill left Brian and started off with Yen Ling, his Chinese interpreter, to find them. Enquiring along the road, he was continually directed to proceed still farther forward. Suddenly a bullet whipped through the windshield just where he would have been sitting if he had been driving a Lend-Lease truck instead of a Canadian-manufactured right-hand drive. Bill decided he must already be between the Chinese and Japanese lines, and shouting to Yen Ling to jump, he stopped the car and bent over to open the door. As he bent, a bullet whizzed over his head. He and Yen Ling dropped down the embankment into the ditch as shells began to find their range, one of them demolishing the truck. On all fours the two men hurried up toward the Chinese lines, the Japanese dropping a series of shells into the ditch behind them. Contacting the Chinese casualties and their stretcher bearers at the upper end of the ditch, the men led them to Brian's remaining truck, and so back to us. Bill drank some coffee and went over to wake Tom and have him accompany him back to the front for the remainder of the casualties.

"Tom, Tom, wake up," said Bill, shaking Tom's shoulder. "I need you for an ambulance trip. I have lost another truck. The Japanese have been shelling me."

"What, did you lose my extra pair of socks?"

"Yes, Tom, I'm afraid I did. I didn't dare go back to the truck for them." That was a major catastrophe to the Friends, who had so few clothes that I had to lend them all of mine while the nurses washed theirs out at Shwemyo Cliff.

"Did you say you lost another truck?" said Martin, waking up sleepily. "You salvaged the tires, didn't you?"

"No, Martin, I couldn't." The air became blue with profanity.

April 10th—Time after time the ambulances went back to the front yesterday, until by three this morning we had had to operate on a hundred and twenty patients more. Grindlay and the nurses and I were falling asleep in spite of ourselves about one in the morning, so Eric volunteered to make us some tea. Coffee, he felt, would be too much of an undertaking. When he came back with the tea it was burned! The first and last burned tea I ever drank—and made by an Englishman!

We used up all our sterile supplies yesterday, so the nurses turned out at dawn to wash out the bloody towels and gauze. They were just as tired as I, so I got up and joined them in washing out the stuff in the near-by stream where we could take cover and still enjoy the sight of the bombers. Those crazy sores I got on my feet at Pyinmana just won't get well. The nurses dress them several times a day, but the foul discharges from the wounds of the several-day-old casualties keep my shoes wet and the sores dirty.

On our return for lunch I found that Grindlay and O'Hara had been scrubbing out the operating room themselves with cresol. Grindlay had found pieces of amputated fingers and toes in the plaster of Paris and wound refuse on the floor! No sooner had we finished lunch than the Friends brought in another thirty-five patients. One of them had his enlarged spleen shattered by a shell fragment. Insects were so numerous that they kept dropping into the wounds of the abdominal cases. Planes were over us all afternoon, but we had no time to stop and take a look.

April 11th—Twenty-five more cases arrived at eight-thirty this morning. No more can be brought till after dark as the shelling is so incessant that the stretcher bearers can't evacuate them from the front lines till then. We all decided to have a good sleep during the day, but it didn't work very well. It's too hot! Today is Bill Brough's twenty-third birthday. Wherever we set up, regiments of Chinese soon move in beside us. They are moving in next door. They won't get out of sight when observation planes come over; but the pollution of our precious wells is distressing. These wells were never supposed to supply water to so many hundreds. Now we have to send Tun Shein for water to a monastery a mile away. He brings it back in a jeep. Captain Eldridge and Fabian Chow dropped in for a chat. Personnel of the Air Force is reported to have reached Karachi, but they have no planes.

April 12th—Friends couldn't locate the new casualties, so we had a baseball game. It wasn't too much of a success. Emily scalded her arm badly with steam from the sterilizer. The sterilizer truck does not permit free movement. It is too full.

Colonel Williams brought Major General "Bobby" Lim and Colonel Chen down to visit us. They brought some flashlights and a couple of revolvers to chase away the Burmese who are continually putting barriers across the roads at night and then popping at whoever gets out to remove the barriers. Bobby Lim had some Red Cross money along to help us pay our bills. Colonel Williams is certainly going to town securing medicines and supplies for us, flying in a lot of stuff from India. He has a very sympathetic understanding of our problems here.

Seven Japanese bombers passed over us this afternoon. On their way back seven A.V.G. planes suddenly appeared hot on their trail. We heard later that they caught up with the Japs just before they reached Toungoo and shot down three. Everyone in the unit shouted and screamed with joy that the A.V.G. scorpion still had a sting left in its tail! Report says A.V.G. got eighteen out of twenty-one planes over the Namkham valley today.

Had only thirty-five cases today. We have been burning up the bloody remnants of clothes we have had to cut off our patients and cleaning up the grounds and the little hut next door where we place postoperative cases until the ambulances can cart them off. My, what a stink!

Things were so quiet I got a sudden inspiration to find out whether or not I had guts to drive one of the ambulances to the front. All the men objected; but I would have gone if the silly nurses hadn't fastened on to my shirt and stowed away in the ambulances to go along too! Even at that I could have made it, for Bill Brough promised to wait for me out on the road. I had an idea I could sneak out in a jeep when no one was looking, but those confounded nurses beat me to it and hid the keys!

April 13th—We were just dropping asleep at night when Paul drove in with three more nurses from Loilem. Jap raiders were strafing the Taunggyi-Kalaw road as he came along. He made a record trip to Namkham and back—up in a jeep and back in a "pregnant" truck. We had quite a time delivering that jeep from the body of the truck. Wished I had had my obstetrical instruments! Paul had brought along Tiny's cache of Waldorf toilet paper. I was almost as glad to see it as I was to see the nurses! E Hla had written me a nice long letter with all the news of the crowd. Hkawn Tawng, angry at not yet having been brought to the front, had run off with a Chinese shopkeeper. All the wards were comfortably full. Dr. Grey had flown back from India and she and Dr. Ahma were busily at work, leaving E Hla in charge of the hospital finances. Japanese planes had brought the front to Namkham, as they tried to wipe the A.V.G. out of Loiwing. So far the A.V.G. had had the best of it, shooting down Jap planes in dogfights over the valley. The nurses had had a ringside seat for the whole show. Some of them had been at Nawng Tao delivering a baby during one of the attacks and on their way home had passed two Japanese planes that had crashed.

Tun Shein made us a lot of bel-fruit juice. Most refreshing.

MEDICAL MAJOR

April 14th—Just got to bed last night when twenty more casualties were brought in. We worked on them till two in the morning. Terribly hot and dry today! They brought in three Indians who had been shot by the Burmese. Tun Shein has located several nice thin Shan pants for Grindlay and me. They are so comfortable to work in. The F.A.U. brought in a lot of loot they had salvaged from Pyinmana. A lot of Burmese are burning their homes so as not to have them commandeered by the Chinese.

April 15th—Between the heat and the bombers we can't get much sleep in the daytime, and the nights are full of work. Last night at ten-thirty, thirty-five cases arrived, two of them belly cases which Grindlay greatly enjoyed. One had a hole in his liver, but is doing very well indeed. While the captain was enjoying himself to his heart's content I had a most extraordinary case—a shell fragment had torn right across a soldier's buttocks without touching bone, laying the buttocks wide open. The wound was like two isosceles triangles with the apices turned in. The rectum had been dissected completely away from the other structures and was hanging down, without perforation or injury to the sphincter, like the udder of a cow. There was very little actual loss of tissue, so that after debriding and filling up with sulfanilamide powder I could get the structures loosely together. I wish I could keep him here, but our staff isn't sufficient. Two more truckloads arrived while we were working, and we did not finish till nine-thirty this morning, when we had one hour of sleep before we had to start washing out last night's gauze and linen. They brought in a

Chinese officer who had been shot in the arm by a Burmese who thought he was too overbearing when he asked for food. It is 136° in the sun. Villages are burning all around us. I was finishing a bath at sunset when a plane circled over us and then made a forced landing west of town. We started off in jeeps to catch the pilot if he were a Jap or help him if he were an A.V.G. man. We must have made a complete circle around the plane without locating it, while the pilot had made the edge of the town under his own steam when we got back.

"Are you an A.V.G. pilot?" we asked.

"Yes, I had to make a forced landing in a dry river bed, and the plane cracked up. My name is Patech."

"Come on over to our 'Little America,' " I said, and he jumped in.

We gave him a lot of coffee and a little snake poison. He almost sobbed at finding friends so soon. He had lost sight of his buddy and had circled around looking for him until his gas gave out. We sent him on into Pyawbwe with a truckload of patients.

Eric was out burying Chinese all afternoon. It was "high" time!

April 16th—Soon after Patech left, the trucks came in with seventy cases which kept us busy till 8:00 A. M. Grindlay had a Chinese who had been attacked by Burmese. He had had a lot of parallel chops with a dah on the top of his head. The wounds went down into the bone but not through. It was too hot to sleep, so we had a discussion as to what to do. The Japanese had been advancing rapidly along the Irrawaddy and their soldiers were said to have been on the main road north of Meiktila. Other Japanese patrols were reported trying to cut the Shan States road at Kalaw, while two drives were being made toward the Sixth Army headquarters at Loikaw, one from Toungoo on the Thandaung-Mawchi road and one westward from Chiengmai in Siam. If these drives succeeded we would be encircled. That would not matter for our personnel, as we could sneak out on the same mountain paths; but we would certainly lose all our precious equipment. Grindlay and I went to Pyawbwe to see General Stilwell and contact Dr. Mei for information about our ex-patients.

A British liaison officer, Captain Crouch, came to us to get some rest. He had been isolated in a Chinese trench for seven days with practically no food and only muddy water to drink. Almost continuous shelling had kept him from getting any sleep. We got off his filthy clothes, gave him a bath and some good food, and after a few hours of sleep he was a new man.

April 18th—General Sibert dropped in at dawn and ordered us to retreat to the first decent place beyond the junction of the two roads to Mandalay from Myingyan and Meiktila. We began to pack at six-thirty, had breakfast, and after a little fun smashing up all the furniture and windows to let off steam, were off at nine just in time to avoid the retreating Chinese. Burmese fifth columnists had been attacking the Chinese. So far all the Burmese villagers have been very good and kind to our group, recognizing us as the Americans and "Burmese" that we are.

It was ghastly hot! We nearly perished of thirst before we got to Kyaukse, the first place beyond the junction General Sibert mentioned. In Kyaukse we found a couple of tiny shops still open, so we tanked up on all the tea and coffee—if you can call it that—that they had. Kyaukse had already been bombed, and inevitably would be bombed again. A few miles south of the road junction, and perhaps three miles away from the nearest railway station, I had noticed a couple of bungalows by the side of the road. Leaving the nurses bathing in a lovely deep river near Kyaukse, we officers explored near-by roads; but finding nothing we decided to set up at the bungalows—Kume Town. Ko Nyunt had a lot of nice tea ready, but when we unloaded at Kume bungalow he went on his first and last strike and refused to get dinner. Poor chap! He was as tired out from the heat and lack of water as we were. The nurses, as usual, turned in, so that we finally got a meal late at night.

Kume Town, April 19th—Grindlay, O'Hara, and I kept thinking we were too far back, and the F.A.U. had no idea where to go to pick up casualties; so Grindlay and O'Hara went off to Maymyo in a jeep to contact Colonel Williams. Things had been moving so rapidly during the last twenty-four hours that no information had yet reached the colonel. But their trip was not in vain. O'Hara, who was nauseated every time he took a mouthful of rice and was thin and ill, had had a very hard time eating anything at all those last days at Tatkon. Once in a while some thoughtful soul had left him a can of beans or a tin of soup and that had been all he could eat. In Maymyo he had a grand American dinner, bought sixty pints of fresh strawberries, and arrived in Kume at midnight so happy that he woke the whole crowd and fed them the strawberries. Dr. Mei went through today on his way with his unit to set up at Sakhantha and Hsipaw. That means the Friends will have a sixty-mile trip to the front and another ninety miles or so back to the base hospital from here.

April 20th—Grindlay was quite friendly this morning. In Maymyo yesterday he discovered his old pal of Chungking, Sergeant Chesley, whom he describes as the only really good laboratory man in the world! He spent a lot of time telling Chesley what a fine bunch of girls our nurses were and how expert they were at their nursing. Chesley, who had seen the smoke screen of profanity that Grindlay had laid over the historic city of Chungking when he received orders to work under an ex-missionary, and who himself was a most confirmed misogynist, laughed in scorn. O'Hara also joked about the way he had received his orders to join our unit!

"Boys," he said to his fellow officers, "I'm going to get terribly sick with something right away and be back here in four days." He was sick now, all right, from our horrible food! But, though tempted by the taste of a real American dinner and strawberries, he could not persuade himself to remain away from our unit.

Rumors of a break through the Sixth Army at Loikaw came to us this morning, so I impregnated a truck with a jeep, and with a nurse-driver and Bill Brough in his ambulance, we went back to Pyawbwe to get orders direct from General Stilwell as to where the casualties could be found. The general had been working steadily for several days without rest and had just started to take a much needed nap when we arrived. Hearing I was there, he came down, told us where to find the patients, confirmed the news of the Japanese break-through, and had me sworn in as a major in the Medical Corps. I told him that the break-through would negative the value of our Sixth Army unit to a great extent and asked for permission to rush to Loilem at once and bring back five nurses to Kume.

"How do you plan to get to Loilem? By the Maymyo road?"

"No, sir, I prefer to take the direct road through Thazi and Kalaw."

The general's tired face became grim. "If you go by Kalaw you will have to start at once and drive like hell or the Japs will reach Hopong before you!"

"I am starting at once, sir."

"Good-by, Major." Gosh! was I really a United States major?

That pregnant truck certainly covered the ground! Thazi had been bombed twice since we had that delightful Chinese lunch in the restaurant there on our way down. Less than four weeks ago! And now not a building remains! Desolation, absolute and complete!

While we were driving along tonight I kept thinking of the way General Stilwell came down to see me today. It was the same way the first time I met him. Someone introduced me to Colonel Dorn, explaining about our work with the Sixth Army. Colonel Dorn went into the general's room, and almost immediately he came out and shook hands, asked a lot of friendly questions and then was very apologetic because some Chinese generals had come in for a big banquet and he couldn't continue his conversation with me. Some bootlickers that I knew tried to act as though they had known the general all their lives and didn't even get a "good morning." They say that he turns down invitations at important places right and left because "there is a war on," and yet he always has time for anyone who is trying to do a good job. Bill Cummings also got to see him, and the general spent a long time talking with him. He is most fun of all when you are talking business with him for he gets the point before you are half through with your sentence and his decision is as quick as lightning. You certainly get the idea right away that it wouldn't pay to start any bootlicking. He had a big laugh today when I told him our unit had three gears forward and only one in reverse! Even the nurses see through him. This morning before I left several of them told me to give their love to "Granddaddy Joe."

"Why, who on earth is 'Granddaddy Joe?'" I asked.

"Why, General Stilwell, of course."

"I suppose you have a name for Colonel Williams, too?"

"Yes, he is our '*dooteah* daddy'—'second daddy.'"

Thinking of Stilwell made me think of Fogarty. That grand fellow is dead. The plane that was taking him to Chungking crashed and he got a compound fracture of the thigh, dying some time later.

April 21st—Lunch beside the road at sunset yesterday was our only stop. We couldn't see whether Kalaw had been bombed or not. About midnight as we were approaching Heho, a group of Punjabi soldiers stopped us with leveled guns—which surprised me since we were coming from the west, about the only direction the Japs would not be coming from! I stopped, obligingly removed the canvas, and offered the soldiers a ride. They climbed in, sat around and in and on the baby jeep, and rode with us as far as Shwenyaung. We didn't discover, until we got to Loilem, that they made off with all our personal possessions when they descended! Taunggyi was in ruins around us as we drove through. Hurrying down the Taunggyi hill into Hopong we were racing the Japanese. Would we find them already at Hopong? If so, I was not going to stop so obligingly for them as I had for the Punjabis! I forced the nurse to lie down, held my revolver out of the window with one hand while I rushed down the road. I didn't expect to hit anything with my automatic, but if I met Japs, the noise of the gun plus the terrific speed with which I intended to plunge through them might startle them into letting the old fool by! But they had not arrived, and did not arrive for an hour or so. The total population of Hopong visible that night was one lone Chinese soldier, stumbling around with a rather dazed expression on his face!

We got to Loilem at dawn. Bill was as glad to see me as he would have been to see Hazel. Gladder, perhaps! He would not have been glad at Hazel's presence in Loilem that morning.

16

Helping the A.V.G.

WHEN OUR surgical unit left for Pyinmana and the Toungoo front, Bill had gone back to a double job. The government had ordered him to organize extensive truck farms throughout the Shan States so that a sufficient supply of vegetables might be raised for the Sixth Army. He secured upward of sixty pounds of vegetable seeds in Lashio, Hsipaw, and Taunggyi, and, receiving wholehearted support from the sawbwas, had the seed planted in all suitable localities. Ted Gurney and Stanley Short had taken their families to Lashio as ordered by the government. Learning that the earliest plane available would leave in four days, they went to Kutkai, on the invitation of friends there, and just got out of Lashio before the town was bombed. Ted and Stanley saw their families off to India on a comfortable passenger plane (instead of the usual troop carrier, which was delayed on account of engine trouble), and then hurried back to Langkhu. During the days that followed they were incessantly on the move, going from their own hospital (now full of Chinese soldiers) back and forth to Mong Pan, Wan Hat, and Loilem, at each of which towns many Chinese troops were stationed. At Mong Pan, casualties from raids across the Siam border were constantly coming in. Mawkmai was bombed, and military and civilian casualties were brought for hospitalization. On top of the surgical work, there were always the usual cases of malaria, dysentery, pneumonia, and so forth, which kept them fully occupied. Though Gurney and Short had only two nurses to help, and a minimum of equipment with which to work, they felt well supplied, as previously they had been doing the whole work of the hospital alone.

On the night of April 10 an urgent message came from Loilem asking for help with a patient who had a bayonet wound of the chest. There was no doctor there at the time as Bill had taken Dr. Tu down to Loikaw where action had already begun. As they left, the nurses pleaded with Bill to bring back some patients—which he promised to do. Just as they got out of Loikaw they came upon an upturned truck in which there were a number of casualties. These they sent straight back to the hospital. That was the first installment for those nurses who were clamoring for work! When they arrived at Loikaw, they found the first lot of patients already waiting, having just arrived from the front. Bill thought that some of these were too difficult for Dr. Tu, so he took them back to Loilem, where there were more facilities, and sent for Dr. Gurney to come up immediately. Gurney and Short went to Loilem at once, arriving about midnight. The next morning, having done what was necessary, they were about to leave when a convoy of trucks brought in a hundred and twenty Chinese casualties from the recent bombing of Thazi—the railway junction a hundred and sixty miles west. The next twenty-four hours were busy ones for all concerned. Short gave the anesthetics while Gurney and the nurses operated on the worst cases. There was no time to pay much attention to the planes that came and went—some, no doubt, on their way to Taunggyi, and others reconnoitering Loilem itself. The next morning

Ba Saw arrived from Namkham and helped finish up the surgery. The relief of working in the base hospital with a relative sufficiency of nurses was unspeakable!

Gurney and Short returned to their own work in Langkhu, leaving Ba Saw in charge of Loilem. On the seventeenth, Graham suddenly appeared in Langkhu saying that the British liaison officer had ordered the evacuation of the nurses at Mong Pan, and that General Stilwell had requested that Gurney go to Loikaw. So Graham and Gurney went on to Mong Pan at once to collect the nurses and all hospital equipment. On their return they left those nurses at Langkhu and took the two younger ones from there on to Loilem the next morning. Then Bill, Gurney, and four nurses went on to Loikaw with a view to handling the casualties from the action that was expected very soon. They set up on arrival that night, and were snatching a short sleep when they were awakened by an officer who ordered them to retreat early in the morning. Bill remained behind for more definite information and to salvage anything useful he could find in town, while Gurney and the nurses pushed back a few miles and set up once more, by the side of the road. Soon Bill appeared.

"It's no use," said Bill. "The Japs arc only eight miles away and we have been ordered to evacuate all our hospitals back to Lashio. We will have to hurry if we are to rescue the Langkhu nurses."

This packing up and retreating was getting to be a nuisance. When they reached Loilem, Graham and Whittington were loading the trucks. While Gurney went straight on to Langkhu to rescue the personnel, hospital equipment, and three hundred gallons of petrol from the local dump, Bill, who had received reports of abandoned missionaries on the Taunggyi road and of sawbwas whose transportation had broken down, went back to rescue them and send them on to Lashio in trucks he had commandeered. It was an overloaded truck that reached Loilem from Langkhu late that night! A little more sorting out of equipment and equalizing of loads, and the remaining trucks left Loilem for Lashio at three o'clock in the morning. Owing to a shortage of vehicles, Bill, Ba Saw, Theodore, and four nurses were left behind, together with a jeep and four tons of hospital stuff. It was hoped that Graham and Whittington might be able to dump their loads in Lashio and return for them before the Japs reached Loilem. Colonel McCabe and Colonel Aldrich drove in at four, while I arrived at five with the pregnant truck they needed. No wonder Bill was glad to see me. If I had not brought the truck they would have been in the hands of the Japs in less than twenty-four hours. The safety of all the other nurses except those at Kengtung, whom Bill had ordered by radio to retreat by the short cut to Lashio, greatly relieved me. The base-hospital patients had all been evacuated by the Sixth Army, so we did not need to worry about them.

They let us have three hours' sleep, and then as a squadron of bombers flew over we started packing. I had just delivered my truck of her jeep when a car drove up and an A.V.G. groundman, an old friend of mine at Loiwing, stepped out.

"Lord! If it isn't Doc Seagrave! I never thought I would have as good luck as this! Listen, Doc, those bombers machine-gunned one of our pilots back at Namsang. He is in a bad way. Will you go and see him?"

"Nobody in the world I would rather help than one of you A.V.G. boys," I said. "I'll start at once with a couple of nurses in a jeep and operate on him there. Will you ride with me?"

"No, I have to take this truck back, and as it runs on only half its cylinders you can get there much faster than I can."

Sterile equipment was available, so we started at once. Halfway to Namsang a car passed us. The driver saw our red crosses and stopped. I walked back.

"I have a machine-gun casualty here," said the driver. "Will you take care of him?"

"I was coming out to get him. I can do the surgery, all right, but I am worried about his after-treatment. I have been ordered to evacuate my Loilem hospital. What shall we do with the patient after the operation?"

"Don't worry about that. I'll fly him back to Loiwing where he will be in the hands of a real surgeon."

I felt that that was an unkind thing for an A.V.G. man to say to me after all I had been trying to do, but my loss of face didn't matter if I could only give this injured pilot the help he needed! We turned back to Namsang. In the pilot's room the nurses boiled instruments and laid out sterile goods.

"That is a wonderful doctor you A.V.G. men have in Loiwing," I ventured.

"You bet he is. Dr. Richards is a grand man!" The pilot's buddy was grim.

"How long have you boys been stationed at Loiwing?" I asked, as I started to scrub.

"Two months."

"Then you must have seen that little 'show' of mine across the valley from you," I said.

"What do you mean?"

"Haven't you ever seen the Namkham hospital buildings?"

"Say, who in hell are you?"

"I'm Seagrave."

"Doc Seagrave? Hell! All right, Doc, go ahead and do what you can for my pal. I have another job on. I've got to blow up a bomb dump the R.A.F. left here," and the self-appointed chaperon went out, covered with smiles.

The patient on the rude bed also was smiling with contentment as Than Shwe adjusted the chloroform mask. One bullet had gone right through the thumb. Two others were in his legs, and I recovered several bits of airplane metal from various parts of his body.

As soon as the patient recovered from the anesthetic we hurried back to Loilem. Bill was stamping around in great disgust.

"You'd better get going right away," he shouted. "The Japs are reported at the divide over there eight miles away and may be here any minute. I have sent the nurses along with Dr. Ba Saw and Theodore to wait on the Laikha road."

17

First Retreat

April 22nd—That *was* a trip! I was driving the jeep in which Htulum was killed, and it had no windshield. In the late afternoon it began to rain, and I nearly froze to death. We got to Pangkitu at dusk and had dinner in a little Indian restaurant there—or what was left of it. Everyone was on the road that day, whizzing north. Chinese Sixth Army trucks were the only decent vehicles. British civil officers and their clerks were packed tightly in undersized English cars. Trucks that should have been burned before the war began had been made to run somehow and were heavily overloaded with fleeing Karens and Shans. Nowhere was there any sign of effort to plan resistance to the Japanese advance. Theodore took pity on me as we started again, loading the stuff from my jeep into his and driving the one without the windshield, since he had a thick overcoat of English Army issue. The trip on from there was one mad struggle to keep awake. If we could have found a hut to sleep in after ten o'clock, we would have stopped; but we went past the last hut of which we knew and had to keep driving until about two in the morning. I went off sound asleep for as long as three or four seconds at a time, waking up startled to find I was driving a jeep, and still more astonished to discover the jeep was still on the road! Bawk, in the jeep behind, later said that she had done the same thing. Bill, ahead in his truck, was also having trouble. At last, about thirty miles from Hsipaw, Bill saw a broken down *zayat*, or monastery resthouse, and we went in to sleep. The joists had given way at one side, and the floor was thirty degrees off horizontal and covered with refuse and various excreta; but it seemed like paradise. We fell asleep immediately.

Sometime before dawn one of our own trucks drew up, recognized our caravan and stopped. It was Graham and Whittington on their way to pick up Bill and the nurses. We had a joyful reunion, made a huge pot of American coffee which was disposed of in most efficient style, and went on, much refreshed. At the junction with the Lashio-Hsipaw road we parted company, Bill and the other boys going on to Lashio to contact Gurney and bring him back with a team of nurses to set up in Hsipaw, while Bawk in her jeep and I in mine took the four Sixth Army girls with us west.

In Hsipaw we had breakfast, and finding a few stores still open, bought a lot of cotton *longyis* and other things for our unit girls. In Maymyo all the stores were closed. We were horribly hungry, and hunted up and down every street to find a restaurant of some sort. There was nothing. But, also hunting, were Brian and George of our own F.A.U. They were returning from Hsipaw, where they had taken a lot of our casualties, and were just as hungry as we were. We gave up, finally, and set out for Mandalay, discovering, about five miles out of Maymyo, that the shopkeepers had set up stalls by the side of the road out of the reach of bombers. We had a wonderful meal: three different kinds of hot Burmese curry and the most delicious rice I had had since my last trip to Namkham. The ration rice we had been eating wasn't fit for the pig!

Mandalay was a ghastly mess. There wasn't a thing left within sight of the road but the two leper asylums. Fire had wiped out every bombed building. As we turned south, Bawk's petrol feed pipe kept getting clogged up with dirt. We were in the middle of a tremendous convoy of Chinese troops rushing south to reinforce the Fifth Army. Every time we stopped to blow out the petrol pipe another convoy went past. We were filthy with dust in a way possible only when you ride a jeep in convoy. At that swimming hole south of Kyaukse we stopped and had a gorgeous time getting clean again, scrubbing each other's backs with real joy. Smelling less like an eight-day casualty, we pulled in at the Kume bungalow and were at once smothered in a screaming, sobbing, laughing blanket of hysterical nurses. The crazy girls had been convinced, on our failure to return that morning, that we had fallen into the hands of the Japs!

Grindlay had had himself a time! The day I left, Tun Shein had built us an operating room of mat and thatch which had gone into action at once when, at 4:30 P. M., Bill Brough and Brian had come back with the first load of casualties from the south. Up again before daylight yesterday, Grindlay had begun work on a Gurkha, who eight days before had been chopped through the jaw, face, and neck, his fingers cut off and his arms dangling as the result of wounds that had severed the bones at the elbows. With those awful wounds, which he had received at the hands of the Burmese, the Gurkha had walked eight days, until he accidentally stumbled upon our little setup. Load after load of Chinese casualties were brought in all day and all night. O'Hara was busy, too, as there were several jaw injuries. Grindlay's thin Shan pants stuck to him by sweat and began to rip. Unconscious of calamity, he operated on, occasionally wondering what the hell the nurses were giggling at! Then Koi took pity on her beloved uncle and got two long strips of adhesive plaster to repair temporarily the damaged pants.

"So that's what you girls were laughing at, is it? Well, never mind now—you've seen all I have got already!" Grindlay turned back to the plaster cast he was applying and continued to mix profanity with "that damned plaster," in hopes it might set a little better!

With one hour's rest he continued operating till two o'clock this morning—a hundred and twenty cases in thirty hours. The only good news during the day came when Colonel Williams ordered us to take our cases, not to Hsipaw, but to the river steamer *Assam* at Mandalay. With only eight ounces of chloroform left there was nothing further to be done.

The baskets of strawberries we had brought down with us from Maymyo were just disappearing when Captain Jones appeared with two hundred pounds of chloroform that Colonel Williams had had flown in from Calcutta.

April 23rd—At midnight Bill Cummings turned up with Kaw Naw whom he had picked up in Lashio. This morning we had a powwow with the nurses.

"The 'son-in-law' says that today is the last day cars can get back to Hsipaw and Lashio," I said. "We are not going to be able to get out of Burma through Namkham as we planned. When we go, we will undoubtedly follow the general up the west bank of the Irrawaddy, and we may have to walk out into Assam. If any of you girls want to quit and go back to your people to hide out with them until the war is over, you will have to go now. If you go along with us into India, you will have to count on a lot of hard and perhaps disagreeable work in a strange country for nobody knows how long! Nobody will say or think anything unkind about you if you stop now, and I will furnish you transportation back to Namkham. Stick up your hands if you want to leave."

Not a nurse moved. Only my Lahu orderly wanted to return to rescue his wife and child.

"Well, Bill," I said, "I guess they really mean it! I will have to leave the Namkham-Hsipaw groups entirely in your hands. Let any of the girls leave that want to join their families. Dispose, as you see fit, of all our Namkham equipment and medicines, and the trucks and jeeps of the Sixth Army crowd. If you can get out to Myitkyina, perhaps we may meet you there."

Koi wanted to borrow a hundred rupees on her salary to send back to her father and mother by Bill. I offered to give her twice the amount, but she wouldn't take it. She didn't want her folks killed for the sake of their money. Amid a shower of tears the "son-in-law" disappeared around the bend in the road.

Bombers bombed the Kume Road station today, and the Friends picked up a few casualties. Right behind them came General Sibert. The Jap machine-gun bullets had just missed him. There is another one of those rumors running around to the effect that there is a regiment of Japs, on the other side of the river, which has been lost sight of. If anyone who knows his map of Burma wants to figure out what the Japs are up to, all he has to do is make up his mind what the meanest move in a certain area would be, and a few days later news arrives that the Japs have done just that thing. In this case they are undoubtedly heading for the Chindwin to cut off retreat into Assam by the southern route. It is known that the Japs are not too proud to hire ordinary Burmese coolies to show them paths unknown even to the British.

April 24th—While we were eating dinner last night, patients began to arrive from Yamethin. In all there were eighty-five of them. We finished operating at seven-thirty this morning, and after two hours of sleep I began again. Grindlay has a ureteral stone which began to torture him during the night. He has spent most of the day in the bathtub, soaking. We had a nice swim in the irrigation canal that flows by our compound, and while I was enjoying it a real cyclone came on. Bits of gravel and sand stung my skin unless I submerged. Could hardly breathe for dust before the rain finally arrived. The wind blew our stuff all around the house, and we had only begun to straighten things up when a truckload of British troops were brought in. The sergeant said they had been traveling in convoy up the Myingyan road when the storm broke and a tree crashed down on their truck. He had heard of our unit being at Kume and would appreciate our taking them in. Several of the cases were horribly injured. It was odd to have the men lie quiet on our six operating tables, each waiting his turn. One of the men had his scalp torn off. Another's skull had cracked like an eggshell. There were three long lines of fracture and two areas where the fracture was comminuted, some fragments piercing the brain. Of the sixteen British, only three had relatively minor injuries.

FIRST RETREAT

April 25th—They woke me at night for sixty more Chinese. Grindlay insisted on helping with a few, though he could hardly stand. Worked all night, using two shifts of nurses as we did the night before. The girls are so tired that two of them dropped asleep on their feet, and then cried when I ordered them off to bed. So far we have had no patients today. An ambulance came for the English. I wish I could follow up that skull case. I let Emily go along with Paul when he took the Chinese to the hospital ship at Mandalay. When there, she heard somehow that her brother Gilbert was in trouble at Aungbinle, a few miles away; so Paul drove her there. Gilbert, being part Indian, was terrified at what the Burmese might do to him, and thought he might avoid being chopped to pieces if he toadied up to the local *hpongyi*. He had no sooner chummed up with these Buddhist priests than the Chinese Army began to round them up for their fifth-column activities. Gilbert, like a foolish boy, began to run when the Chinese came to interrogate him, and received three bayonet wounds. Because of his effort to escape, the Chinese were convinced he was guilty, too, and put him in jail to await trial.

When Paul told me the story I sent him to General Stilwell at Kyaukse, offering to go bond for Gilbert and guaranteeing to take him with us as a member of our unit until he was safely out of Burma. With the general's influence Gilbert was soon released, and Grindlay took care of his wounds.

Sagaing, April 26th—About five o'clock yesterday afternoon Lieutenant Young came in with orders for us to move to Sagaing at once. We were packed up and off by nine, weaving in and out of columns of British trucks and tanks that had been using the road all day. Case has joined our party. We nearly missed the turn to the Ava bridge in the traffic jam. It was long after midnight when we located the A.B.M. compound at Sagaing. The only empty building was the church, and most of the girls slept on the pews. I slept on the front seat of my truck. Soon after dawn a lot of Japanese bombers flew over and bombed Mandalay and the bridge, and for the first time I heard the sound of antiaircraft guns. Nobody hit anything. Beyond Sagaing the road was jammed with British and Indian troops. I kept my eyes peeled for some decent place for us to set up, and just happened to see a lovely bungalow, half a mile away from the road, almost completely hidden by pride of India trees and palms. It would certainly be invisible from the air. We settled down for some rest. All of us are pleased. There is a large irrigation canal beside us with a high dike that jeeps can travel on very nicely. There is only one fault to find with the place—the well water is full of alkali and has a ghastly taste! Spoils the coffee! This is the hot, dry belt and the water wouldn't be better anywhere else near by. It is so hot that the nurses and the villagers are bathing continually. We decided not to unload as we have things so arranged now that we can get out the necessary supplies and be operating in fifteen minutes if casualties come in.

April 27th—Grindlay, Bill Brough, and O'Hara went off to the general's new headquarters at Shwebo, twelve miles away. They saw General Stilwell sitting on the verandah looking terribly tired. No one knew what the next move would be, nor will they until orders come in from Washington and Chungking. No further resistance is being given to the Japanese, except for a few Chinese troops that are in danger of being cut off. Everyone is talking about the action in which the company of General Sun's troops cut through the Japanese lines north of Yenangyaung and rescued a regiment of British. General Stilwell sent for Grindlay to have a friendly talk, and outlined plans for dumping our comparatively useless stuff. The next move will be toward India. Grindlay heard that Major Wilson was killed yesterday in the Mandalay bombing. First American casualty! Bombers bombed Shwebo as Grindlay and O'Hara started back, then circled around and began machine-gunning. O'Hara jumped under a culvert, and to his unspeakable disgust found that someone with diarrhea had been there before him!

While the boys were at headquarters I took the girls for a shopping expedition. In none of the cities through which we had passed since Pyinmana had there been a single shop where the girls could spend their pitiful Namkham allowance of one or two dollars a month for the little bits of finery so dear to their hearts. The Red Cross now allowed them about ten rupees each, and there was no place to spend it! Some of them were pretty ragged, for these Burmese voile jackets are flimsy and the shoes are still more so. Tun Shein had heard of a few shops open eight miles west of Shwebo, so we went there. Every door was barricaded, but a few people were on the street.

"Fellows," I said to the F.A.U. boys who went along with us, "don't get out of the truck or the people will all run away. Let the nurses browse around by themselves for fifteen minutes, and those barred doors will open."

The nurses chattered in Burmese, laughed, and acted just as any bevy of normal Burmese girls would when they have a shopping spree ahead of them. After ten minutes I began to call out to them in Burmese, letting the people know they weren't dealing with a stranger. My Burmese is sometimes quite good and it was particularly good today! In the fifteen-minute time limit some of the stolid villagers admitted there were a few things for sale at a certain shop. I walked along with the nurses. There was a bolt of voile on the counter. The nurses asked the price, and then, true orientals as they were, began to bargain with the shopkeeper.

"Girls," I said, "don't try to beat that man down. Pay him whatever he asks and if you can't afford it, I will buy the stuff for you. You are lucky to find anything suitable, and these poor people are going to have a hard enough time as it is these next few months."

I spoke purposely in Burmese. A few minutes after we left that shop a rumor spread among the villagers that here was a group of people that had a slight touch of humanity in them! Bars were removed from doors, shops opened, and the nurses became quite happy as they exchanged their pitiful stipends for feminine finery.

When we got back to our charming bungalow we found that the surgical team of the Friends Ambulance Unit, China Convoy, had arrived. I will never be able to understand why these men came down. By the time they reached Lashio the Battle of Burma was over. We were doing no surgery now. They had come through, knowing that bridges were to be blown up behind them. Peter Tennant, their boss, was with them, and he had brought with him Lu Shang, one of their Chinese interpreters, the only F.A.U. man we did not like. However, the surgeon, Handley Laycock, is the sort of man one ought to have a chance to meet: conscientious objector? Yes. But any sensible man objects to the things he objected to. He certainly never objected to war because of fear, nor yet through dread of hardship.

Colonel Williams came down that afternoon to look over our stock, and advised us to get rid of the bulky things that would certainly not be needed on a swift retreat. We dumped several boxes of Kotex that some misguided soul had sent us, not realizing that the Chinese Army was composed of men! Colonel Williams says that the present plan is for us to go by river or train to Myitkyina and then by plane to India, walking out if planes are not available.

I asked Colonel Williams if we might not send Paul and a couple of nurses by that evening's train to Myitkyina with one of our trucks, so that they could hurry to Namkham by the motor road and warn Bill Cummings to leave at once and join us. He gave us permission, and we prepared everything, choosing nurses who could kiss their folks good-by en route. It was an awful disappointment when Paul returned to say that there had been a collision and the train was not going. The news is that Lashio and Hsipaw are already in the hands of the Japs.

Tonight the Friends had a big powwow. Tennant doesn't want them to remain with us. The Friends who have been with us don't want to be taken away. Bill Brough finally got permission for them to remain. Williams has suggested that Laycock and his surgical team join the British on their trek out, while we go along with the Americans. I think that is the best solution. There are so few doctors that it seems useless to keep so many in the same place.

April 29th—I went into Shwebo with Grindlay today to see if Colonel Williams had any orders for us. We are not getting any casualties, except for an occasional man that jumps out of his truck when he sees our flag by the side of the road and comes in for treatment. I met Grindlay's friend, Sergeant Chesley! While we were talking to him the bombers came over again. They sure went to town on Shwebo. Why didn't they realize that the most important part of Shwebo that day was General Stilwell's headquarters, a mile out of town? If the Japs had any sense they would know that the American general they hoped to kill was as astute as they were and had not located his headquarters in the town itself. We started back as soon as the bombers disappeared, finding the whole town burning, trees across the road, electric mains torn and impeding our way. We wove in and out through the streets looking for casualties, but there were none. None of the natives had remained in the town; they had too much sense! The only casualties from the Jap bombing that day were some pigeons. They looked so pitiful that we did not pick them up to take home for dinner!

We have had so little work to do that the nurses are going wild. Two of them got into a big fight today. Just before supper I found Roi Tsai out on the verandah sewing and crooning songs to herself, the way she does when she is homesick. I stopped it right away because whenever she does that for very long at a time she works herself up into hysterics. None of this crowd likes peace and quiet.

April 30th—Terribly hot again. We had a few minor casualties. Brian and Kenneth drove in toward Mandalay for some stuff, but couldn't get there. There was some rain, and Brian was driving like mad, as usual. He skidded, turned over, and now has a broken collarbone. Bill Brough is down with severe dysentery. Tennant has ordered them off to Myitkyina by train, as soon as the railway line is cleared, and they are to be flown to Calcutta. Darn it, those are the two that really led our Friends Ambulance. How on earth will we get along without them? This talk of our tramping out of Burma has me worried. It has been a long, long time since I have had to do much foot work in the jungles, and I feel much older than forty-five with this confounded malaria that keeps returning. And no treatment of any sort helps these four sores on my feet. The only thing that gives me hope that I may be able to make it over the mountains is that the Friends brought me a pair of English Army Issue boots today. They are as heavy as lead, but they permit me to wear two pairs of thick woolen socks, and that ought to pad my sores! Plans for evacuation change daily. We understand the idea at the moment is for us to go to Myitkyina by truck. Unless the government has been rushing construction of new roads that I don't know about, we will have ourselves a real trip.

18

Pulling Out

May 1st—Colonel Williams was downstairs in his jeep just as we woke up. Somewhere north of Mandalay is a regiment of Chinese who couldn't get across the Ava bridge. Colonel Williams wanted Grindlay, a couple of Friends, Lieng Sing, and Low Wang to go east to Kyaukmyaung, where one takes the ferry for the Mogok Ruby Mines, and set up a surgical station there to take care of casualties when this regiment arrives. The rest of us were to go north to Zigon. We hurriedly selected a lot of equipment for Grindlay and loaded it on a separate truck, and they set off with the truck and a jeep. Grindlay is afraid this means he is going to be permanently separated from our unit, which makes him swear as badly as he did when he was first ordered to join us! The rest of us started north. We have enough men to drive all our trucks and jeeps except for one jeep, and Big Bawk is driving that one. Koi is too tired for me to make her drive it, while Big Bawk is as strong as a horse. The road north of Shwebo is nothing but a graveled dike along the canal and so narrow that you can hardly pass anyone else, so it takes hours to cover a few miles. About forty miles north the road stopped suddenly. Our two generals were there, and they ordered us to strike west a couple of miles and find a place to sleep in that was not too near a railway station. The next station south of us got plastered this morning. It was rather pitiful. A company of English "Lancs" had been badly shot up at Prome and sent to Calcutta to recover. The other day, far too late for them to be of any use, they were flown into Myitkyina, with orders to come down as reinforcements. Their train reached this station just in time for them to be bombed, and lots were killed. Laycock and his Friends took care of their casualties.

General Stilwell has set up three miles beyond us on the "Mu" River. Since there is nothing further to do until tomorrow, I am going back to Kyaukmyaung to see how Grindlay is getting along. Maybe we can contact Colonel Williams again. He has remained in Shwebo.

May 2nd—What a day, what a day! We got to Kyaukmyaung about nine last night. Eric was beside the road looking for me, by George! Those boys seem to know my psychology! Told me Grindlay was down at the river since there was a lot of trouble about steamers. Only available ones had no crew. Kyaukmyaung had been bombed the day before, and everything was in a turmoil. Eric had a lot of cold rice and sardines and—of all things—S and W coffee. Grindlay had found any number of cases of the stuff, abandoned on the dock, and had salvaged a couple of cases for us. I did not trust Eric to burn the coffee as he did the tea, so I made it myself, and it was unspeakably delicious. Real American coffee! Grindlay came in stomping angrily. He had to go right in to Shwebo and contact my old friend General Martin and have the English cough up some steamer crews, or the Chinese Army would not be able to get across the river. The Japanese are already at Kalewa, and that means that all these English troops that are trying to get out of Burma by the "comfortable" southern route will have to cut their way through. As I thought, that is where that "lost battalion" of the Japs was heading for all this time.

We went back together in our jeeps. General Martin is nothing but a walking skeleton. Still calls me Colonel! There is no way he can find crews, so we went on and found Colonel Williams still up. He had been burning everything at headquarters. When he heard Grindlay's story he decided it was a useless gesture to send him back on the original mission, to wait with his arms folded until the Japs surrounded and killed him; so the captain left at once to pick up the truck and his personnel and rejoin us at dawn. When the colonel heard that I knew where the new general headquarters were, he decided to come along with me. Not all of the general's papers had been destroyed yet, so he got rid of them all—plus the house—by means of a tin of gas and a judicious match. He certainly never could have found the right road in the dark. There was slightly less traffic on the road. I got him to headquarters at four-thirty, and, after contacting the general, got orders for our unit to fall in line at dawn when the general's echelon passed us. I got fifteen minutes' sleep while our boys and the girls loaded up. Grindlay, the old truck driver, got to camp just as we were pulling out. Three Anglo-Indian refugees hitched themselves onto us at the last moment. I am sure I will get into trouble about their being along. Never should have been given a commission in this man's Army. I am not tough enough; but there is hope. I am getting tougher and tougher every day!

Who told Big Bawk to lead our echelon, I don't know, and I don't want to find out, for I wouldn't have time to repair his shattered jaw. Just beyond the road's end we had to drive across the bed of a stream and then up a sharply sloping bank onto the dike again. Bawk is a wonderful driver, but she had not had enough experience to know there would be less chance of tipping over if she attacked the bank at right angles; so her jeep rolled over. None of the girls was hurt. The officers wanted me to take the jeep away from her, but I refused, and told Bawk to get back in and drive. She has guts, all right! The road from that point on was ghastly; nothing but cart track here and there, and occasionally nothing but a blazed trail through the jungle where the general's advance guard had chopped down small trees to open up a path. We are having a contest to see who can keep the roof supports of his truck the longest. Grindlay, who told me this morning that he was "exhausted," is finding out that he has reserves he never knew about, driving his jeep through this kind of jungle! O'Hara is driving a jeep too. Martin insists on dragging that useless jeep that Lieutenant Haymaker was riding in when it turned over and skinned him in such a way that he had to lie on his tummy for weeks! Martin and Tom take turns driving the tug jeep and the tugged jeep. I think they have a bet on to see who can eat the most dirt and not holler!

At bombing time the Japs came over and bombed the echelon of Chinese immediately behind us. We heard them in time and hugged the filthy ground in our most approved manner. Stopped at dusk at Pintha, a town with the expressive name of "beautiful fanny." There was a well across the railway line, and we had a gorgeous time washing off dirt. Grindlay began to bathe after the nurses had left and, thinking himself alone, did it in the nude. He could not reach the caked dust and sweat on his back so he yelled, "Hey, somebody, come and scrub my back." Little Bawk heard him and, quite unconsciously, went over and began to scrub. As soon as Grindlay could get the soap out of his eyes he looked around to see who was obliging him, and there was General Stilwell standing near, chuckling! We had some most delicious bananas to eat at dinner. Just as we were getting into "bed," the last train to run north from Shwebo pulled in beside us and kept us awake, chugging around for hours. Two of the nurses were hugging themselves to sleep in the cab of my truck, so I am going to sleep on top of the sterile goods in the back. Rather lumpy!

May 3rd—We followed the general out at dawn. Traveled all day, but only managed to cover about forty miles. What imitation bamboo bridges there were had been crushed by the Chinese six-wheelers ahead of us. Tennant, who is supposed to be an English racing-car driver, distinguished himself by getting embedded in the sand of a river bank and holding up the procession for hours in the awful heat. My years of misery on these Burma roads are coming in handy now. This is old stuff to me, and if it were not for the terrible heat and lack of sleep I would be perfectly happy.

One of General Stilwell's cars caught fire. Of course, it was the one with a lot of small-arms ammunition on board. We had to cut a new road around it to avoid the popping shells. Sometime during the day we must have circled that town of Zigon which we were supposed to reach the day before yesterday. In the afternoon there was a twelve-mile stretch of fairly good road leading into Wuntho. Actually sped up to thirty-five miles an hour. Before, we had had miles of rice fields and their dikes to negotiate. I kept awake by clowning around with the truck, and talking Shan at the top of my voice. The natives thought I was drunk! Lilly, the A.T.G. expert on cars, is with us—the chap who diagnosed the trouble with my jeep that day in Maymyo after one second's examination. That chap has an extraordinary way with a bottle. He never draws the cork from a bottle but pushes it in with his thumb—and then, to keep the stuff from spilling, he just has to drink it up! But I haven't seen him tight yet.

Martin got fed up with the broken jeep at last, so we had a grand time burning it up. We dragged it off into the woods a hundred yards from the road and built a little fire a yard away from it and then I blew a hole in the gas tank with my revolver. Only time I can remember hitting what I was aiming at! The Japanese will never be able to use that jeep. Martin loaded all the spare tires onto my truck. I still have a couple of roof trusses left. That is more than the other truck drivers can say.

The general is parked on the edge of Wuntho near some monasteries. Our crowd slept on the ground before the bridge. This is the best swimming hole in Burma, barring none. There is a little dam below us, and the water is clear and deep. Our crowd has become the best bunch of back-scrubbers in Christendom. If only those girls wouldn't use their fingernails on me!

I went over to headquarters to chum around with our fellow officers for the first time. Colonel St. John was at his best. That chap can certainly tell a story. Jack Belden, *Life* reporter, was there. He seemed to think it was his unfortunate duty to try to get a story out of me.

May 4th—We lost the whole morning waiting around for orders. Japs are reported to have taken Wanting. That means they are in Namkham right now looting the house and hospital and nurses' home. Why have I worked so hard all these years to build up that plant? I shall never be able to do it again, old and tired as I am. Well, I have had me a darned happy time out of it! I still keep on thinking there must have been some PLAN behind it all. If all that background of mine has molded this unit into the sort of machine that can do the special sort of nasty tasks that General Stilwell needs to have done, I won't shed any tears!

Now they have a new plan for Grindlay. He is to go along as medical officer for a convoy of jeeps that will cross into Assam by the northern route from Mogaung, Roi Tsai's home. We shifted our loads around again, getting out the stuff he would need and discarding all our excess supplies. The heat was worse than ever, and we were parched with thirst and hungry. Didn't dare cook for fear we would be late when orders came to start. You can't relax in this awful heat. No food all day.

They say Brigadier General Martin has started west from Wuntho with the idea of connecting with the southern route into Assam above the Japs. General Stilwell feels certain he will be cut off. We are to try to get through to Myitkyina. Colonel Williams drove up to order us to be ready to leave at four. Koi and Paul Geren have had a fight. Koi felt he was working too hard and wouldn't let him lift heavy boxes from truck to truck. Tried to make him let her take his place. Paul felt insulted to have an eighty-pound nurse try to do his work!

PULLING OUT

May 5th—We started off at four in three echelons. General Stilwell commanded the first, Colonel St. John the second, and Captain Grindlay the third. I brought up the rear, determined to see that none of our crowd was left behind. I was a minute late getting started and took the wrong turn in town and then had a hell of a time catching up with the others. We had a graveled road for a while but went past the north turn and would have been at the Irrawaddy again in no time if Case had not interrogated some Burmans. The road north was one of those things. Some government official had existed in this district with the vision to know that if the Japs attacked Burma, it would be advisable, even this far north, to have means of communication available to replace the railroad when it was cut. The road began all of a sudden at the boundary line of his district. We got lost trying to find it, but the general's luck held, for he discovered, near the turn, the man who had built the road. We backed up in the dark and got onto the road. Even then it was not easy, for there were bits of elephant roads and paved roads here and there leading off into the jungle. With the P.W.D. man to guide us we managed fairly well. At every crossing the general left some officer behind to direct the traffic, and we carried him along with us in our truck. There was one place where the general did not feel it necessary to leave a traffic cop; but Tennant, who had gotten to the van of our group, somehow, decided to leave Ruby there so the rest of us wouldn't get lost. Famed tiger country! But Ruby got down meekly and stood there in the dark, directing traffic, until Grindlay came along. "Oh, uncle," said Ruby, "I am so glad to see you! I have been expecting a tiger on my back any minute." Grindlay cursed and swore and picked her up. The rest of us might get lost if we didn't have any damned sense, but that girl was not to be left on traffic-cop duty in the middle of a jungle!

The general found a forest bungalow abo midnight. We have three hours here to get some food and sleep. All the food we have time for is rice and sardines. All the other pews are occupied so I am going to relax on the roof of my cab.

Off again on the dot of three. Same kind of roads as yesterday! Grindlay was so sleepy he decided to wake himself up by scaring the sleep out of O'Hara. On a little strip of good road he sped up to sixty miles an hour, sweeping past O'Hara and bumping him over toward the other side of the road. The ruse was very effective. O'Hara will never get sleepy again when Grindlay's jeep is behind him! At dawn we got to the Maza River near Naba. The big railway bridge was right beside us, and we had to wait there for hours because a Chinese six-wheeler had broken through the flimsy bamboo bridge. We went swimming while Chinese repaired the bridge under Colonel Holcombe's direction. General Stilwell promised the men he would give them a hundred rupees if they had the bridge ready under three hours. We expected the Japs to bomb us and the railway bridge any minute, so we did not get any real sleep.

Between that bridge and Indaw some Burmese dacoits fired on Colonel St. John. Many of the villages are deserted. We had a long wait in one of them while the general went into Indaw for information. Rumor says the Japs will be in Myitkyina tomorrow, so we are cut off. We were ordered to start west from Indaw to take the middle route into Assam. A group of British joined us.

Indaw was jammed with refugees, and the road, ankle deep in dust, was so crowded that we had to do a great deal of it in low to keep from hitting someone. Those poor people! Mothers trudging along, pregnant, but carrying children on their backs. Blind people. Lame and wounded soldiers—saw and recognized a few of the Chinese casualties we had operated on. Children and ancients walking along hand in hand. Punjabi cavalrymen on lovely horses. British officers on foot with their men. Chin soldiers of the Burma Rifles walking home with their families, looking as though they had been discharged from their regiments. Easy to see that the road into Assam is going to be lined with graves—or, more probably, skeletons—soon! We got a big laugh out of one group of refugee Indians dressed in the yellow robes of *hpongyis*. They must have taken a monastery by storm, to pay back a small part of the mistreatment they have received from fifth-column *hpongyis*. I hope the group of *hpongyis* they beat up were not the perfectly innocent variety.

Fifteen miles of this, and then we had to ford streams. Paul's truck sank in up to the hubs in the first ford and something went wrong with General Stilwell's own car. The general must have heard some bad news in Indaw, because he has ordered us to move forward continually at all costs, abandoning vehicles at once if anything goes wrong. He abandoned his own car there, and we hurriedly salvaged our surgical instruments out of Paul's truck and went on. At the next ford they ordered Lilly, the American Technical Group man with the powerful thumbs and leather stomach, to drive the trucks across so there would be no more mired down. Tun Shein forgot to tell him that his truck had trick brakes, so when Lilly got across the other side and jammed down on the brakes the truck plunged into the body of the one in front and crushed the radiator. We had to abandon it also. Mine was the only one of the original trucks of our unit that got through. The Friends have lost one of theirs. Even Lilly could not have driven the trucks up the steep bank on the west shore if Grindlay and other American officers had not stood beside the truck and thrown sand under the wheels as they started spinning. Several times a jeep had to come to the rescue and pull.

Some time after dark we passed a lot of Chinese troops quartered in a refugee camp. We kept on over one more ridge along a very narrow road where it was all we could do to get by a lot of oxcarts that were being used by refugees. At 2:00 A. M. we stopped to camp for an hour by a stream. Heard there was some talk about the advisability of paying the nurses off and leaving them there so they wouldn't be a drag on the party as we marched over the mountains! But General Stilwell heard about it too and squelched it at once.

19

On Foot

May 6th—I fell asleep at the last minute and darn near didn't get into my place in our echelon when the general started at three. That would have finished me once and for all! We passed through a big Hkamti Shan village called Mansi, and, five miles farther along, the road ended at a flimsy bridge which nothing but a jeep could negotiate. The general got us all together around him and made us a speech. All the different groups were to turn in their food supplies into a pool, then abandon everything they had except what they felt they would be able to carry themselves. I got the nurses together, after that, and told them the Chin Hills and Naga Hills which our trail would cross were famous for their steepness and therefore they certainly could not carry so much stuff as to make them lag on the march. We must vindicate ourselves by covering the ground as fast and as far as the long-legged Americans. Furthermore, we would certainly be called on to care for the sick en route; so each girl must take a little first-aid kit, with the drugs for malaria, dysentery, headaches, etc. My speech was very effective; for tonight I find the silly girls threw away their blankets and have only enough for one to every group of three. They even threw away their silk *longyis* and kept one extra cotton outfit each.

While the Americans were shuttling back and forth to the

end of the jeep road eight miles away, transporting the food supplies, we set out on foot. I find my feet don't hurt much if the ground is fairly smooth and I can set my feet down squarely. It is this ghastly heat! I noticed the girls were carrying water in sulfathiazole bottles. About fifteen thousand tablets of the only sulfathiazole in India must be all over the ground back there! After four miles I was exhausted and lay down for a half hour under a mango tree and soothed my parched tongue with green mangoes. There is no shade, but at least we did not have to climb mountains. That guy Grindlay has got guts. He carried Ruby's pack as well as his own. Colonel Williams did this trip on foot with us, though he could have hopped one of the food-carrying jeeps. He seemed to have made up his mind to take things the hard way with his medical unit. He is ten years older than I am, but he can walk circles all around me. The Americans have a tiny bungalow, and Mr. Case had persuaded the *hpongyis* to let our unit have their monastery. There is a world of difference between these Hkamti Shan *hpongyis* and the variety between Mandalay and Rangoon. The people were very kind to us and cooked us a wonderful dinner. We heard a mule train was passing the bungalow, and the general persuaded the muleteers to go with us to Assam. That will make it possible to take all the food along, and we won't starve. Major Barton, an English commando officer whom we used to see in Namkham and Lashio fifteen years ago and who speaks most of the languages of the orient, has joined us to act as a guide. He has lived most of his life in the jungles and is built like a bull. He has an Edward VII beard. The nurses have been bathing my feet and putting dressings on the sores.

May 7th—Up at dawn, but the Chinese muleteers, as usual, took an extra hour or more to get the loads tied on the saddles; so the sun was fairly high when we started. We followed a path that passed through jungle crossing a stream they call the Chaunggyi several times until we came to a sort of gorge; and then there was no road at all. The general and his Hkamti Shan guide led us splashing right down the stream bed. The general sets the pace and is followed by the American officers; then comes a small group of heterogeneous officers; then the English; then our group; and finally the general's Chinese bodyguard. The general has been carrying one of the tommyguns. From ten minutes to until the hour we have a rest, and then fifty minutes of marching. When we started down the river, the Americans at first stopped and snatched off their shoes and rolled up their trouser-legs. Later they gave up in disgust, and all plodded right through. One or two have cut off their trouser-legs and made shorts of them.

We are all worried about Than Shwe and how she can stand the trip. It is less than a year since I opened her abdomen for appendicitis symptoms and discovered the peritoneal cavity full of tuberculosis and the appendix tight to the horn of the uterus. She looks well and is carrying absolutely no pack at all. About ten o'clock one of the Friends saw a rubber air mattress that had been discarded by an officer, inflated it, put Than Shwe on board, and dragged her along. As soon as the girls got tired they began to sing. I was scared that the general might think this a breach of discipline, but no bullets hit me from his tommygun and their singing put new life into me, as it always does, so I let them go to it. About noon Colonel Holcombe, who has been ill for weeks, had a heat stroke, and they brought him down slowly behind us. About a mile farther on Major Merrill fainted from the heat right in front of Bawk and me, and we fell out of line of march with Colonel Dorn and gave him first aid. He should not have had such a heavy pack! Than Shwe and her air mattress gave me a sudden inspiration. When Merrill's condition improved, Bawk and I hurried on to send Paul and Tom back with it. They dragged Merrill into our noon camp where the general was having two small bamboo rafts built while we were cooking. Colonel Dorn has given us permission to cook our own mess separately from the officers, as the girls like chillies and things in their food that the Americans can't eat. I had an hour's sleep until the ants biting me had had a good meal, and then we all had a bath. I asked the general for permission for four of our Friends Ambulance men to drag the hospital rafts down the river. Colonel Williams has assigned Than Shwe to ride on Colonel Holcombe's raft, and a Chinese lieutenant, who also collapsed with the heat, to Major Merrill's. It was dark before we stopped for the night. The general would have kept on if there were not so much chance of his men getting badly hurt stumbling around in the dark. The Friends didn't get in with the rafts till midnight. They were sopping wet, since, without light, they had been unable to avoid deep places and had sunk in up to their necks. One of them stepped on me as he was trying to find us in the dark. They are dead tired.

May 8th—Grindlay has been detailed to bring up the rear with the sick who are to travel at their own rate of speed. The river is running in a sort of gorge. On some of the sandbanks there is tiger spoor. Some group of refugees had driven jeeps down the river but gave up and abandoned them. I have never seen jungles so full of monkeys! The minute they spot us they start whooping and hollering. Nurses claim they are yelling, "daddy, daddy, daddy!" They can get a laugh out of anything! Jack Belden dropped back to walk with us and find out something about these nurses who laugh and sing when we white people are cussing our sore feet and the sand in our shoes. He was surprised to hear them strike up one of the modern Chinese national songs and wondered where they picked it up. Hadn't heard of our Sixth Army work, I guess. We crossed short bits of jungle here and there, and the girls insisted that some of the plants beside the road were edible. I have forbidden them to eat anything, though, until Tun Shein passes on it. I don't want any of them poisoned. We stopped for our noon meal on a high bank above the river, where there were some big trees and shade. Bawk spread out a rubber sheet she is lugging along so I could lie down and get some rest; but the shade moved away from me so fast that I had to get up and move every few minutes. Thorns were everywhere, and the girls kept picking them out of their bare feet. But the ants were positively vicious! Grindlay didn't turn up until we had finished our food, really delicious with some wild gooseberrylike fruit and some boiled wild greens that Tun Shein recognized. We are all vegetable hungry. Grindlay had been lost. He had had to go very slowly until a Chinese mule was sent back for Major Nowakowski to ride, and then the mule had a much faster gait than Grindlay, so Grindlay gave up and wandered along behind, finally noticing a village on the bank of the stream. Just about then he must have passed out from heat exhaustion, for when he came to, he was lying under a house with a Hkamti woman peeking down at him through the floor slats. He couldn't decide whether to go up or down stream and must have dropped asleep again. When he awoke he saw a uniform in the distance, and found us. The nurses made him lie down and took off his shoes and stockings, bathed his feet, and put dressings on his broken, bloody blisters while Tun Shein fed him his lunch. We are camped for the night by a big Hkamti village on the river bank. It took Tun Shein about fifteen minutes to make the villagers fall in love with him and cook us a dinner.

May 9th—The coolies the general secured to carry stuff at the first village refused to go any farther, so Case had to round up a new group. Took us that much longer to get started. Some of our packs are being carried and we distribute the rest around so that each person's load is fairly light. The Friends' packs are still rather heavy, but they are the type we all really need —they hang from the shoulders without constricting the chest. The rest of us have the ordinary Kachin and Shan bags and their straps make it hard to breathe.

Our trip today was across the neck of land between the Chaunggyi and the Uru, into which it flows. Just before the noon halt there was a huge elephant standing just off the road looking at us. The general and several other officers stopped with tommyguns to shoot if he charged—until our whole line of march went by into safety—and then rejoined us. The hill climbing, however, had been too much for Than Shwe, and she, with Kenneth and Eric, had had to drop behind unofficially. They passed the elephant after the guard had gone on. Our camp was covered with elephant spoor. It was hard to find room to lie down, and the ants and thorns were worse than yesterday. There was a little creek beside us with a sandy bottom, and the nurses scooped out hollows and lay down in them to cool off after they had gathered a lot more wild vegetables. We had three vegetables today. Some are rather coarse and some have a bitter tang, but the nurses like them all the better for that. As far as I am concerned, as long as the chillies and salt last I can eat any vegetable and enjoy it! An airplane flew over us a couple of times but we hid. A mile before we reached Maing Kaing there was a graveled road, too narrow for cars. The gravel was so sharp it cut the feet of the nurses, whose shoes had worn out and been thrown away, until the blood ran and finished off the flimsy shoes of the girls who still had them. We stopped for a long rest in Maing Kaing eating dozens of bananas and drinking gallons of coconut milk, then came on to the Uru River bank where we are bedding down on the sands. Tun Shein persuaded the local people to cook us another meal, and, of all things, they produced some boiled potatoes. O'Hara is ordered to camp with the Americans, so Grindlay went over to invite him to dine with us. How that rice hater did attack the potatoes!

20

Floating Down the Uru

May 10th—They say it is Sunday again, but you can't prove it by me! The general had secured three large rafts and one small one, and we are to float down the Uru to the Chindwin. Each of the rafts consists of three sections fastened together with rattan. The Burmese had several hours' more work to do on one of the rafts, so we had a long wait ahead of us. The sight of those bare bamboo rafts worried me, for I hate the hot sun, and there were occasional dark clouds that looked like rain in the offing. Tun Shein scouted around and found a lot of thatch piled up under a native house, so I went over and stood near the general until he noticed me.

"Sir," I said, "if we may have your permission, our nurses will build shelters of thatch on each of those rafts to protect the whole group from sun and rain. We can complete them by the time the last raft is ready."

"O.K., get going!"

The Friends and orderlies split bamboos, some of the nurses cut rattan into twine and others wove framework under Tun Shein's direction. As the shelter went up some of the American officers got interested, watching the way the girls twisted the rattan knots, and then began to help. We did our raft last, putting on the thatch after we had begun floating down the river. The raft assigned to us was the largest and had been tied nearest the bank. As the other groups loaded supplies onto their rafts, they had to carry heavy loads across ours and many of the rotten bamboos had broken before we started our historic trip. The small raft with Colonels McCabe, St. John, Wyman and Major Merrill went first, with orders to explore Homalin for Japanese. The Americans went next, then the English, and finally our group. Grindlay is with us as my second in command. And Jack Belden elected to come with us too! He doesn't dislike us as much as he thought he did. He spent the time chatting with first one and then another of the girls, who speak English freely, and is getting their life stories.

Eric is going to be the ruin of us all. He is so big and clumsy! He can't sit still, and keeps plunging around here and there, and you can tell where he has been by the broken bamboos he leaves behind. This afternoon I had to cuss him and order him to stay put. We men live in our underpants and the girls in nothing but a single *longyi* strapped up under their armpits. Every time we get hot we drop over the side and have a swim. It is nice to be able to sleep again. If we aren't swimming we are sleeping. Tun Shein has built us a little native fireplace of mud amidships, and we have weak tea and a bit of black sticky rice, which he begged off a native, every so often when our tummies rumble. We are better off than the others who don't know the customs of the country. We are all growing beards. Koi has adopted Grindlay as her own very special uncle and won't let him do a thing for himself.

The first hours were easy. We had a Hkamti captain at the bow and a helmsman at the stern. We men only had to jump to action when we got into shallow water. The Hkamti have taught us to be patient and not try to pole faster than the current, for when we pole too rapidly, the several sections of the raft tend to pull apart. We had to pull them together once during the morning and attach them with reinforcements of full-thickness rattan. An hour before sunset we caught up with the general who had stopped at a sandy bank to cook dinner. The minute the girls set foot on land they scattered into the jungle. This time they were unusually successful and came back with five different wild vegetables. The variety of which they had secured the most was a tender leaf with a slightly sour taste. I took some of it to Colonel Dorn.

"Have a taste, Colonel," I invited. "Tun Shein guarantees that it is edible and the nurses have brought in far too much for us to eat. How about boiling some up like spinach for the general's mess?"

Colonel Dorn took a taste, decided the leaves had possibilities, and gave instructions to the cooks. He told me later that they had really enjoyed it. It was something like spinach with the vinegar already added.

Since we always make a point of it, we were done with dinner and ready to move before the others were, so we sat around and sang while the others ate. It was dark when we started off again. We arranged shifts of two men each, since we were to travel all night and our Hkamti friends were tired. Grindlay and I took the first shift, I on the bow and he on the stern. The batteries in my flashlight were almost gone, and we kept grazing snags that appeared out of nowhere. Grindlay was cussing me from the stern.

"Damn it, Doc, why don't you push us off those snags?"

"Damn it yourself! If I had a flashlight that would work I

would keep us off them." I had the advantage of him, for I could cuss him roundly in Burmese and Shan, and make a good effort of it in Chinese, without his even knowing I was cussing! I could have done a better job of it also if there had been anything for me to stand on. There were only one or two sound bamboos left at the bow. I couldn't keep my shoes on for fear of slipping into the water, and as I moved from port to starboard and back again with my long bamboo pole, those confounded broken bamboos kept piercing my feet and often they ran right into those blasted sores of mine.

After three hours of cussing I turned my pole over to Paul with a sigh of relief. I found my bed was partly under water, so I moved over to a six-inch-wide stretch between a couple of nurses on the other side. But I hadn't had more than a beauty nap when I was wakened.

"God damn. God damn. God damn!" Breathless, fervent, a real prayer! Was that Paul? It certainly was none other! Something must really have happened if that most discreet, self-contained, he-man saint, Paul Geren, was cussing! Aching in every joint I got up and looked out.

"What's the matter, Paul?"

"This damned river is so deep I can't reach the bottom with my pole and there is a little creek falling into the river over there that makes a kind of whirlpool, and the raft just keeps running round and round in the same place. I can't paddle with this bamboo fast enough to get us past."

"Just let me find another bamboo pole and maybe both of us, working together, can get us by."

It was another hour—two hours and a half in all—before we

managed to inch the raft beyond the interference of that little creek. Then we both went to bed and turned the job over to the Anglo-Indian refugee.

May 11th—Tun Shein cooked us some red sticky rice for breakfast. We caught up with the other rafts at ten. Even with the extra food that Tun Shein wangles out of the natives we are still half starved. I don't know how the others stand it! Soon after we caught up with them a bomber flew over us and swerved back and down toward us again. We expected to be machine-gunned any minute, till someone spotted the English insignia. When only a hundred feet off the ground the plane began to drop bags on the sandbank and we all plunged overboard, General Stilwell included, and raced for the sacks. Natives of the near-by village also were racing, but aside from a sack or two we got the whole shipment. Inside the sacks were bully beef, many of the tins cracked, ration biscuits, and cigarettes. The general carried back his own sack. The beef in the cracked tins had to be eaten immediately, so for once we had our fill.

We found a lot of bamboos at one of the villages and have spent a lot of time today splitting them and repairing our raft which is fast going to pieces. There are not many places where you can stand with safety, and the floor level is not much above water. In the afternoon we got to another stretch of deep water just as a strong head wind came up. The rafts just kept turning round and round until some officers swam to shore with a rope and drew us in. We stopped there for a meal. It was dark when we started again with orders to keep in sight of each other. Our flashlights are all worn out and the snags are worse than ever. To make matters still more difficult, the current is now much stronger. Time after time it was almost impossible to keep the raft from breaking up. All hands had to plunge overboard and pull the entire length of the eighty-foot raft with every ounce of strength, the sand washing away from under our feet as we struggled. Once the water was too deep for the men at the stern, and the raft got away and did the next few miles stern first. For several hours we saw nothing of the other rafts and then suddenly discovered their lights right in front as we swung around a corner. Captain Eldridge shouted back that the Burmese steersman had let the general's raft get into the wrong channel and we were all to remain where we were. "Where we were" was good! There were the usual crosscurrents of the river's bend and if we held the stern in the front, the raft would break loose and float off by itself with no men on board. We had to get all the stronger nurses out to help us. Finally Martin explored in the dark and found a place a hundred yards farther on where the currents were less confused, and we poled in there and "anchored" ourselves with bamboo poles driven into the bottom. The next shift is on duty now to keep us from breaking loose, and I am going to try to get some sleep. It is long after midnight.

May 12th—The night shift went to sleep, too, and the raft broke away again. The front and center sections held together by only one bamboo. It began to pour rain, but I was sopping wet as it was, the place where I lay being six inches under water. From then till dawn all we could do was let the raft take its own course while we tried to keep the various sections somewhere near one another. As soon as there was light enough Tun Shein got some more rattan and tied us together again. Then it was a question whether the raft would stay afloat long enough for us to catch up with the general, who had vanished during the night. It rained again this morning and we had a time trying to get our clothes dry. The funniest thing that happened the whole trip was when we came around a bend and found Lieutenant Belknap sitting on a snag right in the middle of the stream hoping someone would find him! He had started off across country with the mule caravan, but his feet were so covered with sores he couldn't make it in to Homalin. Tun Shein found some potatoes and cooked them for breakfast —one tiny potato each!

Just before three this afternoon we found the other rafts tied up to the bank behind a huge boat with high carved teak stern. The officers on the scout raft and those with the mule train had explored Homalin and had found no Japanese there. While we were eating some bully beef and the biscuits, I heard there were some shops still open in Homalin, so, with the general's permission, sent Tun Shein, Grindlay, Martin, and Eric on ahead to try to buy shoes for the nurses. When they got to Homalin everything was closed; but Tun Shein started kidding the Burmese until he got them laughing, and then one of them admitted he had some shoes for sale. They bought ten pairs of tennis shoes and two pairs of oxfords, a lot of cigarettes, and some flashlight batteries. By this time the Burmese had fallen so much in love with Tun Shein that they invited the party into the headman's house and gave them tea. They were drinking the tea as we marched through. The rest of the party is sleeping the night in a Buddhist monastery and our unit is in the "nunnery." The floor is full of holes. Grindlay distributed the shoes, and all were fits except Ruby's. Her feet are as big as a man's and we had to cut holes for her big toes.

21

Over the Mountains

May 13th—Off at daybreak, marching north two and a half miles to the Chindwin. Over to the west were the terrible mountains to be marched over. The top of the range was wreathed in clouds. We had to cross a half-mile of deep sand before we got to the river itself. There were only two or three small dugouts available for the crossing when we arrived. The nurses crossed over in one of these, crouching on the bottom and balancing carefully to keep the thing from rolling over. Later, larger dugouts came along and one Burmese cabin boat with a hold and everything. Someone had found a little pony for the sick men to ride, and the general ordered me to swim him over. I held on the stern as the boat started off, leading the pony by the bridle. At first the animal went willingly, being used to fording small streams; but when he got tired and saw no farther bank in sight he got wild and tried to swim back. For ten minutes the boatmen could make no progress at all and then, catching a glimpse of the bank, the pony became docile again.

We waited on the far bank, where there was no room to stretch out and no real shade, until two this afternoon, wondering where the pack train had disappeared. It finally turned up beyond us, having crossed the river some distance below. There was a good trail through teak forest. As we climbed the ridge we saw our first Chins, villagers with heavy loads of thatch grass they had been ordered to produce for construction of shacks for refugees. They are quite like the Kachins and some of their words have a resemblance. After only a short march we passed a burned village and descended to a small stream whose banks were very rocky. We found enough patches of sand for us all to have just enough room for a small bed. The water is very cold and very refreshing after the awful heat we have been through. My sores are much worse. While we were bathing, a tremendous storm blew up and we could see rain pouring down all around us. It missed us completely, much to everyone's delight, for there was no possible shelter for us and we would have been set for a cold wet night. The nurses burst forth into song again. They say we made only ten miles today.

May 14th—Case had to get a lot of Chin carriers to replace the Hkamti, and so, since Chins carry their loads suspended from their foreheads and not on yokes like Hkamti, there was a lot of repacking to do. The road today was steep from the start, and the swarms of monkeys everywhere kept laughing at us as we panted and sweated. Our noon camp was by a clear mountain stream rushing madly over gigantic boulders. I had a malarial chill while the boys were cooking and the nurses fixed me a place where I could stretch out in a sort of arbor and rolled me up in a blanket. Of course, the general had to catch me at it just as the chill passed off.

"What's the matter, Seagrave, got fever?"

"No, sir, I got wet and felt a little cold so was warming up."

"How are your feet?"

"Better, sir."

"You are lying."

"Yes, sir."

The general laughed and walked off to give orders to start. Grindlay saw a lot of otters playing in the stream, but I wasn't interested. Today was the first without elephant spoor. They say the road was built by the government of India in 1918 to suppress a rebellion among the Chins who did not understand why they should form a labor corps to work in France. It is being repaired for the first time since then. The reason why there are not the motorable roads needed now so badly to connect Burma and Assam is that the Burma-India Steam Navigation Company wanted the monopoly of Indo-Burma trade for their Calcutta-Rangoon steamers. Only six people have used this road ahead of us.

We have outdistanced everyone else. Jack Belden is still with us on the march and sleeps with our unit at night too. There is supposed to be only one more day's march before we reach the top. The afternoon climb was worse than the morning one. I got so angry with the girls for singing and talking at the tops of their voices as we climbed. Couldn't stand the idea of anyone wasting breath while I was dying on my feet, as it seemed to me. I asked them to confine their singing to the few slopes down. Maran Lu wouldn't listen to me and I had to give her a direct order. The last hour the road was horribly steep and a drenching rain came on. My morale was at very low ebb. We finally reached some half-finished grass shacks at an elevation of thirty-nine hundred feet. That means that we have climbed three thousand feet today, for Homalin is only four hundred and fifty feet and we went down almost as much yesterday as we climbed up. A Mr. Sharpe, secretary to the maharajah of Manipur, was waiting in camp. He was sent out by the government of India to meet General Stilwell. He has a few ponies here and about a hundred Naga coolies. There are more ponies and anything up to four hundred more coolies a few miles farther on. Now, at least, we won't have to carry our packs any farther. The sick are to ride the ponies. The party brought large quantities of food with them and we have to be on half rations no longer. There are only five to eight more days of travel ahead of us, depending on how fast we travel. The general knows the rains are due to break suddenly and effectively soon, and he has rightly determined to push us along to the limit of our endurance. It would be terrible to have to climb these mountains if we had rain all day long, and the Assam rainfall is so heavy they measure it in feet and not in inches. Case found a couple of pigs and gave our mess the smaller one. It couldn't have been very large, for we ate up every scrap in one meal. The girls have been drying my clothes as well as theirs. I have done nothing but roll up in my blanket and pray for a sudden easy death! Thirty-nine of us have to sleep in two small huts on muddy ground. The rest of our party have been cutting grass to spread out. Grindlay has picked up a severe conjunctivitis. The smoke of the fires—the rain compelled the boys to cook inside the hut—makes his eyes burn terribly.

May 15th—We were up at dawn but couldn't get off till seven-thirty as the loads all had to be arranged again to suit the Naga carrying customs. Colonel Williams ordered me to take command of the sick cavalcade. Lord, what a break! I honestly don't think I could have taken another step. There were only eight ponies at the start but I managed to wangle two of them for Than Shwe and Esther. Grindlay now commands our unit. He will not ride a pony and yet I have seen his feet and they are a terrible sight. He insists he is younger than I, and that, of course, is a self-evident fact.

The trail was very steep and hard on the ponies, but until my noon chill started, I enjoyed gazing in awe at the Nagas. When we first saw them, last night, they were wrapped in blankets. This morning they were stripped for action, and never in my life have I seen such beautiful men in such large numbers. They were perfectly shaped with well-developed muscles. Lovely proportions! There wasn't much of them that you couldn't see, for almost all were naked except for a tiny apron and a little bag, about six inches long and two wide, for the most important part of their anatomy. There was no trying to avoid the heavier loads. Their chief anxiety seemed to be to beat the other man to the load and get going first. They had their heads shaved except for a ridge of hair down the middle. Their ear lobes were stretched to great lengths by heavy ornaments.

There was no shade from the hot sun and the heat was damp. We covered only six miles before the noon halt, where our meal consisted of tin willie and biscuits. We had tea, though, and that washes anything down! Had to climb another two thousand feet in the afternoon to the border ridge at an elevation of six thousand feet. During all this latter part we could look back and see across the entire country that we had taken seven days to cross spread out in panorama below us. On the horizon were the low hills of the jungle where we had abandoned our trucks and supplies. We passed a border pillar and the girls burst into song again as they crossed into India. Everyone began talking about the huge quantities of ice cream she was going to consume and the numbers of movies she was going to see when she reached Calcutta. To hear them carry on you would think we were going to sleep in Calcutta tonight with no further miseries before us! We are now in *taungya* country again, the first we have seen since we left the Shan States. The Nagas are more like Kachins in some ways than the Chins are. They burn down the hillsides to plant their rice for three or four years until the soil is no longer fertile and then move on to another spot and burn down some more. Between these patches of *taungyas* are stretches of thick forest. There were three hundred and fifty more Nagas waiting for us as we rode on for a time along the ridge. Clouds came up from the west, and then as the rain broke, we had a last glimpse of the Chindwin before we plunged down into the valley. There were now twenty-eight ponies, but only eighteen were usable. Many had no saddles. Most of the saddles were in pretty poor condition, without decent girths or stirrup leathers, and my stirrups today were so narrow I could just get the tips of my Army boots into them and no more. I am glad Than Shwe and Esther had a chance to ride up the steep section. Going down in the rain we had to lead our ponies and walk a good bit of the way. Our refugee friend begged for one of the new ponies and I let him have it. Then the big scab rushed along with it, not waiting for the people who were really sick! The two women refugees are not so bad, but all three of them manage to slip in a squeeze when there are any favors to be had, while the nurses don't like to accept any favors for fear the Americans will get the idea they haven't got guts! The Naga village where we are spending the night is back in Burma again! When the nurses heard that, they didn't continue to brag quite as much about what they were going to do in Calcutta! There is only one hut for us and we had to dry out our clothes. Maran Lu is completely all in and in a rotten humor and acts like a cat. Grindlay says she insisted on talking and singing all by herself while they were climbing the worst stretch. Now she and all the rest of us have to pay for it. Several of the girls are distinctly pooped. The ones who usually take care of me could do nothing but change into drier clothes and drop down on the floor, so I have been trying to dry their wet things, holding them in my hands over the fire. Everyone is talking about how Bill Duncombe can laugh. He has always been very reserved around me, since he took his place in our Friends Ambulance at Kume, but he and Paul have become fast friends, and today, when the morale was low, Paul told him something funny and his laugh roared out so loud that all the Americans turned and laughed in sympathy. Grindlay was greatly impressed with a herd of miffin that he would have missed entirely if the girls hadn't seen them and called his attention. They are wild cows that look something like buffaloes but have a white tufted tail. They were grazing along the border ridge. I, of course, missed them entirely.

May 16th—Up at 4:00 A. M. and off at 5:30 to the sound of a wild elephant trumpeting in the distance. I made Koi and Bawk ride with me today and they kept me busy answering all sorts of fool questions. I wish I had a phonograph record with me to say, *"Nga m'thi, nga m'thi.* I don't know, I don't know." Maran Lu had to ride, too, but she is still provoked with me and didn't say a thing. We went over a mountain shoulder with gorgeous scenery—just like the woods in Ohio—and then down a deep chasm, losing most of the height we struggled so hard to gain yesterday. Why did I put my movie camera onto the mules? The road up the other side of the chasm wound back and forth on the face of the precipices and the whole line of march was spread out in front of us, certainly a full mile in length. This was the first very steep climb since the last group of Nagas joined us, so I heard something new and very impressive. The Nagas travel in groups from the same village, keeping step as they walk in single file. At every step one or another lets out a grunt, each grunt in a different key, up and down the line until each has had his grunt, and the leader begins again. It makes a weird tune something like this:

Leader	Unnhh
No. 7	Hump
No. 3	Ugh
No. 8	Heep
No. 2	Hic
No. 5	Hah
No. 6	Ho
Nos. 4 & 9	Hay

Not a chance of our riding the ponies up that stretch! We had to get off and lead them. At the top of the precipice I found several of the girls and a couple of men waiting. Grindlay had ordered them to wait for me and have a ride because they had been on the verge of collapse. We hitchhiked from there on. The grades were not quite so steep but they were enough. Thank goodness it was not much farther till we came to the little village where the general had set up the noon camp! Red-blanketed chiefs carrying rifles met us there with their formal present of rice wine. The blankets and rifles are a gift from the government and are the royal marks of the chief. Nobody has any trouble persuading the Nagas to carry his rifle or tommygun. The Naga lucky enough to carry one is the envy of the whole tribe for the day! We left at two this afternoon and walked downhill for a couple of hours. I had had more than my share of riding, so I put one of the girls on my pony. Giant Eric caught a tiny pony without a saddle and rode him bareback. Eric's legs are covered with sores from the thighs down. Of the eighteen ponies only four or five are ridden by our unit, though our unit is 40 per cent of the whole party. Ruby's feet have been so badly torn by those tight shoes that she is walking barefoot again, and the path now is covered with broken shale. The girls think they lose face when ordered to ride.

We stopped for the night by another rushing mountain stream. Our whole crowd had to get into one narrow hut. I made the nurses spread out a single layer of blanket on the top of the rough saplings that the floor of the hut is made of, and we are all going to sleep in the one huge bed. I was selfish and picked my spot at the farther end where various portions of my anatomy can bulge out of the side wall of thatch if I don't have enough room—and provided it doesn't continue to rain! All the menfolks dropped down to rest, but those silly girls rushed off to the river, bathed, washed their own and our clothes, came back and have been powdering their noses and even putting on a touch of rouge! Now they are singing as they serve up our food! All sorts of fellow sufferers have been coming to us for dressings for their feet, and the adhesive is running short; but I overheard two girls laughingly tell each other that they each had a roll hidden out, which I wasn't to be told about until I had gotten properly frantic!

22

Through to Imphal

May 17th—What a night! What a night! By actual count we were each entitled to five saplings to lie on; but as the crowd in the middle twisted and turned in sleep, made restless by branches and knots pushing into them, they gradually pushed me out until I had only two saplings left. I tried so hard to stay on those two that I got horrible cramps in my legs and kicked out the side wall beside me—and then it rained! Tun Shein and Ko Nyunt got up long before dawn and cooked us some breakfast. The coolies had slept on the path, and the ponies were a mile beyond us. The sick party had to walk to the ponies and then the pony *syces* had got mad because they were not given a chance to cook food on the trip at their usual times, and refused to co-operate. They hid stirrups and girths and pretended they were lost. General Sibert rode with us today. One of my stirrup leathers was very short and the other long and there was nothing to be done about it. I dangled my feet most of the time. The road was so narrow we could hardly pass the carriers. We climbed steadily for hours. Veins of coal had been exposed everywhere cutting the road. First we went through a forest of firs and then, near the top, came to pines. This, they said, was the real top. I don't believe them. I got permission from General Sibert to remain behind at "the top" with the two nurses who were riding until the lost ponies turned up. Our ponies had a chance to graze and we found a hut where we could stretch out on a couple of banana leaves. Colonel St. John and Major Barton caught up with us there with the whole mule team and they straightened out the *syces* so we could have decent saddles at least.

The rest of the party was an hour ahead of us on the trail, but the road now was smooth and comfortably wide and so well graded that we made wonderful speed, even running and trotting in spots! We got to the afternoon camp just five minutes after the others. General Sibert is fed up with his pony and would rather walk no matter how sick he is. The nurses were laughing about how on the way down they took the wrong turn onto a path that turned out to be a short cut, and the first thing they knew, they were ahead of the general! There was an occasional drizzle. One thing that impressed me today, as we passed through the Naga villages, was the absence of women anywhere near the road. We made eighteen miles today, pushing on after lunch to a Naga village of fourteen houses built of heavy planks carved with all sorts of figures. There were totem poles here and there with the mounded graves of the dead in front of the houses. The houses are decorated with miffin skulls instead of the human skulls of not so long ago. There are pigs and dogs everywhere. All this in an alpine setting. We were given one of the Naga houses to sleep in. The front room had a nicely packed floor covered with straw, and it looked so inviting that our three refugee parasites were, of course, already parked there when we looked for a place to sleep. Five of us have found a sloping platform of planks in a corner just about big enough for us if we don't try to turn over. It is clear and cold. While the boys were cooking dinner we had our usual foot clinic, treating each other's sores and then the sore feet of others of the party. On the whole we have done rather well in not letting the sores get worse. Most of them started that first day's march down the Chaunggyi.

May 18th—Got up in the dark and were off by 5:15. It wasn't hard to get up. Everyone but myself had been chewed all night by innumerable dog fleas! While the darn things never bit me I was having my own troubles, for I was on the highest edge of the sloping platform and had to cling to the edge with my fingers and toes to keep from rolling the others off onto the ground.

Today the hills were drier and there were fewer streams. The valleys were a bit wider and there were terraced paddy fields here and there. I knew they were lying to us yesterday when they said we had reached the real top, for we climbed up again until we went over a pass seventy-five hundred feet high, where there was a very strong breeze and we had to get off and walk, sick and sore-footed though we were, to keep warm. The rainfall here when the season starts must be very heavy, for the trees are shaggy with orchids, lichens, and moss and parasites of all sorts. Ghostly appearance! Two railway men from India, who were sent to Burma to help out during the war and were about the only two men who stayed and helped Captain Jones with his impossible job to the very end, are sick with malaria. Today they couldn't balance themselves on their horses; so Colonel Williams is having them carried by the Nagas on stretchers. We had tea and biscuits for lunch at a camp in the next valley. That was the most wonderful valley of all, for around the camp were six brand new latrines—the only ones on this whole trip. The nurses were so pleased that they practically lived in them! From that camp on we had glimpses of Ukhrul, the town on the top of the distant ridge to which all the mile posts of the past four days had been pointing. When we started to climb again we came to a village with a church in it. Gosh, are there still things like churches in this Godforsaken world? A Naga chief who was walking beside me and knew a few words of English pointed to it and said, "American Baptist Mission." Well, we certainly were reaching civilization again!

As we climbed up to Ukhrul I chatted quite a bit with the British officers who had been assigned to my sick cavalcade for the day. They had held various civil and military positions in Burma and had actually heard about me and about Namkham! I didn't feel quite so lonely—no, I think I felt more lonely as my mind went back to Namkham again: Namkham in the hands of the Japs! Where was Bill Cummings? Where were the nurses?

They assigned us the government bungalow at Ukhrul. It actually had a flower garden around it. The nurses had been trying to teach me for months how to "say it with flowers" in Burmese. One flower meant "I hate you," and three meant "I love you." I could not find enough flowers available for me to give three to each, so I let them pick the darn things themselves and take the consequences! These girls like nothing better than to deck themselves out with flowers in their hair. With black hair, such as they all have, any flower looks wonderful!

Although Ukhrul is sixty-five hundred feet high and the water cold, those crazy girls were bathing till dark. I can't understand it! I am going to stay dirty.

The government officer escorting us, Mr. Sharpe, had arranged for a miffin barbecue and a Naga song-and-dance festival in the general's honor, but they had to call it off. Imphal has been bombed and all the local people have run away. They run faster in India than they did in Burma! And farther, too! They found a butcher who didn't run away and he butchered two steers for our crowd, and we have all the meat we can eat! There is a fireplace in the bungalow, so we cut our meat into steaks and grilled them in the fire on sticks. Didn't eat anything but meat tonight. My steaks were partly burned and partly raw, but I don't think I ever tasted anything so heavenly!

Two A.B.M. preachers came to talk to me when they heard I was a missionary. I was so awfully tired that I turned them over to Case. He is a much better missionary than I am!

May 19th—We spread out our single blanket on the floor, but the cement was horribly cold and I was on the edge as usual and couldn't keep the upper blanket on me when the other four rolled, so I got mad, built up the fire, and slept on a chair beside it. They say we made twenty-one miles yesterday. I certainly felt like it, and yet I had that pony! How do the others stand it?

We got off at 5:30 and for miles were passing swarms of Nagas of a different tribe from our carriers. Their hair is cut in a different pattern and they wear different clothes—if you can call those aprons and bags clothes! There has been a cold drizzle all day. The nurses are so tired now that they have lost all sense of shame and don't even bother to leave the road to answer the call of nature. And nobody cares about it either! At noon we had a "dry" halt. Yeah! It was "dry" as far as having any fluid to make tea was concerned; but there was plenty of water falling from the skies on us! I never saw anything so funny as the efforts of the various members of our group to keep dry. I had a sweater which made me imagine I was keeping warm. Roi Tsai had on Kenneth's trench coat. The girls who brought rubber sheets with them instead of blankets had them fastened over their shoulders; but funniest of all were Lilly and Little Bawk. Lilly cut two holes in his blanket, put his head through one and Bawk's head through the other and they walked along together looking like a couple of ghosts. Everyone got a good laugh out of them, so they were an invaluable asset to our morale! Grindlay looks just what he says he is: absolutely exhausted. Yet he won't ride my pony. He is so afraid that he will lose one of the nurses that he walks backward at every corner counting them! In the state of half coma we are all in, it isn't possible to tell, except by counting, that anyone is missing. That darned jackass, Maran Lu, was demon-possessed again today and went off into the jungle saying she was going to hide out there till the end of the war!

My saddle kept slipping off as I went down that last awful descent. Finally the pony put his foot in a deep hole and fell just as the saddle slipped up on his neck and made me turn a full somersault on the rocks. Then I got mad and finished the trip on foot! We got into camp late. Colonel Williams met us at a narrow suspension bridge beyond which was the motor road into Imphal, and informed me that the general had ordered our unit to set up in Imphal and help the government with the refugee problem until he had another job ready for us. Near the general's camp was a shack occupied by refugees. They were a healthy lot—probably the last healthy lot to come through—so they moved out quite willingly when they heard there were a bunch of nurses who needed shelter for the night. Maybe you can call it shelter! Grindlay had his hands full, for he had been ordered to leave our unit and remain with the other American officers. His friends, Sergeant Chesley and Colonel St. John, had arrived in camp with high fever, and Grindlay hadn't the slightest idea how to treat malaria.

Sometime after dark Colonel Eckert and Lieutenant Arnold arrived in a jeep to meet the general. We were all ordered into the bungalow to listen to the news. Tokio, Colonel Eckert said, had been bombed by the United States Air Force. Well, we can stand anything now!

May 20th—We slept late this morning. Didn't get off until 7:30! We were quite ready to leave, for it had poured all night, the roof of our shack had not been repaired for years, and we were all sopping wet. To make matters worse, when the rain began to pour, refugees had all pushed back into the hut and lay in the aisle and on top of our feet. The government sent out a number of trucks and ambulances to fetch us. In my ambulance we had Colonel St. John and Sergeant Chesley, both looking more dead than alive, though their high fever had temporarily subsided. As soon as we left the mountains and started across the huge Imphal plain we began to have difficulty with mud. There was no gravel on the road and the trucks had ploughed deep ruts. Our ambulance had huge desert tires and they would not fit into the ruts of the trucks ahead, causing us to skid more than ever. Every time we slipped off the road it was a case of all hands getting out in the mud to push. The driver had a peculiar habit of doing everything in low, even when the ambulance could have gone on quite well in high with an occasional shift into second gear. I suppose he was afraid for his safety in high, not realizing that high gear doesn't cause skidding on a muddy road nearly as much as low. Martin finally got peeved, pushed him out and began to drive for us. The cars all had to be hauled across a detour, necessitated by a broken bridge, and General Stilwell pulled just like the other officers. There were sixteen miles of this and then ten miles of graveled road into Imphal. Our ambulance pulled in last after the nurses had disappeared, so leaving Grindlay at the old fort, built in memory of British officers and men massacred during the early years of British rule, we began to explore the town. There were bomb holes everywhere, the tiny ones caused by antipersonnel bombs. Not a shop was open. Aside from troops there were no inhabitants to be seen.

I finally located the nurses and Friends in the English Casualty Clearing Station. The English captain in charge of the station is one of the finest men I ever met. His father, it seems, was a medical missionary at Quetta, in Baluchistan, and a very famous man. The buildings of a separate hospital unit in the compound had just been vacated and he told us to set up in them. There were beds there, and mattresses! How many weeks is it since I last slept on a bed?

With a sigh of relief I pulled off my boots for the last time and started soaking my feet in the puddles of rain water, when suddenly one of the nurses let out an awful scream.

"Mr. Cummings! Mr. Cummings!"

There was Bill coming on the run, tears streaming down his cheeks! What a bedlam broke loose, sobs and cheers, tears and laughter. The girls threw themselves on him and fairly mauled him, firing questions at him so rapidly he had no chance to answer. They would have torn him apart if the food ordered for us had not that minute arrived. The nurses were so starved they finally consented to pack their mouths with rice and dal and give Bill a chance to answer my questions. Gurney had brought out fourteen nurses with him, traveling by plane from Loiwing to Dinjan. Several of our orderlies had also come by plane, among them Theodore and Judson. Bill, Graham, Whittington, Ba Saw, and Bella had driven to Kunming in trucks and jeeps and had then flown to Dinjan. They located Dr. Gurney's crowd at Jorhat in the A.B.M. hospital where the crazy girls were already attending classes in the nurses' training school and trying to help on the wards. While they were worrying about what had happened to us, Bill bumped into my old friend Colonel Ottaway, who used to be a tin-mine manager near Tavoy. Ottaway told him he had been supplying foodstuffs to R.A.F. planes to be dropped to General Stilwell and that the general would probably reach Imphal in another three days.

Bill and Ted Gurney talked over the new information with Colonel Ottaway, and they decided that if our unit had come out with General Stilwell, Gauhati would be the logical place to wait for us. Ted would take the nurses there by train while Bill rode in Ottaway's jeep to Imphal. Kyang Tswi was afraid

Bill would slip away in the jeep without her, so she hid all his clothes and Bill had to leave in the things he stood up in! They drove all day and all night and got to Imphal yesterday. Just a few minutes ago Bill, wandering hopelessly around, had bumped into Colonel McCabe and learned we had arrived!

23

Bill's Story

THAT EVENING Bill and I had a chance to talk. He told me quite a tale:

After leaving us in Kume, Bill traveled back to Hsipaw, seeing no sign of a stand being made against the Jap advance which could cut them off on either of the two roads from the south. There was nothing to do but evacuate Gurney and the nurses, who had been operating steadily, to Namkham. After they were safely off, Bill commandeered a Chinese Red Cross truck and followed with the rest of our equipment. A few miles along, he met a puzzled Colonel Boatner who wanted to know where the hell that damned bridge was that General Stilwell had ordered him to blow up! Bill stopped a minute to enlighten him, made it into Lashio at midnight, and then, with breakfast at Kutkai, managed to reach Namkham at noon. Next morning Ted insisted on going back to Kutkai with four nurses to set up, but they found Major Lindsay already there doing what little there was to do, so they rushed back to salvage Namkham. At Kutkai they heard that our base hospital at Loilem had received a present of twenty-eight bombs the morning after we left, and Hsipaw also had been plastered.

At Namkham the woman's surgical ward was full of R.A.F. men. Dr. Grey and Dr. Ahma, who had been doing my Namkham hospital work, had flown out that day from Loiwing with two women missionaries. Bill's house was full of government officials, and Gurney and the Grahams and Whittingtons and Dr. Barr-Johnston were in my bungalow; so Bill slept on the big table in the nurses' home. Dr. Barr-Johnston had brought out two of the Kengtung nurses. The others elected to remain with their families.

The next morning Mrs. Graham, Mrs. Whittington, and other missionaries flew out from Loiwing. Bill made a rush trip to Kutkai with two nurses who wanted to rejoin their people, and returned with five huge sacks of salt to distribute to Kachin and Shan teachers to help them through the months of Japanese occupation. Loiwing had been bombed again the day before and the stabilizer of one of the big United States Army transport planes had been injured. The plane was now repaired and had no passengers. Bill was hopeless of ever reaching Myitkyina ahead of the Japs, so he arranged for the nurses to take passage. At the last minute Bill and Ted had a fight, for Ted was determined to be the last to leave; but Bill finally persuaded him that the nurses would be lost in India without him, and pushed him on board just in time. Two patients went along with them.

After the plane left, Bill asked an A.V.G. officer if he knew when Hsipaw had fallen.

"Yes, the Japs took it two days ago."

"In that case," said Bill, "they will be here day after tomorrow morning."

"How can they? The Namkai bridge has been blown."

Bill got a map and showed the officer the short cut from Hsipaw through Namtu Silver Mines to Namkham.

"God! We'd better get out of here."

Dr. Richards of the A.V.G. went back to Namkham with Bill and was presented with one of our trucks, two of my sterilizers, my Oldsmobile sedan, and all the medicines he could carry. He took some of our surgical instruments, too. Then Bill went over to the nurses' home and discovered that the Shans had stolen most of the suitcases that the nurses had left ready packed for Bill to put on his truck. Bill doesn't get profane very often!

That historic afternoon Dr. Tu and Nang Leng found a few minutes to get married. Bill pleaded with E Hla to go along with him, but her mother refused to budge and E Hla had to stay behind. What do you suppose the Japs have done to that charming girl and her baby?

Bill called in all the mission staff and paid them three months' salary in advance. To E Hla he gave six months' salary —God bless him!—and huge quantities of salt, kerosene, rice, and sesamine oil. Koi's poor old father and mother got the same. Then he had an argument with Ba Saw.

"What is the advantage of my going with you?" asked Ba Saw.

"If you stick out this thing with Dr. Seagrave, then, at the end of the war, you can build up the Namkham hospital again while he goes home to America for money."

"O.K. I'm going."

Ba Saw arranged to meet Bill at Kyuhkok on the border that night and hurried off in a jeep to get Bella and the baby and return by the road on the other side of the river. Graham, Whittington, and Bill left Namkham in relays as they got their trucks loaded. Bill thought the others had salvaged my clothes and more precious possessions, so he brought along only my family photographs. Somehow or other he didn't find the Kaisar-i-Hind medal the viceroy gave me. When he left, the Shans were waiting to loot our entire setup. Myers of the American Red Cross came through Namkham the next night and went to our bungalow for a couple of hours of sleep and found everything looted and no bed to lie on. At the hospital, also, everything had been stolen. The Japs appeared a few hours later at the precise time that Bill had predicted, one party on each side of the Shweli suspension bridge, surprising and shooting the British captain and men detailed to destroy the bridge.

Bill's memory of the once great Burma Road was of one long, continuous traffic jam. It took him six hours to get from one side of Chefang Town to the other. He refused to sleep in Paoshan because it looked ripe for a bombing; and, sure enough, it was plastered the next morning. A spring on the ambulance that Nang Leng was driving broke, and Bill repaired it with a rear jeep spring, filing extra threads on the shackle bolts, and making a lot of washers out of a biscuit tin. At the side of the road they passed my Oldsmobile, abandoned because of a broken axle shaft; and there was the end of another of my dreams.

During the night at Shiaokuan, two of Bill's companions got tight, and one threw a lighted cigarette which dropped on top of a sweater containing a lot of .22-caliber shells. Bill, dreaming happily of a Japanese attack, found his dream had a sound accompaniment. The two drunks "put out" the fire by throwing the sweater onto a straw mattress which then blazed up merrily.

White rhododendrons were blooming along the road as if

there were no war on; but war traffic jams lengthened the time for the trip to ten days. Casualties on the road asked for treatment when they saw the ambulance, and Dr. Ba Saw and Dr. Tu cared for them. The chief nuisance of the trip, however, was Nang Leng's adopted son, one of our hospital orphans, so spoiled that he remained constipated the whole trip because Nang Leng had forgotten to bring along his pet chamberpot!

At Kunming, Nang Leng and Tu went off to his relatives, keeping the ambulance to help them set up in a new practice. One of our trucks Bill gave to the Friends Ambulance, and then turned the rest of them and the jeeps over to the United States Army. A.V.G. influence got them passage by plane to Dinjan the next morning. At Dinjan, half starved, they made a wonderful meal of sauerkraut and sausages which they ate with hemostats, having no other cutlery. Ba Saw's baby boy thought the whole trip was grand fun!

24

Assignment in Assam

May 21st—This place is lousy with mosquitoes. Worst we have seen. The Casualty Clearing Station captain has produced some mosquito nets for us today and a few extra blankets, but last night was pretty bad. This morning I went up to see Grindlay and O'Hara at the fort, and the general was there looking quite fresh. I believe he stood the trip better, tired as he was, than any of us. He could have made much better time if others had been as capable of marching as he. He appointed a board of three colonels to meet with me at two o'clock and decide rate of salaries for each of the groups of nurses and orderlies.

The three officers who appeared were our old friends Colonel Holcombe, Colonel McCabe, and Colonel Williams, who had more firsthand information with regard to the build-up of our unit than the other officers. The policy approved by the board was not to attempt to pay the girls on the same basis as American Army nurses, because of the difference in living standards, but to pay them sufficiently large salaries to cover the cost of messing and refit, and leave enough over to permit them to save against the very rainy days that would come to Burma in the postwar period. While discussions were going on, Colonel Holcombe began to have a malarial chill, and we put him to bed in one of our new wards. Colonel St. John and Sergeant

Chesley were already in the wards with three Chinese, for, aside from myself, none of the American medical officers was prepared to take care of malaria patients. Two nurses went on day duty at once, and two more are on night duty now. Sergeant Chesley was so nauseated that we had to give him his medicine by hypo; and Colonel St. John, besides the nausea he is suffering from, is sensitive to both quinine and atabrine. I have decided to treat him with only one dose of five grains of quinine given very accurately at the time he feels the chill begin to come on. He is so fed up with being ill that he co-operates wonderfully.

Colonel Ottaway came in to chat. I told him Imphal, on closer acquaintance, seemed the last place where we would be of real service to the government in handling evacuees. There were government medical units coming out continually with troops and remaining in Imphal for a week or two, and even they were unable to get supplies to do effective work for the sick. Furthermore, it was a policy not to keep refugees at Imphal one minute more than absolutely necessary, for it was too close to the border, and food was almost unobtainable. Colonel Ottaway agreed and added the fact that the hundred-and-thirty-mile motor road connecting Imphal with the railway at Manipur Road Station was very narrow and the mountain sections were particularly subject to landslides during the heavy rains. He suggested that we get permission to set up in Gauhati, a day's journey by train below Manipur Road. Gauhati was on the banks of the Brahmaputra River and the meeting place for the three routes that refugees would follow out of Burma. Manipur Road, he said, was worse even than Imphal, because it was a very malarious spot, so full of swamps that space was limited and refugees were permitted to remain there only overnight. He told me he could furnish our unit two trucks in the morning if I could get permission from Colonel Williams and General Stilwell to move on from Imphal.

I reminded General Stilwell of the wide latitude he had given me in Burma in the selection of locations for our unit and asked for permission now to choose the spot in Assam where we could really accomplish the purpose of his orders. He agreed immediately.

After twenty-four hours' separation from us, Grindlay walked down this afternoon to say good-by, for he follows the general to Delhi tomorrow and won't see us again unless our roads lead to the same place after our Assam assignment has been carried out. The nurses spotted him as he entered our compound and, yelling "Uncle Grindlay, Uncle Grindlay," rushed on him and flung their arms around whatever part of him they could reach. Grindlay had tears streaming down his cheeks and the nurses were sobbing quite openly. That fellow has made himself so essential a part of our unit that it is going to be pretty hard to get along without him; but with Gurney and Ba Saw to help me I had no argument wherewith to ask Colonel Williams to continue to detail him to service with us in Assam. I have learned a lot during these twenty years. If you want the confidence of your superiors so that they will give you what you need, you always ask for the very least that you can possibly get along with. If you find out later that you asked for too little, you go to town and turn out the best job you can anyway.

My fever came back on me again this evening and the nice Casualty Clearing Station captain came over and gave me an intravenous injection of quinine. We have just enough ampoules left to get Colonel St. John safely to Delhi.

May 22nd—Off early this morning. Our Chinese patients went down in an ambulance. We borrowed three air mattresses and spread them on the floor of the two trucks, which Ottaway assigned to us, and put our three Americans on them. There were twenty in each truck. The three refugees have at last been persuaded to leave us and go down in the regular refugee caravans. I wonder if those three feel the slightest appreciation of the fact that, coming with General Stilwell and our crowd, they are about the luckiest refugees out of Burma. I was horribly ill the whole way down, but there was no place to lie. It was a most monotonous trip. With the side curtains down we couldn't see a thing except that our driver didn't know where his back wheels were and seemed determined to drop them over the edge. There were car wrecks everywhere and a lot of trucks had been bombed by the Japs. The nurses tried to sing, but the rough road jolted the songs out of them and they quit. Grindlay told me yesterday afternoon that General Stilwell said that the singing and laughter of the nurses on the trek out was the most marvelous morale-boosting device he had ever come across. We turned our patients over to Colonel Williams in Manipur Road. Chesley has got over his misogyny. He asked permission to send back presents to the nurses from Delhi.

May 23rd—It was midnight before we found a camp to stay in at Manipur Road. Everything was crowded. We got two tents finally, with string beds to sleep on. Had less food to eat yesterday than for some time. This morning we all had breakfast in the British officers' mess and ate several times what we should have been allowed. Since we are a United States Army unit the British are more polite and anxious to please than they would be if we were English. I told them we had our own cooks, so they have supplied us with rations, and we cooked our own lunch and dinner. This camp is on the site of some ancient Hindu temple. There are many phallic symbols set up in groups, huge rock carvings showing signs of great antiquity. The nurses couldn't figure out what they were, and that is perhaps just as well! I had fever till two this afternoon and then contacted the British colonels in charge of the local C.C.S.'s. They insist that Gauhati is the place for us, for here even they are able to do nothing constructive. Every available foot of ground is covered with patients for whom they cannot furnish tents. The refugee patients are so ill they can't make use of the toilet facilities and the sanitary condition is awful. Nine died on the way down from Imphal yesterday in our truck convoy. They die every night here before they can be put onto the trains. The only thing to do is get them out of this bottleneck and down to Gauhati for real treatment, before sending them on by boat and train to their homes. The officers were convinced that the Army as well as the government would welcome us at Gauhati with open arms. To facilitate our rapid arrival in Gauhati they have given us a third-class coach and one first-class compartment on the hospital train this evening. They were very apologetic about the third class, but I assured them that our only anxiety was to get going on our new assignment and we would go in a freight truck with pleasure! Now I have settled down in the first class myself with Bill and three nurses. That is no way for me to act, but I feel so sick I don't believe my morale would be equal to the third-class coach. It is a two-berth compartment, so I am going to ease my conscience by sleeping on the floor.

May 24th—We slept in the station all night. They say that after the Imphal bombing all the train crews ran away and they are running the train with volunteer crews. Guess that must be right, for we had not covered more than seven miles this morning when, going around a siding, our driver failed to apply brakes, plunged into the train on the main line and derailed our engine and tender. We have been near the tiny station all day. I have slept almost continually, but the nurses have been running around picking flowers. Tun Shein got on the job again, so we have had enough to eat including delicious bananas. Paul, whose favorite brand of poison they are, disposed of a whole bunch all by himself. I made a couple of trips to see sick British soldiers on board and the nurses have been taking care of them. We have almost no medicine left. This evening they began to push the cars of our train around to make way for the wrecker train. The English soldiers turned out and so did the nurses and Friends. Maran Lu got off a statement today that will go down into history. "I hope we never have to travel by airplane like the Sixth Army girls," she said. "We traveled by jeep and had to get out and push the jeep. We traveled by truck and pushed the truck, by raft and had to push the raft, by train and had to push the train. I shouldn't like to have to get out and push an airplane!"

May 25th—They finally got the wrecked engine out of the way and we started off after a delay of twenty-four hours. Assam is very much like Burma, though not nearly so rich a country nor so picturesque. Perhaps I am a bit prejudiced. Got to Gauhati just before dusk. I expected a city, but it is nothing but a town. There was just one gharry and one cart available at the station, so we used them for our baggage and marched over in our best manner to the A.B.M. compound. Several Sixth Army girls were walking around in the cool of the evening and stood paralyzed with astonishment for a full minute when they saw us marching in. Then there was a most joyful reunion.

The A.B.M. has a fifty-bed women's hospital here, with one American woman doctor, Dr. Randall, and three American nurses. They say there are two Indian women doctors, too, a lot of staff and pupil nurses. There are three other women missionaries in charge of a high school and orphanage and they have a large dormitory for college girls studying in the local university. They all made us very welcome. The Educational Mission House has taken over the six Friends Ambulance boys and the girls are parked in some of the smaller buildings. Bill and Gurney are in the downstairs part of the medical bungalow. Paul is across town at the evangelistic mission. The ladies have given me a private room in the hospital which has a bath and a lovely bed with inner-spring mattress.

May 26th—This morning I wandered around the compound, making plans. I asked the mission ladies to let us use their college dormitory for cleaner patients and the high-school building for the others. Both these buildings are unused because the school and college have closed down since the Imphal bombing. The ladies were glad to co-operate, for their own civilian work has almost ceased and they have been wanting to get into the very sort of work we are planning. With their permission I drove around to the Casualty Clearing Station to contact Colonel Meneces, informing him of General Stilwell's orders and asking him if he could use us in his refugee program. He was delighted at our arrival, but needed us more in the care of military evacuees at the moment as the other refugees had not yet swamped the hospitals arranged for them by the government. Colonel Meneces wondered how long it would be before we could accept patients, and I said we would be ready at once if he could find us any medicines. With the mission hospital beside us we could borrow equipment until the supplies Colonel Williams had promised to send us arrived. Meneces took us right over to his stores and told his officer to give us anything up to half his supply of each article we desired. The good Lord has certainly given me some decent men to work with!

Later—That evening the C.C.S. ambulance brought us twelve Indian troops and I put them in the high-school building with nurses from the Sixth Army group on duty, since they had had quite a rest after their easy trip out. The next day some British soldiers arrived and by the third day we had a hundred patients, and the Fifth Army girls were back to work again. By the end of a week we were up to two hundred patients, which was the capacity of the two buildings. It was a relief to have two such hounds for work as Gurney and Ba Saw again with me, for I could not stand on my feet more than half an hour at a time. My room was on the ground floor of the building we were using for British troops, and I spent my days in a large comfortable chair with my feet propped up, at last getting the treatment and rest I needed for a cure. Nurses and doctors came to me for orders and I made rounds of the most seriously ill patients once a day.

About ten days after we arrived one of the Lahu orderlies whom Case had turned over to us came down with a virulent attack of cerebral malaria and died in twenty-four hours. Several nurses also broke down with the disease, one of them having an atabrine psychosis as a result of our needing to use that drug. She had a mania for climbing trees and stayed up in one all one night, singing, praying, and saying naughty things about everyone who came in sight. We have been lucky not to lose any nurses. The troops we have had have been horribly ill with malaria, dysentery, and skin disease acquired on the way out. Many had had to cut their way through the Japs.

My old friend, Brigadier General Thompson, director of the Medical Services for the British Army in Burma, was brought to us one night with a temperature of 105° which promptly went up to 106°. It was touch and go with him, but he is well now and off to Shillong for a long rest.

The nurses are playing baseball again every Friday night. At first I could do nothing but referee. In the first game one of the nurses made a hit yet ran to first so slowly that the ball was fielded and she was put out.

"Why don't you run faster?"

"I can't. I left my strength behind in the Naga Hills!"

June 21st—The evacuation of troops is over and we will have no more admissions. But the government hospitals are now swamped with Indian refugees and they want us to help with them.

June 30th—I have never seen anything so pitiful as these poor refugees! They are starved and emaciated and suffering so much from lack of vitamins that they can't swallow. With this starvation background they have picked up the most virulent forms of malaria, amebic and bacillary dysentery. Those who picked up cholera and smallpox died before they got to Manipur Road, so we have had no cases of cholera and only two of smallpox. There have been women dying of puerperal fever as a result of having had abortions on the trip out. It is the most hopeless situation from the medical point of view. We can't get medicines for them for the railway has been washed out in several places and steamers are busy with the transport of reinforcement troops. The supplies Colonel Williams is sending us are still held up. We are trying to treat malaria without atabrine and with very little quinine and our stock of neosalvarsan is almost gone. There is no emetine and almost no stovarsol for amebic dysentery and absolutely no sulfaguanidine for bacillary dysentery. The typhoid cases have done fairly well. But those poor people keep on dying three or four a day.

The dormitory building is screened and we are trying to keep the worst dysenteries there. The other building is not screened and screening is not to be bought; the flies there are impossible to describe. The patients sleep on mats on the floor, which is what they prefer, and in spite of our nurses being on almost full-time duty with flyswatters, in spite of flypaper everywhere, in spite of gallons of Flit, the patients and the floors are black with nasty flies. The flies are all over the patients' faces and even get into their mouths. The dysentery cases are so weak they are incontinent, and that doesn't help matters much! Some of the patients have "Naga sores" which eat down through skin, fascia, and muscle and even into bone, destroying the periosteum. The other day I had to remove the entire femur of a patient with one of these sores. I put him into a cast then, and his temperature immediately dropped to normal and remained normal. The best treatment for the sores seems to be 10 per cent Mag. Sulph. in glycerin after the sloughs have been debrided in the same way we did our war wounds.

July 1st—I can't help but feel that the Japanese were very clever when they decided to let the Indian refugees leave the country. They took pains to see that the refugees would starve by robbing them of their money and food supplies as they went through their lines. One pregnant Indian woman dropped on her knees before the Japanese and begged for the return of just enough money to help her through into India, and she was kicked in the abdomen for her pains. She aborted on the way out and is one of those who died here from puerperal infection. Making starvation en route certain, the Japs thereby also made inevitable the acquisition of the worst forms of contagious disease, and the arrival, in a poorly prepared province of India, of thousands of sick who would each one be a source of contagion to the whole country. It seems like a new variety of bacterial warfare!

Somewhere in India. Later—The newspapers are full of accounts of R.A.F. and United States Air Force activities in Burma, and the nurses, who have seen the destruction the

Japanese wreaked on their home towns, are rather depressed at the certain knowledge that the havoc now caused on those same towns by the allied air forces must mean their final disappearance. I have been comforting them by assuring them that their folks are undoubtedly so sensible that they must have taken to the woods, away from Japanese-occupied sections. Today the matter came closer to home in the announcement that the United States Air Force had bombed Japanese barracks at Namkham. There is nothing at Namkham fit to be used as barracks except the bazaar buildings, the hospital, and nurses' home and the dormitories and school buildings of the Kachin and Shan missions. Well, that is the end of all my dreams and hard work. As I feel now, I wouldn't want to drive broken-down trucks all night to haul stone and go through those other miseries in order to build up those buildings again in the same poverty-controlled way we built up before. The hardest building of the lot to hit would be our bungalow—Tiny's dream house and mine; but if, as they certainly would be, the Japanese High Command were quartered in that house, I hope the Americans busted the daylights out of it!

The number of refugees diminished rapidly at Gauhati, and the government hospitals were able to cope with the situation. Besides, Dr. Martha Gifford, who used to be in Moulmein, came to help Dr. Randall; and the two of them are going to continue the work we began and which they had been helping us to do. The inspector general of civil hospitals and the secretary to the government of Assam have written their formal thanks for the assistance given by this American Army unit. We are at work for the Chinese Army again. We don't know where we are going next, but all of us hope it is going to be to a big job! The last time I saw General Stilwell, I told him we all hoped that when new action developed against the Japs he would save out the meanest, nastiest task of all for us. The general turned on me like a flash with a real sparkle in his eye.

"I can certainly promise you that," he said.